Personal Reminiscences Of A Great Crusade

Josephine E. Butler

Facsimile of 1910 Edition: First published 1896

This Edition: All Rights Reserved.
Copyright © 2002 Portrayer Publishers
Re-published April 2002-Facsimile of 1910 edition: First published 1896
By **Josephine E. Butler**
No part of this edition may be reproduced or transmitted in any form or by any means, graphic, electronic, or mechanical, including photocopying, recording, taping or by any information storage or retrieval system, without the permission in writing from the publisher.

Published by Portrayer Publishers
For information on any of our books, please contact:
Portrayer Publishers, 55 Red Lane, Hill Cliffe, Appleton, Warrington, CHESHIRE, United Kingdom, WA4 5AL.
Telephone: 44 (0) 1925 497783
Facsimile: 44 (0) 1925 497783
e-mail us at : publishing@portrayer.co.uk

ISBN: 0-9542632-1-9
A catalogue record for this book is available from the British Library

Printed in the United Kingdom.

Personal Reminiscences Of A Great Crusade

Josephine E. Butler

Facsimile of 1910 Edition: First Published 1896

Cover Illustration: Ackermann, R., The Microcosm of London, Vol. II, Plate no. 44 (Hospital,Middlesex)

Personal Reminiscences of a Great Crusade

By JOSEPHINE E. BUTLER

NEW EDITION

DEDICATED TO THE MEMORY OF
SIR JAMES STANSFELD

LONDON
HORACE MARSHALL & SON
1910

Introduction

OUR long years of labour and conflict on behalf of this just cause, ought not to be forgotten. A knowledge of, and a reverence for, the principles for which we have striven ought to be kept alive, for these principles are very far from being yet so clearly recognised as that our children and our children's children may not be called upon to rise again and again in their defence.

SECOND EDITION, 1898.

THE system that Mrs. Butler and her coadjutors so successfully combated in England, still exists in various parts of the British Empire and of the Continent of Europe, and in Japan and South America. Enactments similar in principle also threaten from time to time this country and the United States of America.

NEW EDITION, 1910.

Prefatory Biographical Note

A VERY charming *Autobiographical Memoir* of Mrs. Butler has been edited by George W. and Lucy A. Johnson, and may be obtained for 6s. through any bookseller, or from the publishers, Arrowsmiths of Bristol, or Simpkin Marshall of London. This memoir consists mainly of extracts from Mrs. Butler's published works. We are indebted to it for the following facts :—

In an introduction to the Memoir in question, the Rt. Hon. James Stuart, her warm personal friend, and fellow-worker for many years, thus describes her personality : " She was at home in every class of society. She was very beautiful, and of a very gracious presence, and the impression made by first seeing her and hearing her voice has, I expect, been forgotten by none who ever met her. She was of a very artistic temperament. She was a good painter, an extremely good musician. She was a bold rider, and active, though always of a somewhat weak health. Her industry and application were unbounded. She was very full of humour, and, while deeply in earnest, had the faculty of being at times charmingly gay. She dressed with great taste and simplicity. She, above all things, loved her home and her husband, and that love was wholly returned. She was extremely cosmopolitan. At the same time she was a great lover of her own country, and particularly of the borderland between England and Scotland, where she was born, and where she now lies buried in the churchyard of Kirknewton, where many of her ancestors lie. For she came of an old Border family ; and bravery, and the alertness of battle, and the power of self-sacrifice, and the indignation against wrong which characterized her, came to her, perhaps, partly through her descent. She was a great reader of the Bible, and a humble suppliant before the throne of God. But, while her own beliefs were clear and definite, she had no narrowness in her views, and the very names of those who have been her foremost supporters show how wide her sympathies were, and how acceptable she was to people of all creeds, as well as of all politics and all climes."

Josephine Elizabeth Grey was born at Milfield Hill, in the county of Northumberland, on April 13, 1828. She was the fourth daughter of John Grey, and of his wife Hannah Annett. John Grey's ancestors were wardens of the East Marches, and Governors of Norham, Morpeth, Wark, and Berwick Castles in the old Border days, from whom are also descended the Tankervilles and the Greys in the House of Lords.

John Grey was appointed to the charge of the great Greenwich Hospital Estates in Northumberland in 1833, and as a pioneer in the scientific improvement of waste lands, turned it into a very valuable property. Mrs. Butler says of this period, " Our home at Dilston was a very beautiful one. Its romantic historical associations, the wild informal beauty all round its doors, the bright, large family circle, and the kind and hospitable character of its master and mistress, made it an attractive place to many friends and guests. Among our pleasantest visitors there were Swedes, Russians, and French, who came to England on missions of agricultural or other enquiry, and who sometimes spent weeks with us. It was a house the door of which stood wide open, as if to welcome all comers, through the livelong summer day. It was a place where one could glide out of a lower window and be hidden in a moment, plunging straight amongst wild wood paths and beds of fern, or find one's self quickly in some cool concealment, beneath slender birch trees, or by the dry bed of a mountain stream. It was a place where the sweet hushing sound of waterfalls, and clear streams murmuring over shallows, were heard all day and night, though winter storms turned those sweet sounds into an angry roar."

John Grey was a man of wide and deep sympathies, and

PREFATORY BIOGRAPHICAL NOTE vii

besides being a great influence for good in his own immediate neighbourhood, was a personal friend and fellow-worker of Clarkson in the Abolition of the Slave Trade. His daughter speaks of " his large benevolence, his tender compassionateness, and his respect for the rights and liberties of the individual man. His life," she says, " was a sustained effort for the good of others, flowing from these affections. He had no grudge against rank or wealth, no restless desire for change for its own sake, still less any rude love of demolition; but he could not endure to see oppression or wrong of any kind inflicted on man, woman, or child. ' You cannot treat men and women exactly as you do one-pound notes, to be used or rejected as you think proper,' he said in a letter to *The Times*, when that paper was advocating some ill-considered changes, beneficial to one class, but leaving out of account a residue of humble folk upon whom they would entail great suffering. In the cause of any maltreated or neglected creature he was uncompromising to the last, and when brought into opposition with the perpetrators of any social injustice he became an enemy to be feared."

Mrs. Butler's mother was also a fine character, and warmly seconded the efforts of her husband for the general good. She was descended from a Huguenot family.

As Mrs. Butler grew into young womanhood the sad and tragical recitals which came to the family from first sources of the wrongs inflicted by slavery on negro men and women " broke," she says, " her young heart," and keenly awakened her feelings, especially " concerning the injustice to women through this conspiracy of greed and gold, and lust of the flesh, a conspiracy which has its counterpart in the white slave-owning in Europe."

" For one long year of darkness," she says, " the trouble of heart and brain urged me to lay all this at the door of the God, whose name I had learned was Love. I dreaded Him, I fled from Him, until grace was given me to arise and wrestle, as Jacob did, with the mysterious Presence, who must either slay or pronounce deliverance. And then the great questioning again went up from earth to heaven, ' God ! Who art Thou ? Where art Thou ? Why is it thus with the creatures of Thy hand ? ' I fought the battle alone, in deep recesses of the beautiful woods and pine forests around our home, or on some lonely hill-side, among wild thyme and heather, a silent temple where the only sounds were the plaintive cry of the curlew, or the hum of a summer bee, or the distant bleating of sheep. For hours and days and weeks in these retreats I sought the answer to my soul's trouble and the solution of its dark questionings. Looking back, it seems to me the end must have been defeat and death had not the Saviour imparted to the child-wrestler something of the virtue of His own midnight agony, when in Gethsemane His sweat fell like great drops of blood to the ground."

The next stage in the preparation of Mrs. Butler for her great world-wide work was her marriage in 1852 to a man of singularly noble character, George Butler, son of the Dean of Peterborough. It was in this year that the portrait was taken which appears on the cover of this work. The first five years of their married life were spent at Oxford, where Mr. Butler did important work in the University, as tutor, examiner and lecturer. Here they met many leading people, and Mrs. Butler says, " In the frequent social gatherings in our drawing-room in the evenings there was much talk, sometimes serious and weighty, sometimes light, interesting, critical, witty, and brilliant, ranging over many subjects. It was then that I sat silent, the only woman in the company, and listened, sometimes with a sore heart, for these men would speak of things which I had already revolved deeply in my own mind, things of which I was convinced, which I knew, though I had no dialectics at command with which to defend their truth.

" Every instinct of womanhood within me was already in revolt against certain accepted theories in society, and I suffered as only God and the faithful companion of my life

PREFATORY BIOGRAPHICAL NOTE

could ever know. Incidents occurred which brought their contribution to the lessons then sinking into our hearts. A young mother was in Newgate for the murder of her infant, whose father, under cover of the death-like silence prescribed by Oxford philosophers, a silence which is in fact a permanent endorsement of injustice, had perjured himself to her, had forsaken and forgotten her, and fallen back, with no accusing conscience, on his easy social life, and possibly his academic honours. I wished to go and speak to her in the prison of the God who saw the injustice done, and who cared for her. My husband suggested that we should write to the chaplain of Newgate, and ask him to send her to us when her sentence had expired. We wanted a servant, and he thought that she might be able to fill that place. She came to us. I think she was the first of the world of unhappy women of a humble class whom he welcomed to his own home. She was not the last."

In 1857 Mr. Butler accepted the post of Vice-Principal of Cheltenham College. Here Mrs. Butler met with a terrible trial in the sudden death by accident, of her only little daughter Evangeline, in the year 1864. This was followed by a long period of darkness and intense depression of spirits, which was only dispelled by visiting amongst the four thousand poor women in the jails and workhouses of Liverpool, where she sat amongst them and picked oakum, until she gained their confidence. Her husband had previously taken the Principalship of Liverpool College, following the celebrated Dr. Howson, who vacated it to take the position of Dean of Chester. The result of her work here was, she says, " to draw down upon my head an avalanche of miserable, but grateful womanhood." She first of all filled the basement and attics of her house with " as many as possible of the most friendless girls who were anxious to make a fresh start." This becoming inconvenient, a " House of Rest " was started, which continued for many years, and was finally taken over by the town as a municipal institution.

PREFATORY BIOGRAPHICAL NOTE

1864 was the date of the commencement of the last stage of the preparation of Mrs. Butler for her great life-work of attacking and undermining the world-wide evil of State Regulated Vice. 1864 was likewise the date of the introduction of State Regulated Vice into England, which was the last of the countries of Europe to adopt it, as it was also the first, in 1886, to abolish it. Mrs. Butler's part in the great Abolitionist Struggle is detailed in the following pages in her own words.

Mrs. Butler lived the last few years of her life at Wooler, near Milfield, the place of her birth. There she died peacefully in her sleep, on December 30, 1906, and was buried in the churchyard at Kirknewton, where many of her ancestors had been buried.

The editors of her biography conclude, " Surely we may say of her, but very slightly altering the words of Bunyan : As she drew nigh unto the beautiful gate of the City, she asked, ' What must I do in the Holy Place ? ' and the shining ones answered, ' Thou must there receive the comfort of all thy toil, and have joy for all thy sorrow ; thou must reap what thou hast sown, even the fruit of all thy prayers and tears, and suffering for the King by the way. There also thou shalt serve Him continually, whom thou desiredst to serve in the world, though with much difficulty because of the infirmity of thy flesh, There thine eyes shall be delighted with seeing, and thine ears with hearing, the pleasant voice of the Mighty One. There thou shalt enjoy thy friends again, that are gone thither before thee ; and there thou shalt with joy receive even every one that follows into the Holy Place after thee.' As she entered in at the gate, then I heard in my dream that all the bells in the City rang again for joy, and that it was said unto her, ' Enter thou into the joy of thy Lord.' "

CHAPTER I

ORIGIN OF THE SYSTEM OF STATE REGULATION OF VICE

"Our fathers to their graves have gone;
Their strife is past—their triumph won;
But sterner trials wait the race
Which rises in their honoured place—
A moral warfare with the crime
And folly of an evil time."

"So let it be. In God's own might
We gird us for the coming fight,
And, strong in Him whose cause is ours,
In conflict with unholy powers,
We grasp the weapons He has given—
The light, and truth, and love of Heaven."

THE late Professor Emile de Laveleye, at our International Conference at the Hague, in September, 1883, gave some account of the inauguration of this system, which took its rise in France under the auspices of Napoleon I. The system was first suggested by Aulas in 1762, and by Restif de la Bretonne in 1790. It was brought into full operation on the eve of the establishment of the French Empire in 1802. "It could only have had its birth," said Professor de Laveleye, "at a period of disturbance, when the rights of human dignity and individual liberty were forgotten or misunderstood. History, in recounting the saturnalia of vice in Asia Minor, in Greece, and especially in Imperial Rome, narrates horrors which cause us to shudder. But never, either in Rome, or in Athens, or even in Corinth, was the spectacle witnessed of public abodes of shame kept open by the State. Juvenal paints Messalina gliding thither under cover of night. But even Heliogabalus never constituted himself their patron as nowadays do the Municipal and State authorities of our Christian communities in the full sunshine of the 19th century."

Then the same accomplished speaker, in a very forcible address, showed what the legalising of vice has been and has produced in all those nations which, following the example of France, have adopted it. "It has been the source of profound disorders, both moral and physical: of moral disorders, by destroying the aversion which vice should inspire, and thereby strengthening its power; of physical disorders, by exciting incontinence, and all its concurrent evils, with proffered facilities and promises of immunity."

I shall have occasion later to draw attention to the different dates and methods in which this system was introduced into the several countries of Europe. England was the last country in which it found a foothold. When, in 1872, I was summoned to give evidence before a Royal Commission to inquire into this question, I stated on the authority of Mrs. Harriet Martineau and other venerable writers and politicians, a fact which has never been contradicted in any way, *i.e.*, than an attempt was made during the Melbourne Ministry to introduce this Parisian system into England. It was deemed impossible, however, to place such an Act of Parliament in the hands of a young virgin Queen for signature, and the attempt was dropped. There was a renewed endeavour during the life of the Prince Consort, but this was also abandoned, from the knowledge that was obtained of the Prince's distinct disapproval of this Continental system. Prince Albert died, and it was during the first year of Queen Victoria's widowhood, when she was presumably absorbed in her private grief, that the promoters of this system in England succeeded in pushing an Act through Parliament, and obtaining for it the Royal signature.

There were four Acts; the first, tentative, in 1864. This was repealed when the Act of 1866 was passed, and this, after verbal amendment in 1868, was still further extended by the Act of 1869. This last Act was not allowed much peace, for it was in the autumn of the same year that the opposition arose; in fact, a powerful protest had been raised shortly before the passing of this complete Act. Mrs. Harriet Martineau, with all the shrewdness and enlightenment of a true woman and an able politician, had seen the tendency of a certain busy medical and military clique in this direction. The then editor of the *Daily News*, who was favourable to our views, asked Mrs. Martineau to write a series of letters in his paper. This she did, and her letters are extremely weighty, and wonderful to read at this day, when we have an immense accumulation of evidence to support her and our views, which she, of course, did not possess. Her advice on this matter concerning our army is admirable. Speaking of our poor soldiers, she says:—" But while favouring the element of brutality in him (the soldier), we had not need go further and assume in practice that his animalism is a necessity which must be provided for. This is the fatal step which it is now hoped that the English Parliament and the English people may be induced to take. If the soldier is more immoral than his contemporaries of the working class, it must be because the standard of morality is lower in the army than out of it. Shall we then raise it to what we clearly see it might be, or degrade it further by a practical avowal that vice is in the soldier's case a necessity to be provided for, like his need of food and clothing? This admission of the necessity of vice is the point on which the whole argument turns, and on which irretrievable consequences depend. Once admitted, the necessity of a long series of fearful evils follows of course. There can be no resistance to seduction, procuration, disease, regulation, *when once the original necessity is granted.* Further, the admission involves civil as well as military society, and starts them together on the road which leads down to what moralists of all ages and nations have called the lowest hell. . . . It is a national disgrace that our people should have even been asked to regard and treat their soldiers and sailors as pre-destined fornicators." And in another of her letters to the *Daily News* Mrs. Martineau, writing of her experience of Continental cities, said: "There is evidence accessible to all that the Regulation System creates horrors worse than those which it is supposed to restrain. Vice once stimulated by such a system imagines and dares all unutterable things. And such things perplex with misery the lives of parents of missing children in Continental cities, and daunt the courage of rulers, and madden the moral sense, and gnaw the conscience of whole orders of sinners and sufferers, of whom we can form no conception here. We shall have entered upon our national decline whenever we agree to the introduction of such a system."

We, the women of England, were not the first to arise in opposition to this iniquity. For at least fifteen years before our call to the work, warning lights had been held out from time to time by persons or societies who thoroughly knew the system, and dreaded the disastrous effects for our country of its establishment in our midst.

A group of Baptist and other Nonconformist Ministers, in which my relative, the late Charles Birrell, took a leading part, early went to the Government, conveying an earnest warning and protest on the subject. I cannot fix the exact date of this event; but I have a vivid recollection of the account of it given to me by Mr. Birrell. I believe it was during the Administration of Lord John Russell.

In 1860 a Committee of the House of Lords sat to consider the question of introducing the Acts for the regulation of vice into India, or establishing a more complete form of Acts already existing there. The majority of the witnesses examined by that Committee were wholly opposed to the system. Miss Florence Nightingale was one of those witnesses. Her recorded evidence and expression of opinion are lengthy, and exactly what we might expect from a truehearted and an experienced woman. Lord Frederick Fitz-Clarence, Commander-in-Chief of the forces in India, said that "after giving the whole subject his best attention, he concurred with his predecessors in command of the army in believing that police measures of the kind in question could not be carried on without involving the certain degradation and oppression of many innocent women, and occasioning other evils which, in his opinion, would be very much greater than that which it was their object to remedy." Dr. Grierson (of the Indian Army) said that when the natives of India saw the authorities making such careful provision for the protection of immoral persons, and at the same time doing little for the good of the other classes, they were "sorely perplexed." General Jacob said : "The proper and only wise method of dealing with this question is to improve the condition and moral well-being of the army. Coercion of any kind always increases the evil. Moral forces alone are of any value."

A third strong protest was that of the officers of the Rescue Society in London. They made a series of very strong efforts against the threatened introduction of the regulation system.

The late Mr. Daniel Cooper, the well-known and respected Secretary of the Rescue Society, wrote to me in 1870: " You ask me to tell you what the Rescue Society did to bring this infamous legislation under public notice. In 1868 we published a pamphlet and waited on the Home Secretary. With the pamphlet we presented a copy of a 'Memorandum of Objections' to this legislation. This Memorandum was circulated by thousands. We placed it in the hands of every member of both Houses of Parliament; we forwarded it to all the principal clergy of the Metropolis and other important towns in England, and also to the leading Nonconformist ministers. We spent more than £100 in the circulation of our papers, and with what result? I am ashamed to say that very little effect was produced. The utmost apathy prevailed; people would not believe our words and would not stir. The infamous Act of 1869 was passed in spite of all our efforts.

"At this crisis we learned that the *Women* of England were taking this question in hand. We were rejoiced beyond measure when we saw the announcement of your Ladies' National Association.

"I tell you candidly I had felt an almost utter despair in seeing that, after putting forth our pamphlet, and writing thousands of letters, imploring our legislators, clergy, principal public men and philanthropists to look into the question, such a stoical indifference remained. We felt, on hearing of your Association, that Providence had well chosen the means for the defeat of these wicked Acts. The ladies of England will save the country from this fearful curse; for I fully believe that through them it has even now had its death blow. The men who charge the ladies foremost in the struggle with indelicacy are not worthy the name of men. As to our Members of Parliament, pray do not excuse their ignorance; do not try to palliate their error by saying the Act was passed at the fag end of the session. The papers placed in their hands by ourselves, the letters of warning we addressed to them, leave them no excuse. Knowing, as none but ourselves can know, what was done to arouse them, I cannot but conclude that, with a few honourable exceptions, our Members of Parliament cared nothing about the matter until public opinion forced them to look into it. But for the Ladies' National Association we should have had no discussion, and the Acts would by this date have probably been extended throughout the country. I say this solemnly, and from an intimate knowledge of all the plans of the Association formed to extend these Acts. Go on; give the country no rest till this law is abolished.—Yours truly, DANIEL COOPER."

The names of Dr. Charles Bell Taylor and Dr. Worth, of Nottingham, must be gratefully remembered, for it was to those gentlemen that we, the women of England, owed our first clear information of the nature and the passing of the Act of 1869. I had been on the Continent with my family in that year, and had been learning much there concerning the disastrous effects of this system. On the journey home I found a telegram awaiting me at Dover, begging an interview, and this was followed by a somewhat mysterious appeal from these alert friends at Nottingham to " haste to the rescue." In a few days the whole state of the case was put before me and a small group of friends. No organised action, however, was taken by us until the close of December of that year. In fact, there was much preparation of heart, nerve, and mind necessary for such a task as was now opening out before us. It was not a thing to be taken up hastily.

Meanwhile, in September of this same year (1869), some other watchful friends had taken occasion of the Social Science Congress meeting at Bristol to introduce again a strong warning note, or rather now a protest, against the legislation in question. The Rev. Dr. Hooppell, of Northumberland, Mr. George Charleton, of the Society of Friends, and Mr. Banks, afterwards for so many years the able and indefatigable secretary of the National Association, proved themselves on this occasion already well-armed and staunch advocates of the abolition movement, of which they themselves were amongst the earliest initiators. They formed there a local association, which was afterwards merged into the National Association, which had its office in London.

I have already, in the "Recollections of George Butler," recorded sufficiently my own and my husband's first call to this great work, the inward preparation for which had been going on for many years previously. I have spoken there of the horror, the dismay we felt on the first full knowledge that this iniquity had been established by law in England, of the weeks of self-questioning and hesitation which followed for myself, of the tardy but firm resolution at last formed to imitate, if I may use the simile, the example of Quintus Curtius of old Roman fame, and to leap into this yawning gulf in order that the nation's wound might close again. But this Roman hero, I had read, met his fate fully equipped, armed from head to foot, fearless, and in the perfection of self-renunciation. I felt that, for such an enterprise, I should require nothing less than "the whole armour of God." I have recorded also in that book the noble and unselfish part which my husband took from the beginning in this warfare ; and to some extent I there also indicated the sacrifices he made, and the anxieties he silently endured for many years, after he had spoken to me that momentous word (to me a consecration for the work), "Go, and the Lord be with you."

This word was spoken after we had conferred fully together on the action we should adopt, and after our conclusion that we must make an immediate appeal to the great public.

Many persons, honestly judging the matter from the outside, have mistakenly imagined that the persecution which had to be endured, the ridicule by which we were constantly assailed in the Press, the social ostracism, the coldness of many who had before been friends and companions, the obloquy, false accusations, abuse and violence, continued for years, must have been the greatest of the trials incident to the part we were called to take in so dreadful an enterprise. So far as my own experience bears witness, those who judge so are mistaken. These things were for me light and easy to bear in comparison with the deep and silent sorrow, the bitterness of soul of the years which preceded. I recall those years of painful thinking, and of questionings which seemed to receive no answer and to be susceptible of no solution ; those years in which I saw this great social iniquity (based on the shameful inequality of judgment concerning sexual sin in man and woman) devastating the world, contentedly acquiesced in, no great revolt proclaimed against it, a dead silence reigning concerning it, a voice feebly raised perhaps now and again, but quickly rebuked and silenced. The call to action, the field of battle entered, with all its perils and trials clearly set out before us, were a joyful relief, a place of free breathing, compared with the oppression and the heart-woe which went before.

Those alone who have trod the silent and secret " way of Calvary " will fully understand me. Those who have not may well think the discipline of being traduced, slandered, threatened, and "spitefully entreated " a very hard discipline. But one who has endured the deeper and keener spiritual discipline, when there seemed no escape, no ray of hope, must regard the outward persecution and violence only as a welcome sign that the battle is set in array, and that the enemy is roused to bitterest hatred because his claims are disputed and his sovereignty is about to be overthrown. The inward sorrow I believe to have been necessary for the vitalising of righteous action, and the insuring of depth, reality and constancy.

On the 1st January, 1870, was published the famous Women's Protest, as follows :

" We, the undersigned, enter our solemn protest against these Acts.

" 1st.—Because, involving as they do such a momentous change in the legal safeguards hitherto enjoyed by women in common with men, they have been passed, not only without the knowledge of the country, but unknown, in a great measure, to Parliament itself ; and we hold that neither the Representatives of the People, nor the Press, fulfil the duties which are expected of them, when they allow such legislation to take place without the fullest discussion.

" 2nd.—Because, so far as women are concerned, they remove every guarantee of personal security which the law has established and held sacred, and put their reputation, their freedom, and their persons absolutely in the power of the police.

" 3rd.—Because the law is bound, in any country professing to give civil liberty to its subjects, to define clearly an offence which it punishes.

" 4th.—Because it is unjust to punish the sex who are the victims of a vice, and leave unpunished the sex who are the main cause, both of the vice and its dreaded consequences; and we consider that liability to arrest, forced medical treatment, and (where this is resisted) imprisonment with hard labour, to which these Acts subject women, are punishments of the most degrading kind.

"5th.—Because, by such a system, the path of evil is made more easy to our sons, and to the whole of the youth of England; inasmuch as a moral restraint is withdrawn the moment the State recognises, and provides convenience for, the practice of a vice which it thereby declares to be necessary and venial.

"6th.—Because these measures are cruel to the women who come under their action—violating the feelings of those whose sense of shame is not wholly lost, and further brutalising even the most abandoned.

"7th.—Because the disease which these Acts seek to remove has never been removed by any such legislation. The advocates of the system have utterly failed to show, by statistics or otherwise, that these regulations have in any case, after several years' trial, and when applied to one sex only, diminished disease, reclaimed the fallen, or improved the general morality of the country. We have, on the contrary, the strongest evidence to show that in Paris and other Continental cities where women have long been outraged by this system, the public health and morals are worse than at home.

"8th.—Because the conditions of this disease, in the first instance, are moral, not physical. The moral evil through which the disease makes its way separates the case entirely from that of the plague, or other scourges, which have been placed under police control or sanitary care. We hold that we are bound, before rushing into experiments of legalising a revolting vice, to try to deal with the *causes* of the evil, and we dare to believe that with wiser teaching and more capable legislation, those causes would not be beyond control."

This Protest was published in the *Daily News*, and the fact of its appearance was flashed by telegram to the remotest parts of the Kingdom. The local press largely reproduced it.

Among the two thousand signatures which it obtained in a short time there were those of Florence Nightingale, Harriet Martineau, Mary Carpenter, the sisters and other relatives of the late Mr. John Bright, all the leading ladies of the Society of Friends, and many well-known in the literary and philanthropic world.

A pause ensued, a silence on the part of our opponents and undecided or critical lookers on, induced by the first shock of this unexpected and powerful manifesto. A member of Parliament, fully sympathetic with us, said to me: "Your manifesto has shaken us very badly in the House of Commons; a leading man in the House remarked to me, 'We know how to manage any other opposition in the House or in the country, but this is very awkward for us—this revolt of the women. It is quite a new thing; what are we to do with such an opposition as this?'"

But this temporary pause was succeeded by signs of much agitation and business among our opponents in preparation for an organised stand against our attitude and claims; and simultaneously was inaugurated the great "Conspiracy of Silence" in the press, which continued unbroken until the autumn of 1874, when a well-known Ex-Cabinet Minister spoke powerfully at a public meeting on our behalf. After this one occasion, however, the press, as if by common consent, fell back into its old attitude of silence. This silence could not be in most cases attributed to a regard for the feelings of readers, for statements in favour of the Acts were continually admitted. We had, however, great encouragement from many and often unexpected parts of the world.

Many persons on the Continent, working for social reforms, were even then rejoicing in the trumpet-blast which had been sounded from England, in open opposition to this vicious system. We had inaugurated a line of action to the continuance of which we were pledged by sacred duty in regard to the hopes which it had awakened throughout Europe.

Amongst the reforms which, it was hoped, would be aided by the present agitation was one connected with the army, in the substitution of some better system of national defence than that of a military army of celibates, kept as a distinct class, and demoralized by unnatural provisions, supposed to be needful for their exceptional existence.

The purification of the medical profession was also hoped for, and the exposure and defeat of those deadly materialist doctrines respecting the necessity of unchastity, which had been secretly and widely promulgated, and which, together with the dogmatism and despotism of certain doctors, had begun to exercise so fatal an influence over our legislative counsels. The condition of the womanhood of our country for some time past we often compared with that of the afflicted woman of whom we read in the Gospels, of whom it was said, "She had endured many things of many physicians," and that she grew no better, but rather worse. The afflicted woman alluded to, approaching the person of the great Spiritual Physician, was healed by the touch of faith. A similar faith was coming to the succour of the womanhood of the present day. Their hearts were lifted up to God, with whom are the issues of life and death, and they were taught to scorn the perversions of physicians who, in the supposed interests of the body, trampled under foot the claims of decency and the inalienable rights of every woman, chaste or unchaste, over her own person. God would henceforth, we trusted, place His gifts of healing in holy hands, and say to the poor afflicted womanhood of this day, "Daughter, be of good cheer."

The purification we hoped for was already indicated by the fact that, among the men who gradually rallied around us in this cause, from all ranks and all professions, pure-hearted physicians were among the foremost, both in action and in indignant denunciation of the theories and practices which we abhorred.

Not many weeks after the publication of our Protest, Mr. Gladstone, then Prime Minister, received a Memorial from women of Geneva on the subject; a beautiful and distinct echo from afar of our own cry for justice.

Even earlier than this, more than one sympathetic voice reached us from Paris itself, the birthplace of the evil thing against which we were allied.

Victor Hugo wrote:—

"PARIS, *March* 20, 1870.

"I am with you, madame and ladies. I am with you to the fullest extent of my power. In reading your eloquent letter, I have felt a burning sympathy rise in me for the feeble, and a corresponding indignation against the oppressor. France is apparently about to borrow from England an evil institution, that of chamber executions—legal murders done behind closed doors; and, in her turn, England prepares to adopt from France a detestable system, that, namely, of a police dealing with women as outlaws. Protest! resist! show your indignation! All noble hearts and all lofty spirits will be on your side. The slavery of black women is abolished in America, but the slavery of white women continues in Europe; and laws are still made by men in order to tyrannise over women. Nothing more hateful could be seen than the sight to-day—France copying the feudalism of England, and England reproducing the medical tyranny of Paris. It is a rivalry of retrogression—a miserable spectacle. It disgraces justice in France, and the Executive power in England. Publish this letter if you think fit, and be assured of my earnest sympathy and respect.

"VICTOR HUGO."

From Mazzini, to a member of our Ladies' Association:—

"ITALY, *February*, 1870.

"MY DEAR FRIEND,—

"Can you doubt me? Can you doubt how eagerly I watch from afar, and how heartily I bless the efforts of the brave, earnest British women who are striving for the extension of the suffrage to their sex and for the repeal of the vice-protecting Acts, which last question is but an incident in the great general question of justice to women?

"Is your question less sacred than that of the abolition of slavery in America, or of serfdom elsewhere? Ought it not to be even more sacred to us—in reverence for our mothers,—and if we remember that the most important period of human life—the first—is entrusted to women?

"Are not all questions of equality mere baseless rebellion, unless they are derived from an all-embracing religious principle? and is not that principle—(the oneness of the human family)—the soul of your country's religion?

"Have the men who deny the righteousness of your claims abjured that religion, or forgotten the holy words of Jesus and of Paul:—

"'Neither pray I for these alone, but for them also which shall believe on Me through the Word.'

"'That they all may be one; as Thou, Father, art in Me, and I in Thee, that they also may be one in us.'—John xvii. 20, 21.

"'For ye are all the children of God by faith in Christ Jesus.'

"'There is neither Jew nor Greek, there is neither bond nor free, there is neither male nor female, for ye are all one in Christ Jesus.'—Epistle Galatians iii. 26, 28.

"Do they tell you these words apply to heaven? Ask them Who has taught them to pray that *God's will be done on earth as it is in heaven?*

"No question such as yours ought to be solved without asking *how far does the proposed solution minister to the moral education of society?* The sense of self-dignity, the deep conviction that each of us has a task to fulfil on earth, for our own improvement and that of our fellow-creatures, is the first step in all education. We are bound to start by teaching all whom we seek to educate the words you quoted; *you are a human being; nothing that concerns mankind is alien to you.* If you crush in man his innate sense of self-respect, you decree the helot. If you sanction moral inequality to any extent, you either create rebellion, with all its evils, or indifference, hypocrisy and corruption.

If you punish the accomplice, leaving the sinner untouched, you destroy, by arousing the sense of injustice, every beneficial result of punishment. If you assume the right to legislate for any class, without allowing that class voice or share in the work, you destroy the sacredness of law, and awaken hatred or contempt in the heart of the excluded class.

"In these simple obvious principles lies the justice of your claims.

"In this legislation lies—forget it not—the germ of a moral disease far more terrible than the physical evil they thus brutally and impotently endeavour to 'stamp out'; this first step backwards, taken in selfish fear, will, if not speedily retraced, be followed by others, until the moral sore neglected will become a cancer infecting the very life-blood of your nation.

"In the moral principles I have stated you will conquer. Your cause is a religious one. Do not narrow it down to what is called a right or an interest. Let duty be your ground, both in protecting your unhappy sisters and in urging your political claims. You are children of God. You have the same duty to perform on earth—the progressive discovery and the progressive fulfilment of His law. You cannot renounce that task without sinning against the God who appointed it, and gave to you, as to us, faculties and powers for its accomplishment.

"You cannot fulfil your task without *liberty*, which is the source of responsibility. You cannot fulfil it without *equality*, which is liberty for each and all.

"Your claim to the suffrage is identical with that of the working men. Like them, you seek to bring a new element of progress to the common work; you feel that you, too, have something to say, not merely indirectly, but legally and officially, with regard to the great problems which stir and torture the soul of mankind.

"As for the special cause of which you write, the repeal of these hideous Acts, you will succeed. You have in your

House of Commons men whom surely no giant despair of physical disease can turn aside from the straight path of principle and justice; but even if these should fail you, which I do not believe, you have your people. Your working men have shown us, during the Lancashire famine, how *they* can feel for the down-trodden and oppressed. Appeal to them. I have lived long enough in England to know what their answer would be.

"I am, Dear Friend, Yours,
"GIUSEPPE MAZZINI."

CHAPTER II

"λαμπάδια ἔχοντες, διαδώσουσιν ἀλλήλοις."

"They, bearing torches, will pass them on from hand to hand."
PLATO, *Repub.*, 328.

OUR appeal, we decided, must be made to the Nation. Letters had previously been written by us during the autumn of 1869 to every member of both Houses of Parliament, and to many leading men, lay and ecclesiastical. To all these letters we received only some half-dozen responses which were at all sympathetic. We received others which contained only a strong denunciation of my own and other women's action in the matter. These latter came in some cases from highly esteemed dignitaries in Church and State, several of whom, I am grateful to acknowledge, wrote to me some years afterwards in a wholly different tone.

Having received so little encouragement from the persons whom we had vainly imagined would have taken an interest in the question, we turned to the working populations of the Kingdom. Here our reception was wholly different. I am well aware that the working classes have their faults, and that neither they nor any other class of men are wholly free from the taint of egotism; but of one thing I am profoundly convinced, and that is, that when an appeal is made to the people in the name of justice, they will in general respond in the truest and most loyal manner. Though I had always had confidence in the good sense of the working classes, I was, nevertheless, often surprised to find how readily they were carried up to the highest standard in judging of a moral question, and how almost universally they acknowledged the authority of the ethical truths which we endeavoured to put before them. At times I recollect purposely placing the question on so high a level that I doubted whether the mass of humble people before me would fully apprehend and respond to an appeal based upon motives so lofty. Sometimes a few moments of profound silence would follow such an appeal, and then there would arise that grateful and inspiring sound of the voice of the multitude, deliberately, intelligently and enthusiastically accepting and endorsing the thought which had been presented to them.

Starting from Liverpool with my husband's benediction sounding in my ears, I went first to Crewe, and addressed a meeting prepared in advance by our friend Professor Stuart, of Cambridge, consisting of railway workmen, engine-makers and boiler-fitters. They perfectly understood the message, and acted upon it with intelligence. From there I went (January, 1870) to Leeds, Newcastle, Sunderland, Darlington, and other places, and shortly afterwards a series of visits was paid to Birmingham and other towns of the Midland district. Everywhere the working men themselves organised meetings, writing or telegraphing in advance to friends and acquaintances in other localities to be prepared to give their verdict upon a very urgent question. The meetings were followed by prompt organisation for action, headed in most cases by leading working men. In Leeds, the Trades Union and other leaders worked valiantly with Mr. Algernon Challis at their head, whose ardour and self-sacrifice in this cause deserve to be specially mentioned; and in Newcastle, Lord Armstrong's and Mr. Hawthorne's men, engaged in the engineering works on Tyneside, supported us strongly. In Birmingham a very complete working men's organization was at once formed, an example followed some time after by Sheffield, Liverpool, and other towns. Petitions were poured in upon Parliament, and at bye-elections the candidates were severely questioned by the working men electors. Such was the effect produced by this movement in the Northern and Midland counties, followed by the lessons of the Colchester Election, that the

Government felt obliged to move in the matter. It moved in the direction in which Governments generally move when a question is raised by the people on which the members of the Government themselves have little knowledge and less conviction—they appointed a Commission to consider it. We did not accept the proposal of a Commission at all gratefully, for we felt that although Royal Commissions and Parliamentary Committees are useful, or necessary, in regard to some subjects, the cause we had in hand could not be served, or usefully treated, by a Commission. Great principles cannot be modified by any assembly, even of the wisest men, sitting to consider them. The people had very largely already pronounced their verdict on the principles of Justice, Equality, and Morality involved in our question.

The Abolitionist associations, in presenting a united protest to Government against the appointment of a Commission gave as one of their motives the following:—

"Because we maintain that the great principles which have hitherto protected the freedom, the honour, and the bodily safety of Englishwomen, as well as Englishmen, from the tyrannical control of the Executive, ought not to be referred for discussion to any irresponsible and delegated body: least of all to a Royal Commission. They must be vindicated as axioms, not debated as doubtful questions, and on the floor of Parliament itself, where every word may be heard by the nation."

There was no unanimous conclusion arrived at by the Commission. They produced a Majority Report, which pronounced itself hostile to us, at the same time that it condemned the compulsory treatment of the persons of women, which is the centre and core of the whole system of State Regulation of vice. There was a Minority Report, in our favour; while several of the members of the Commission personally recorded their opinion, apart from, or in addition to either of the Reports.[1]

---

[1] The members of the Commission were: the Right Hon. William

Generally speaking, the evidence given by our opponents served our cause in after years as well as, or better than, anything said by our friends.

It may not be uninteresting to recall the varied character of some of the meetings which were constantly held throughout the country during the first two or three years of our movement. The denial to us of publicity in the press made it of urgent necessity that we should continually address the public in other ways. I will mention briefly one or two of the meetings of those first years which stand out most prominently in my memory. After several large gatherings in Leeds, promoted by the energy and enthusiasm of the working people there, strongly aided by members of the Society of Friends, a larger assembly than any yet held was organised in that town. The Town Hall being found inadequate for the occasion, Mr. Challis and his friends managed to place seats in a considerable portion of the immense Corn Exchange, which in the evening was filled to overflowing, many hundreds standing during the whole time. On the platform we had an encouraging array of M.P.'s, the most prominent as a speaker being Mr. Jacob Bright, who, with his talented wife, was from the first one of the foremost in our cause.

The most interesting speech of the evening was, however, made by the well-known anti-slavery leader, George Thomson. He was then growing old, and was in failing health. His

Nathaniel Massey, the Right Hon. Viscount Hardinge, the Right Rev. the Bishop of Carlisle, the Right Hon. Sir John Pakington, Bart., M.P., the Right Hon. General Peel, the Right Hon. W. F. Cowper-Temple, M.P., Sir John Salisbury Trelawney, Bart, M.P., Sir Walter Charles James, Bart., Vice-Admiral Collinson, C.B., Charles Buxton, Esq., M.P., Major O'Reilly, M.P., Peter Rylands, Esq., M.P., A. J. Mundella, Esq., M.P., Professor T. H. Huxley, the Rev. Canon Gregory, M.A., the Rev. Frederick Denison Maurice, the Rev. John Hannah, D.C.L., S. Wilks, Esq., M.D., John Henry Bridges, Esq., M.D., T. Holmes, Esq., F.R.C.S., George E. Paget, Esq., M.D., Holmes Coote, Esq., F.R.C.S., George Campbell, Esq., D.C.L., George Woodyatt Hastings, Esq., Mr. Robert Applegarth.

zeal for our cause led him to stand upon our platform, but with no idea of speaking. As the evening went on, however, the fire of the old anti-slavery apostolate was re-kindled in his heart, and he could not hold his peace. I recollect his tall and fragile figure as he rose. He supported himself against a pillar, leaning heavily. He began to speak in a low, husky voice, in the midst of hushed attention; for the audience looked upon him as little less than an oracle on any subject connected with the sacredness of the human person and of individual liberty. Before he had spoken many minutes he became perfectly audible, and his voice continued to rise until it sounded forth with the old bell-like, or rather trumpet-like, clearness and power which had so often stirred the heart of multitudes in the United States. That remarkable utterance was one of the last delivered by him; I well recollect the profound emotion which was produced by it.

As a rule we had weighty meetings, and found an excellent spirit, in Scotland; but there was one occasion on which we were for the moment baffled. This was in the great City Hall in Glasgow. The medical students of that town, incited (it was said) by some of their own Professors, came in a body to the hall, determined that we should not have a hearing. There were Town Councillors—or, as they are called in Scotland, Baillies—on the platform. Notwithstanding this, the noise, violence and rudeness of the students continued for about an hour, until the patient chairman made up his mind quietly to call in the police, although we never liked resorting to this measure. The police of Glasgow were a powerful body of men, physically speaking. It was with some amusement, mingled, perhaps, with a little compassion for the misguided boys, that we watched from the platform, where we had been unable to speak a single word, these huge officers entering quietly from the gallery behind, taking the students one by one by the collar, and dropping them over the edge of the galleries as lightly as if they had been kittens. The fall was not a great one, and no one was hurt. The meeting was then continued in peace, though much curtailed.

I asked one of the venerable Baillies on the following day to define for me the exact offence for which some of these students, we were told, had been locked up for the night, or fined. His reply was in broad Scotch, more racy, perhaps, than clearly judicial. " They were punished," he said, " for the offences of barking like dogs, mewing like cats, crowing like cocks, whistling and rattling with their sticks."

From letters written to my husband at home, I take a sketch of some meetings held in my own border county to illustrate the honesty of judgment which we generally found in the North.

" At Berwick-on-Tweed I stayed at the house of the Mayor, Mr. Purvis, a pleasant old gentleman of the old school. There was a great threatening of opposition, which continued even till we drove up to the door of the Town Hall. We were told that the doctors were all ready to fight. The United Presbyterians and other Scottish ministers were my best friends here. The Rev. Dr. Cairns was timid about holding a meeting, although he was wholly in sympathy with us, and he did not at first like the advocacy of ladies. He is a man of much influence in the Scotch Church, and is said to be one of Sir William Hamilton's most distinguished pupils. On reaching the platform he offered up a fervent prayer. It was a full and excellent meeting, and, towards the close, unanimous. The joy of the ministers and kind ladies afterwards was very great. I had heard so much of the approaching opposition that I had prepared my arguments with great care. I quoted the weighty evidence of Lord Frederick FitzClarence against the regulation system in India. You know that he lived at Etal. His name is remembered here in the North, and the audience seemed struck by his verdict, based upon his experience as Commander-in-Chief of the forces in India. Dr. C——, of Berwick, had been put up to oppose us. He came to curse, and lo! he blessed us altogether; that is to say, he came on the platform and applauded as heartily as any one. This so often threatened opposition, which is so often overruled, shows, I think, how slight is the knowledge most people in England have of the subject, and how ready they are to take up the cry initiated by a few experts or great personages in favour of this regulation system. It shows, too, that we need only to appeal to their better judgment and sense of justice. Of course, there are everywhere some bad people as well as good ; but I imagine there are few of the ruffianly class of men in Northumberland who troubled us so much in South Wales. I shall go back to my home with a deeply grateful feeling to my own county.

"I had not thought of visiting other towns in Northumberland, but poor little Alnwick gave me the most pressing invitation which I have had from any town. A leading man there wrote, 'You surely will not leave your own county without visiting us. We should feel much hurt.' I did not expect opposition at Alnwick. I thought the only difficulty might be to keep my audience awake ! When I arrived I found the Town Hall already crowded to excess. I dare say the meeting was an exciting event in the dull old town. A brave doctor took the chair for me. He read a carefully prepared speech which he had written, in which he expressed the fullest sympathy with our cause. He had come into the room with splashed riding boots, as if from a visit to a distant patient, and with a weather-beaten face. I have a great respect for these hard-working country doctors ; they are very unlike some insolent State physicians whom we know, who seem to desire to rule us all on their own materialistic and despotic principles. A strong resolution was passed unanimously at Alnwick. At the end of the meeting I observed a number of pleasant brown faces at the edge of the platform, looking up in the attitude of the cherubs in Raphael's 'Madonna di San Sisto.' They seemed to have some communication for me, and when I came forward they smiled, and one said, 'We all knew your father well—old Mr. Grey.' This was all their communication, but I was pleased with the sympathy expressed in it.

"I then went on to Morpeth. The meeting there had not

been much prepared, for the time was short. We had no Chairman. I met the Hon. and Rev. Vicar walking down the street, and asked him to take the Chair, but he said, with many assurances of respect for you and me, that he had signed a petition in favour of the vice-regulating Acts, and that, therefore, it would not be consistent for him to take the chair. In the ante-room of the hall I saw a very superior working man, a man who bears so high a character, I was told, that although of humble rank, no one, they said, would more recommend the movement in Morpeth by leading it. I asked him to preside. He seemed startled, thought for a moment, and then said, ' Well, if ye'll just wait till I run in and put on my best coat.' He soon returned with his best coat, his face shining with soap, and his hair stiffly brushed. The hall was quite crowded with a very respectable audience —all the tradespeople, many pleasant ladies, ministers, working men, and a few gentlemen. I think I never spoke to so agreeable an audience. Their grave, sensible faces were so intent and full of inquiry. Many of the men stood up and leaned forward, and if the meeting expressed approval of any sentiment there was immediately a sound of ' hush ' through the hall, lest they should lose a single word spoken. The attention did not flag for one moment. An allusion I made to my father, speaking of myself as a Northumbrian, was most affectionately responded to. I felt supremely comfortable, for it was a thoroughly Northumbrian atmosphere. The audience was grave and shrewd, not noisily enthusiastic, but just and fair, and very warm-hearted; and also of superior intelligence; they quickly took up the constitutional and political aspect of the question.

" After the meeting the Chairman took me into his bright kitchen, as there was still an hour to wait for the night mail. I sat by the fire, and a circle sat round—his handsome, comely wife and daughter, and his son, who had all been to the meeting. His wife is a grand, clever woman. What a difference there is between the intellect of such working women and some Society ladies whom I have met! I could make a companion of this woman at any time. I had a lovely walk to the station, and as the train was not due for half an hour I wandered a little way into the fields. It was a perfectly beautiful moonlight night—the air calm, crisp, and not too cold. A light hoar-frost lay like a coating of silver on the fields in the moonlight. The silence, the calm, the pure air, and the beauty around me, with the memory of the kind reception I had had, filled my heart with gratitude. I sent many loving thoughts to you all at home. At last the express broke upon the stillness, bowling along with its red eyes in front, and brought me to Newcastle in little more than half an hour, where I found my kind Quaker friends waiting for me."

Besides influencing electors throughout the country, we felt it our duty to fling ourselves into the midst of contested Parliamentary elections now and again. At this time the question of our army was much before the Government, and there was a strong desire for a more capable administration of military matters, both at home and abroad. An able military man was wanted in the Government. Sir Henry Storks was a man of world-wide experience, and of great reputation as an administrator. He had been Governor of Malta, and had there administered the Regulation system with so strong a hand that he boasted of having practically stamped out in that colony the diseases incident to vice. The Government had a special interest in securing this man for one of the new offices which had been created in the War Department. To this end it was necessary that a seat in the House of Commons should be found for him. His first essay in that direction was at Newark. There he was strongly opposed, even by persons of his own political party, and chiefly by our excellent medical friends Dr. Bell Taylor and Mr. Worth, and a group who followed them. He was signally defeated in his attempt to secure the seat there. Colchester was next regarded as a place which would be easily won for this purpose. It is a military depôt; the system we opposed was **in full operation** there, and a Liberal candidate had been called for. I must give some prominence to this hotly-contested election at Colchester, as it proved to be somewhat of a turning-point in the history of our crusade.

The Shield, commenting on the result, wrote as follows:—
"Sir Henry Storks' name is prominently identified with legislation which is abhorrent to the moral sense of right-thinking people. Our opponents may laugh at the formation of a *new party* on this question, just as their prototypes in America were filled with derision when a 'nigger party' was first organized in that country. This new party here is to the cause of insulted and down-trodden woman what the American Abolitionists were to the despised negro. Our opponents are welcome to their hilarity. All the coarse satire, all the virulent abuse, all the disgraceful rowdyism in the world, will not prevent votes and seats being lost by the party which has employed these ignoble tactics. Mobs were freely employed at Colchester. There was a saturnalia of rioting which those who are so sensitive about the antics of mobs in Paris and New York would do well to take to heart."

The Committee of the National Association in London undertook the formidable business of organizing opposition to the Government candidate. Their tactics and measures were excellent, and ultimately successful. Dr. Baxter Langley very unselfishly consented to be put up as a third candidate in order to divide the votes. The battle was a severe one, for those were the days of hustings harangues, and open voting. The former I have always considered a very useful and healthy outlet for the free expression of opinion and the judgment of the people concerning their candidates and the principles proclaimed by them.

My own personal recollections are chiefly of the numerous meetings which we Abolitionists held for consultation day after day in a modest hotel, the master of which was favourable to our views.

A great public meeting had been arranged for in the theatre. I was with our friends previous to this meeting in a room in this hotel. Already we heard signs of the mob gathering to oppose us. The dangerous portion of this mob was headed and led on by a band of keepers of houses of prostitution in Colchester, who had sworn that we should be defeated and driven from the town. On this occasion the gentlemen who were preparing to go to the meeting left with me all their valuables, watches, etc. I remained alone during the evening. The mob were by this time collected in force in the streets. Their deep-throated yells and oaths, and the horrible words spoken by them, sounded sadly in my ears. I felt more than anything pity for these misguided people. It must be observed that these were not of the class of honest working people, but chiefly a number of hired roughs, and persons directly interested in the maintenance of the vilest of human institutions. The master of the hotel came in, and said in a whisper, "I must turn down the lights; and will you, Madam, consent to go to an attic which I have, a little apart from the house, and remain there until the mob is quieter, in order that I may tell them truly that you are not in the house?" I consented to this for his sake. His words were emphasised at the moment by the crashing in of the window near which I sat, and the noise of heavy stones hurled along the floor, the blows from which I managed to evade. Our friends returned in about an hour, very pitiful objects, covered with mud, flour, and other more unpleasant things, their clothes torn, but their courage not in the least diminished. Professor Stuart, who had come purposely during the intervals of his duties at Cambridge to lend his aid in the conflict, had been roughly handled. Chairs and benches had been flung at him and Dr. Baxter Langley; and a good deal of lint and bandages was quickly in requisition; but the wounds were not severe.

I should have prefaced my recollections of this Election Conflict by saying that on our first arrival in Colchester we went, as was our wont, straight to the house of a Quaker family. Mrs. Marriage, a well-known member of the Society of Friends, received us with the utmost cordiality and self-possession.

At her suggestion we began our campaign with a series of devotional meetings, gathering together chiefly women, in groups, to ask of God that the approaching events might be over-ruled for good, and might open the eyes of our Government to the vital nature of the cause for which we were incurring so much obloquy. Among the women who helped us most bravely were Mrs. King and Mrs. Hampson; there were also many others.

I may be excused, perhaps, for mentioning an amusing incident of the election. I was walking down a bye-street one evening after we had held several meetings with the wives of electors, when I met an immense workman, a stalwart man, trudging along to his home after work hours. By his side trotted his wife—a fragile woman, but with a fierce determination on her small thin face. At that moment she was shaking her little fist in her husband's face, and I heard her say, "Now you know all about it; if you vote for that man Storks, Tom, *I'll kill ye.*" Tom seemed to think that there was some danger of her threat being put in execution. This incident did not represent exactly the kind of influence which we had entreated the working women to use with their husbands who had votes, but I confess it cheered me not a little.

The following letter, which I have found among some preserved by my children, may be interesting. It was written from Colchester to my young sons at home :—

"I have tried several Hotels; each one rejects me after another; at last I came to a respectable Tory Hotel, not giving my name. I had gone to bed, very tired, and was dropping asleep, when I heard some excitement in the street and a rap at my door. It was the master of the hotel; he said, 'I am sorry, madam; I have a very unpleasant announcement to make.' 'Say on,' I replied. He said, 'I find you are Mrs. Josephine Butler, and the mob outside have found out that you are here and have threatened to set fire to the house unless I send you out at once.' I said, 'I will go immediately; but how is it that you get rid of me when you know that though I am a Liberal, I am practically working into the hands of Colonel Learmont, the Conservative candidate?' He replied: 'I would most gladly keep you, madam; undoubtedly your cause is a good one; but there is a party so much incensed against you that my house is not safe while you are in it.' He saw that I was very tired, and I think his heart was touched. He said, 'I will get you quietly out under another name, and will find some little lodging for you.' I packed up my things, and he sent a servant with me down a little bye-street, to a small private house of a working man and his wife. Next day I went to the C—— Inn, the headquarters of our party. It was filled with gentlemen in an atmosphere of stormy canvassing. The master of the inn whispered to me, 'Do not let your friends call you by your name in the streets.' A hurried consultation was held as to whether our party should attempt to hold other public meetings or not. It seemed uncertain whether we should get a hearing, and it was doubtful if I personally would be allowed by the mob to reach the hall where we had planned to hold a women's meeting. Some of the older men said, 'Do not attempt it, Mrs. Butler; it is a grave risk.' For a moment a cowardly feeling came over me as I thought of you all at home; then it suddenly came to me that now was just the time to trust in God and claim His loving care; and I want to tell you, my darlings, how He helped me, and what the message was which He sent to me at that moment. I should like you never to forget it, for it is in such times of trial that we feel Him to be in the midst of us—a living Presence—and that we prove the truth of His promises. As I prayed to Him in my heart, these words came pouring into my soul as if spoken by some heavenly voice: 'I will say of the Lord, He is my refuge and my fortress: my God; in Him will I trust. Surely He shall deliver thee from the snare of the fowler, and from the noisome pestilence. He shall cover thee with His feathers, and under His wings shalt thou trust; His truth shall be thy shield and buckler. Thou shalt not be afraid for the terror by night; nor for the arrow that flieth by day; nor for the pestilence that walketh in darkness; nor for the destruction that wasteth at noonday. A thousand shall fall at thy side, and ten thousand at thy right hand; but it shall not come nigh thee. Because thou hast made the Lord, which is my refuge, thy habitation; there shall no evil befall thee, neither shall any plague come nigh thy dwelling. For He shall give His angels charge over thee, to keep thee in all thy ways.'[1] Are they not beautiful words? I felt no more fear, and, strong in the strength of these words, I went out into the dark street with our friends.

"The London Committee had commissioned the two Mr. Mallesons to come down to help us. I like them much; they are so quiet and firm. Someone had also sent us from London twenty-four strong men of the sandwich class, as a body guard! I did not care much about this 'arm of flesh.' It was thought better that these men should not keep together or be seen, so they were posted about in the crowd near the door of the Hall. Apparently they were yelling with the Regulationist party, but ready to come forward for us at a given signal. The two Mr. Mallesons managed cleverly, just as we arrived, to mislead the crowd into fancying that one of themselves was Dr. Baxter Langley, thus directing all their violence of language and gestures against themselves. Meanwhile Mrs. Hampson and I slipped into the Hall in the guise of some of the humbler women going to the meeting. I had no bonnet or gloves—only an old shawl over my head—and looked quite a poor woman. We passed safely through crowded lines of scoundrel faces and clenched fists, and were unrecognised. It was a solemn meeting. The women listened most attentively while we spoke to them. Every now and then a movement of horror went through the room when the threats and groans outside became very bad. At the close of the meeting some friend said to me, in a low voice, 'Your best plan is to go quietly out by a back window which is not high from the ground, while the mob is waiting for you at the front.' The Mallesons and two friendly constables managed admirably. They made the mob believe I was always coming,

[1] Psalm xci.

though I never came. Mrs. Hampson and I then walked off at a deliberate pace from the back of the Hall, down a narrow, quiet, star-lit street: about thirty or forty kind, sympathising women followed us, but had the tact to disperse quickly, leaving us alone. Neither of us knew the town, and we emerged again upon a main street, where the angry cries of the mob seemed again very near. I could not walk any further, being very tired, and asked Mrs. Hampson to leave me and try to find a cab. She pushed me into a dark, unused warehouse, filled with empty soda-water bottles and broken glass, and closed the gates of it. I stood there in the darkness and alone, hearing some of the violent men tramping past, never guessing that I was so near. Presently one of the gates opened slightly, and I could just see in the dim light the poorly-clad, slight figure of a forlorn woman of the city. She pushed her way in, and said in a low voice, 'Are you the lady the mob are after? Oh, what a shame to treat a lady so! I was not at the meeting, but I heard of you and have been watching you.' The kindness of this poor miserable woman cheered me, and was a striking contrast to the conduct of the roughs. Mrs. Hampson returned, saying, 'There is not a cab to be seen in the streets;' so we walked on again. We took refuge at last in a cheerfully lighted grocer's shop, where a very kind, stout grocer, whose name we knew, a Methodist, welcomed us, and seemed ready to give his life for me! He installed me amongst his bacon, soap, and candles, having sent for a cab; and rubbing his hands, he said, 'Well, this is a capital thing, here you are, safe and sound!' We overheard women going past in groups, who had been at the meeting, and their conversation was mostly of the following description:—'Ah, she's right; depend upon it she's right. Well, what a thing! Well, to be sure! I'm sure I'll vote for her whenever I have a vote!'

"I always expected when it came to an election contest on this question that men's passions would be greatly roused, and that the poorest among women would gather to us; and so it was.

"I went in the cab to the Priory, where all our friends were assembled, looking rather anxious and awed. Mr. Heritage said, 'I prayed for you all the time.' I have now got to my lodgings in the working man's house, which are very small, but clean. I hope to be with you on Saturday. What a blessed Sunday it will be in my quiet home!"

To my husband :—" Dr. Baxter Langley, I hear, has had a letter from Mr. Glyn, on behalf of the Government, entreating him to retire and let Sir Henry Storks get in. Mr. Glyn says the Government are 'quite aware of the vast importance of the question' we are contending about. They have never been aware of its importance till now!! Dr. Langley answers that he will *not* retire, and is ready to be stoned out of the town if it will advance our cause. It is cheering to see the consternation of Sir Henry Storks' party. The Government will have learnt a useful lesson by the dogged and gallant opposition made. Dr. Langley has quite recovered from the effect of the rough handling he has had. And now, do not fear for me, dear husband. My part is over here, so far as public action goes. God bless you all. If I telegraph to you it will be in the name of Grey ; you will understand."

On such occasions as these, my husband's calmness of faith was called into full exercise. His duties as Principal of a great school made it impossible for him always to accompany me to such scenes of labour and difficulty. But his faith was in proportion to his unfailing affection and kindness. On one occasion I was returning home from a distant town in the depth of a very severe winter. The train was delayed by the weather, extra engines having to be obtained to drag it through deep snowdrifts. Due in Liverpool (our home at that time) at seven o'clock, it did not arrive till some time after midnight. He met me at our door, and on my remarking that I feared he must have been very anxious about me (as many accidents had occurred) he replied, with an expression of countenance which was a revelation to me of his implicit trust in God : "No, I was not anxious (though I feared you would feel the cold), for I believe that no evil will happen to you, so long as you are engaged in this mission. God will keep you alive and strengthen you, until you have finished the work to which He has called you."

The day after the Colchester Election I was seated at dinner with my family when the following brief telegram arrived, containing only two words, "Shot dead." We understood that this implied the defeat of Sir Henry Storks. He was defeated by a large majority. Six hundred voters, it was said, who were Liberals, and would have voted for him had they not been enlightened on the subject of his views on our question, left the town on the polling day, or stayed in their houses and abstained altogether from voting.[1]

The moral of this election was not lost on the Government. They learned that this question was not one which they could trifle with or ignore. Some time after, Sir Henry Storks succeeded in getting into Parliament by becoming a candidate for what was then known as " a pocket-borough"; but his advocacy of the unjust and cruel laws in Parliament was reduced to a simple vote. He also had learned his lesson.

On a later occasion Mr. Lewis, of Devonport, a very strong advocate and practical supporter of the system we opposed, was defeated three times at three different places in his attempt to get into Parliament. I think his last defeat was at Oxford. I was not myself present at that election, but the battle was bravely and skilfully fought by Mr. Henry J. Wilson, now M.P., and members of the National Association. These were severe and very needful lessons for our opponents.

Shortly after the Colchester triumph an immense mass

[1] One of the utterances of the defeated candidate did, perhaps, more than anything else to turn the working men's votes against him, viz., this : in a public document regarding his Governorship of Malta, Sir Henry Storks had stated that he much regretted his inability to bring soldier's *wives* under the degrading and disgusting tyranny of this legislation.

meeting was held in the Free Trade Hall, Manchester. Mr. William Fowler, M.P., who was then our leader in Parliament, and had brought in a Bill for the repeal of the vice-regulating Acts, was among those on the platform, and with him were Mr. Jacob Bright, M.P., Rev. Nassau Molesworth, Mr. Thomasson, our true and staunch friend from the first, Professor Sheldon Amos, Rev. Canon Butler, and others. Mr. Bright spoke forcibly on that occasion. The crowded state of that great hall was an indication that the mass of the people were fully awake to the wickedness and danger of the legislation we opposed. We felt more and more that publicity was one of the necessary conditions of success for us. The stratagems of our opponents only raised deeper indignation because they were covert and secret. About 6,000 people attended that meeting, and yet, except in a local and partial manner, it was unnoticed by the Press. A marked feature in the demonstration was the wonderful silence of the assembly between the outbursts of applause which rang now and again through the vast building. Their attention seemed more than usually absorbed, and the temper of the audience was impatient of any interruption, lest a single word or sentence should be lost. There was a resolute earnestness and a sense of conscious power such as could only be manifested by a great audience of more than average intelligence and moral feeling.

My husband was called several times to bear almost alone the brunt of the opposition which arose occasionally at public meetings in which I took no part, or only a subordinate one. The chief of these was the Church Congress, held at Nottingham in October, 1871. It was a very crowded meeting, presided over by the Bishop of Lincoln, Dr. Wordsworth. My husband had prepared very carefully a paper on "The Duty of the Church of England in matters of Morality," in which he introduced, in the most refined and unobjectionable manner, the question of the regulation of vice. Such was the animus against our crusade at that time amongst the upper and more educated classes, that the moment his allusion was understood such a loud and continuous expression of disapprobation arose from that great assembly that he could not proceed. The majority of the clergy present had been carefully trained by evil advisers to consider this legislation an excellent thing, while there was a minority present who were better instructed, and who, the following day, came to tender to us their expressions of sympathy and offers of support. We had many times before heard rough and defiant cries, and noisy opposition at meetings, but never so deep and angry a howl as now arose from the throats of a portion of the clergy of the National Church. I watched my husband's attitude during the prolonged tumult. He continued to stand upright, his paper in his hand, with an expression of combined firmness and gentleness in his face. The President, Dr. Wordsworth, though wishing to do justice to a favourite old pupil of his own and to the subject, was forced to bow to the tempestuous will of the assembly, and to ask my husband to withdraw his paper and to sit down. William Lloyd Garrison once said in the midst of his great anti-slavery conflict, "A shower of brickbats is an excellent tonic." Brickbats are not so much in use in polite and clerical society, but hard words, groans and hisses supply their place to some extent as a tonic to the person at whom they are hurled. I do not think my husband required any such tonic; and as a matter of fact his keen sense of humour led him to recognise a somewhat comic element in this otherwise pitiful outburst of misguided indignation. He afterwards printed his paper in pamphlet form, and continued to labour, during such rare intervals of leisure as his arduous school work afforded him, to win personally the clergy of the Church of England to our cause. In this he was aided by other excellent clergymen, notably Mr. Collingwood, of Sunderland.

Professor Sheldon Amos afterwards said of this meeting: "Mr. Butler alluded to an objection frequently made, that it is not the business of the Church to meddle with politics, or to make the people discontented with the laws by keeping up such an agitation as ours. In other words, it is the business of the Church to encourage political indifferentism, to resist any progressive movement which involves changes in law, and to dissociate herself and her influence from all the most ennobling and invigorating parts of the true citizen's duty. On the contrary, it is a part of the Church's work to refine the critical sagacity of her children. The single-eye for moral purity is hard enough to retain amongst the distorting and blinding colours of earthly interests; it is for the Church and her ministers to be ever calling her children to the acceptation of an absolutely equal standard of purity and goodness."

In 1872, shortly after the Royal Commission had reported, Mr. Bruce, then Home Secretary, gave notice of his intention to bring in a measure as a substitute for the existing Acts. This Bill was printed on March 1, 1872. Its appearance marked an era in the crusade, for the controversy upon it, which arose in our own ranks, resulted in a great sifting of adherents, many of whom were not sufficiently clear-sighted to see its dangers. In fact, it was so cleverly drawn, the good being so mixed with the evil elements, that it required acuteness and careful study in order fully to comprehend its real tendency. It was finally rejected.

CHAPTER III

"Nor dream, nor rest, nor pause
Remains for him who round him draws
The battered mail of Freedom's cause."

IT may surprise some of my readers to learn that the first great uprising against legalised vice had much less of the character of the "revolt of a sex" than has been often supposed. We have heard much of late years, and more than we did when our abolitionist movement began, of the great "Woman Question" in all its various phases and developments. I never myself viewed this question as fundamentally any more a woman's question than it is a man's. The legislation we opposed secured the enslavement of women and the increased immorality of men; and history and experience alike teach us that these two results are never separated. Slavery and License lead to degradation, political ruin, and intellectual decay, and therefore it was that we held that this legislation and the opposition to it were questions for the whole nation at large.

We arose—we women as well as men—in defence of the grand old principles which happily have prevailed and constantly been revived in the Constitution and Government of our country since very early times until recently. It is to those principles, and to the successive noble struggles for their preservation, that England owes, in a large measure, her greatness; if indeed we may venture to use that word. Those principles, I have ever believed, and continue to believe, have their foundation in the Ethics of Christ; and therefore it is that they have endured so long, and prevailed against repeated and violent attacks. But they are being lost to us now. Slowly, gradually, they have ceased to be respected. They do not readily flow on alongside of all the Democratic tendencies of our times. All political parties alike, it seems to me, now more or less regard those principles as out of date, old-fashioned, impossible as a basis of action. My heart is sorrowful as I record this conviction. I recall the past of our country's history, with its loyalty and love for those great constitutional principles for which patriots have suffered and died, and for which we, in our struggle, were also ready to suffer and die. I contrast that loyalty and that love with the present prevailing loose notions concerning the worth of the individual, the sacredness of the human person, and of liberty. As I do so it seems to me that I am standing by the side of a bier, and looking on the *face of a dead friend.* If one writes a word concerning those principles now, there is scarcely a reader who does not turn over to another page, finding the subject dry and uninteresting.

It may be that, when present tendencies have developed into something like the fetichism of Socialistic State-Worship, with its attendant tyrannies and sufferings, there will be a reaction, and that men will be driven, in self-defence, to look back and remember the great moral and political truths, the sound and tried principles which have been lost sight of, and that by reviving respect for these, they will be able to plant them firmly once more even in the very heart of the Democracy of the future. But that time is not yet.

A very old-fashioned statesman, who lived more than a century ago, when urging his countrymen to retrace a false step, spoke the following words in Parliament: "If I had a doubt upon this matter, I would follow the example set us by the Reverend Bishops, with whom I believe it is a maxim, when any doubt in point of faith arises, to appeal at once to the great source and evidence of our religion—I mean the Bible. The English Constitution has its political Bible also, by which, if it be fairly consulted, every political

THE PRINCIPLES WHICH WE DEFENDED

question may and ought to be determined. Magna Charta, the Bill of Rights, and the Petition of Rights, form the Code which I call the Bible of the English Constitution." And so, in 1869 and the following years, seeing, as we did, a direct violation of the principles of just law in the enactments which enslaved the poorest and weakest in the supposed interests of a stronger and a less worthy portion of society, and fearing for the future of our country in consequence, we were driven to search the annals of our past history, to inquire into past crises of danger, and into the motives and character of the champions who fought the battles of Liberty. This we did with the keenness of search and singleness of purpose, with which, in an agony of spiritual danger, a well-nigh ship-wrecked soul may search the Scriptures and the teachings of Christ, believing that in His Word he has Eternal Life.

It is recorded in Whitelock's " Memorials " that in the reign of James I. Sir George Crooke obstinately opposed himself to certain corruptions in the Government, while others, though noble men also, wavered. The historian attributes this steadfastness to the influence of Crooke's wife, Lady Crooke, who continually urged him on, and bade him not fear to do right; and the following words are added by the historian :—" It were well for the country if our daughters as well as our sons were taught and confirmed in the truth, *that public virtue is to the full as important as private morality*, for then we should add a mighty strength to the buttresses of our integrity."

So far as I have been able to study history, I have never found that there was a strong, virtuous and free nation in which the women of that nation were not something more than mere appendages to men in domestic life. They were also strong for public duty, unwavering in principle, and courageous (in crises of danger) for the national defence. In contemplating the present and future of our nation, the dangers ahead, and its resources and means for regeneration, it is impossible not to reckon among the latter the development in the last quarter of a century of a multitude of truly patriotic women, none the less devoted wives and mothers, and an adornment to their homes, because yearning over their country, and far-sighted, not only for *her* vital interests, but for those of the other nations of the world.

The danger which threatened us, and the tyranny which had invaded us at the time of which I am writing, were of a two-fold nature; a moral as well as a very grave political danger. The former, most good men and women instinctively acknowledged. To fully appreciate the latter required probably more instruction in the laws and constitution of our country than most women then possessed; and we were driven continually to urge our fellow-workers to strengthen themselves for the warfare in which we were engaged by trying to master this part of the subject by grave reading and thought. I read again, at that time, attentively, the accounts of the great struggles of our forefathers on behalf of the freedom and purity of our English Commonwealth, and was, more than ever, deeply impressed with the fact that in striving for freedom they ever strove for virtue also, and consciously so, for they knew the vital character of the work they had in hand, and were, for the most part, men who feared God and maintained the purity of private and domestic life, while they defended even unto death, in many cases, the great principles of justice upon which our Constitution was based. And their women stood up side by side with them. Without pausing to wrangle, as has been too much the case in modern times, over the idle controversy concerning woman's "sphere," they simply came forward at the call of duty, armed with some knowledge of law and history, as well as of Christian truth, and were able calmly and clearly to meet and confute all who endeavoured to violate the liberty of the subject in his person or his conscience.

There seemed to have been a retrogression in the public spirit of women since that time. But, happily, in God's Providence, in the early years of our Crusade, the introduction of a great public tyranny again forced upon women equally with men the solemn question, "Where ought human legislation to terminate? At what point are we called on to decide, shall we obey God or man?"

It was clear to us from the first that the character and conduct of our opposition to the immorality and illegality of the vice-regulating laws must be decided by the depth and sincerity of the moral and religious convictions of the mass of our people. It was granted us, in response to the deep desire of our hearts, to perceive already at that time an approaching revival of moral faith and spiritual energy, simultaneously with the rapid advance of a materialism culminating in this frightful expression of medical domination and legislative tyranny. The opposing principles were about to meet in a great encounter; it seemed as if God's voice was calling us to gird on our armour, to watch and be sober. His eye was upon us. We became aware that from the first His hand had been guiding our action in connection with all this movement, and controlling the adverse elements; and we were about to learn more clearly than ever before the force of a spiritual and moral revival as an agency for political reform.

Our struggle, however, though bearing many points of resemblance to former struggles in defence of freedom and virtue, stood almost alone in one striking characteristic, viz., that in our case we had to combat distinctly a double violation of principles. Formerly, encroachments on our liberties did not always involve a direct outrage on public morality and the sanctities of family life. Tyrannical aggressions in former days were indeed ever the fruit of evil principles or passions in one form or another, of the lust of power or of conquest, the greed of gain, or personal indulgence or revenge; but the effect of such aggressions was not so directly to demoralise the people. The immorality was, more or less, confined to the tyrant and his immediate agents. But the legislation which we had risen up to oppose sowed broadcast the seeds of an immoral principle. It was a legistion which not only proceeded from an evil source, but forced evil upon the people.

By the expression of the above thoughts I am anxious to make my readers clearly understand that our early conflict in this cause was—at least for myself and the considerable group of firm and enlightened women with whom I had the happiness to work—much less of a simple woman's war against man's injustice, than it is often supposed to have been. It was wider than that. It was as a citizen of a free country first, and as a woman secondly, that I felt impelled to come forward in defence of the right. At the same time, the fact that this new legislation *directly* and shamefully attacked the dignity and liberties of women, became a powerful means in God's Providence of awakening a deeper sympathy amongst favoured women for their poorer and less fortunate sisters than had probably ever been felt before. It consolidated the women of our country, and gradually of the world, by the infliction on them of a double wrong, an outrage on free citizenship, and an outrage on the sacred rights of womanhood. It helped to conjure up also a great army of good and honourable men through the length and breadth of the land, who, in taking up the cause of the deeply injured class, soon became aware that they were fighting also for themselves, their own liberties, and their own honour.

Thus the peculiar horror and audacity of this legislative movement for the creation of a slave class of women for the supposed benefit of licentious men forced women into a new position. Many, who were formerly timid or bound by conventional ideas to a prescribed sphere of action, faced right round upon the men whose materialism had been embodied in such a ghastly form, and upon the Government which had set its seal upon that iniquity; and so, long before we had approached near to attaining to any political equality with men, a new light was brought by the force of our righteous wrath and aroused sense of justice into the judgment of Society and the Councils of Nations, which encouraged us to hope that we should be able to hand down to our successors a regenerated public spirit concerning the most vital questions of human life, upon which alone, and not upon any expert or opportunist handling of them, the hopes of the future must rest.

My cousin, Charles Birrel, wrote to me at that time as follows :—" You and your companion women have struck a note for which the ages have been waiting, and which even the Church itself, in its organised forms, has never yet intoned."

The year 1873 was not marked by any great event bearing upon our Cause in Parliament or in the country. But, on the other hand, it was marked by an accelerated movement generally on behalf of our principles in every part of the United Kingdom. The seed was abundantly sown during this year which was destined to bear a rich harvest later. At the end of this year there existed some dozen different societies in the United Kingdom working in accord towards the one object, and having committees and correspondents in more than six hundred towns.

First, there was the National Association, which moved its central offices, about this time, nearer to the House of Commons, and which continued to carry on the most active propaganda throughout the Kingdom, and at the same time to bring strong pressure to bear upon Parliament, and to watch every move of our opponents. Secondly, there was the Ladies' National Association, followed by the Northern Counties League, the Midland Counties Electoral Union, the North Eastern Association, the Scottish National Association, the Edinburgh and Glasgow Ladies' Committees, the Dublin Branch of the National Association, the Cork Branch and Belfast Branch of the same, and of the Ladies' National Association ; and, lastly, but not less important than any of the others, was the Friends' Association, consisting of a number of the leading members of the Society of Friends throughout the Kingdom, with the late Mr. Edward Backhouse as President. I recall some of the most prominent and honoured names in this Association, which gave to our cause from the first the weight of those qualities which seem almost peculiar to that body of Christians—great determination and calmness combined ; all the fighting qualities in the highest degree, together with a gentleness of manner and procedure which wins opponents and softens the asperities of conflict. Besides Mr. Edward Backhouse, we had the help and inspiration for many years of the late Mr. George Gillett and Mr. Frederic Wheeler. Many ladies, in fact I may say all the prominent ladies of the Society of Friends, came forward in our work, and those who were less prominent joined heartily and usefully in the rank and file.

This year was also marked by the fact that several other movements were inaugurated which resulted in very important reforms. These movements were begun and carried through by groups of the very same persons who had risen up against the Regulation of vice. The vitality of our Crusade appeared—if I may say so—to cause it to break through the boundaries of its own particular channel, and to create and fructify many movements and reforms of a collateral character. We felt that it was necessary, while combating the State Regulation of vice, and forcing our Government to retrace the false step it had taken, also to work against all those disabilities and injustices which affect the interests of women. Thus a Society was formed, of whom the great mover and promoter was Mrs. Wolstenholme Elmy, for obtaining for the poorer class of married women the right to the possession of wages earned by themselves, and which developed into the Married Women's Property Act. Another reform which we aimed at and attained, and in which Mrs. Elmy also took a prominent part, was the reform of the Mutiny Act. This Act released soldiers, both married and single, from all responsibility in regard to their children, legitimate or illegitimate. This we felt to be a grave injustice, and it was confessed on all sides to be fruitful of much mischief and misery.

Perhaps the most important of the Societies formed at this time was the Association for the Defence of Personal Rights, which embraced a number of points bearing directly upon the interests of women, and aimed at the destruction of many abuses which tended directly or indirectly to foster the great evil of prostitution.

I do not here mention the Women's Suffrage Movement, which took its rise before our Abolitionist Crusade began, and has continued to pursue its own distinct and separate aim unceasingly throughout the years which followed up to the present time, receiving an additional impulse, however, from the enactment of the injustice which the Abolitionists were banded together to overthrow, and from every other enactment which attacked or ignored the interests of one-half of the human race.

I cannot, without departing from the immediate subject of my Reminiscences, enter into the details of these or other movements which were carried on simultaneously with our central one, and only mention them in passing.

In this year an immense number of petitions were sent to Parliament, and also Memorials to individual members of the Government and the House. The working population of the country began to increase their activities, which resulted somewhat later in the formation of the Working Men's League for Repeal, beginning with a list of names of 50,000 working men, who enrolled themselves as members in a very brief time, and of which Mr. Edmond Jones, a working man of Liverpool, was the indefatigable and able President for a number of years.

In the autumn of 1872 an opportunity again arose, through an election at Pontefract, of reminding the Government once more that the claims of the Abolitionists could not safely be ignored. The Right Hon. H. Childers was obliged, by certain changes in the Ministry, to seek re-election. He had been first Lord of the Admiralty, and in that office it had fallen to his lot to administer the obnoxious regulations in connection with our Naval Stations. Several orders had been issued from the Admiralty during his term of office concerning the administration of the system at Plymouth and Portsmouth—orders which had shocked the moral sense of many persons who had not previously been able to see clearly through the conventional wording of the Law itself, the iniquity of the principles on which it was based.

Personally, however, Mr. Childers never seemed to me a very devoted adherent of the evil system. His advocacy of it appeared rather to express a confused comprehension of the matter than perverse moral obliquity. His official responsibility, however, made it impossible for our party to allow him to be re-elected without question or opposition. We did not hope to secure his rejection as a Parliamentary candidate. All we aimed at was the arousing again of the attention of the Government to a sense of the importance of our demands. A certain number of us, therefore, went to Pontefract.

On the first day of his canvass, Mr. Childers having engaged the Town Hall at Knottingley, to address the electors there at nine o'clock on the evening of the 13th August, the Abolitionists, wishing to have the first word, secured the same Hall for seven o'clock, agreeing to move out in time to leave the building clear for their opponents. Then Mr. Childers' party attempted to checkmate them by announcing that he would address the electors at a much earlier hour, and from the windows of the Buck Inn instead of the Town Hall. This enabled us to be present, and to hear what Mr. Childers had to say. He made the customary excuses concerning the delicacy of the subject, and asked those who desired it to be dropped to hold up their hands. Mr. H. J. Wilson here enquired whether he, as a non-elector (for Pontefract), might ask a question, and the reply from the window was, "No! you are not an elector, you are not wanted." Groans followed this answer, and a hubbub ensued. Mr. Wilson would have been roughly handled had not a body of working men placed themselves on each side of him, saying, "Stand still; don't move an inch; you shall be heard; ask your questions; we want to hear the answers." During this time Mr. Childers' chairman, carried away with passion, was trying to reach Mr. Wilson's head

THE PONTEFRACT ELECTION

in order to castigate him with his umbrella. The crowd swayed backwards and forwards, and Mr. Wilson stood firm, with a smile upon his face. Some questions were asked from the crowd, and not at all satisfactorily answered by Mr. Childers.

Suddenly a voice shouted, "To the Town Hall!" (for our meeting). The cry was taken up, and the crowd started in that direction. With some other ladies I had been watching the scene from a window, when several gentlemen came up to us, and proposed to escort us to the Town Hall by way of a quiet back street. Thereupon some of the working men cried out, "No; never go down by a back way. Come along through the middle of the crowd, and before their windows; we will protect you." Our progress to the Town Hall was thus converted into a sort of triumphal procession, Mr. Wilson walking first, with the Blue Book of the Royal Commission under his arm, attended by Mr. Edmondson and others, and loudly cheered by the crowd of men and women in whose midst they moved; while Mr. Childers and his friends looked with perplexed faces from the windows of the Buck Inn upon their retreating audience, which had gone wholly over to the opposition. It was not an encouraging scene for a Parliamentary candidate.

One of Mr. Childers' friends had, however, hurried to the Town Hall, and, reaching the platform before we arrived, offered himself as chairman. Mr. Wilson proposed another chairman, and a new disturbance arose, which lasted for about half an hour. Eventually, however, Mr. Wilson and others were heard with much attention and applause.

Mr. Childers' party retorted by attacking and dispersing a meeting of women the following day. We had arranged to hold this meeting of women in the afternoon, when Mr. Childers was again to address a large concourse from the window of a house. We had decided to hold our meeting at the same hour, thinking we should be unmolested. We had been obliged to go all over the town before we found anyone bold enough to grant us a place to meet in. At last we found a large hay-loft over an empty room on the outskirts of the town. We could only ascend to it by means of a kind of ladder, leading through a trap-door in the floor. However, the place was large enough to hold a good meeting, and was soon filled. Mr. Stuart had run on in advance and paid for the room in his own name, and had again looked in to see that all was right. He found the floor strewn with cayenne pepper in order to make it impossible for us to speak, and there were some bundles of straw in the empty room below. He got a poor woman to help him, and with bucket of water they managed to drench the floor and sweep together the cayenne pepper. Still, when we arrived, it was very unpleasant for eyes and throat. We began our meeting with prayer, and the women were listening to our words with increasing determination never to forsake the good cause, when a smell of burning was perceived, smoke began to curl up through the floor, and a threatening noise was heard below at the door. The bundles of straw beneath had been set on fire, and the smoke much annoyed us. Then, to our horror, looking down the room to the trap-door entrance, we saw appearing head after head of men with countenances full of fury; man after man came in, until they crowded the place. There was no possible exit for us, the windows being too high above the ground, and we women were gathered into one end of the room like a flock of sheep surrounded by wolves. Few of these men, we learned, were Yorkshire people; they were led on by two persons whose *dress* was that of gentlemen.

It is difficult to describe in words what followed. It was a time which required strong faith and calm courage. Mrs. Wilson and I stood in front of the company of women, side by side. She whispered in my ear, " Now is the time to trust in God; do not let us fear "; and a comforting sense of the Divine presence came to us both. It was not personal violence that we feared so much as the mental pain inflicted by the rage, profanity and obscenity of the men, of their words and their

THE PONTEFRACT ELECTION

threats. Their language was hideous. They shook their fists in our faces, with volleys of oaths. This continued for some time, and we had no defence or means of escape. Their chief rage was directed against Mrs. Wilson and me. We understood by their language that certain among them had a personal and vested interest in the evil thing we were opposing. It was clear that they understood that "their craft was in danger." The new teaching and revolt of women had stirred up the very depths of hell. We said nothing, for our voices could not have been heard. We simply stood shoulder to shoulder—Mrs. Wilson and I—and waited and endured; and it seemed all the time as if some strong angel were present; for when these men's hands were literally upon us, they were held back by an unseen power. There was among our audience a young Yorkshire woman, strong and stalwart, with bare muscular arms, and a shawl over her head. She dashed forward, fought her way through the crowd of men, and, running as fast as she could, she found Mr. Stuart on the outskirts of Mr. Childers' meeting, and cried to him, "Come! Run! They are killing the ladies." He did run, and came up the ladder stairs into the midst of the crowd. As soon, however, as they perceived that he was our defender, they turned upon him. A strong man seized him in his arms; another opened the window; and they were apparently about to throw him headlong out. Some of us ran forward between him and the window, thus just giving him time to slip from between the man's arms on to the floor, and glide away to the side where we were. He then asked to be allowed to say a few words to them, and, with good temper and coolness, he argued that he had taken the room, that it was his, and if they would kindly let the ladies go he would hear what they had to say. A fierce argument ensued. Meanwhile stones were thrown into the window, and broken glass flew across the room. While all this was going on (it seemed to us like hours of horrible endurance), hope came at last, in the shape of two or three helmeted policemen, whose heads appeared one by one through the trap-door. "Now," we thought, "we are safe!" *But no!* These were Metropolitans who had come from London for the occasion of the election; they simply looked at the scene with a cynical smile, and left the place without an attempt to defend us. My heart grew sick as I saw them disappear. Our case seemed now to become desperate. Mrs. Wilson and I whispered to each other in the midst of the din, "Let us ask God to help us, and then make a rush for the entrance." Two or three working women placed themselves in front of us, and we pushed our way, I scarcely know how, to the stairs. It was only myself and one or two other ladies that the men really cared to insult and terrify, so if we could get away we felt sure the rest would be safe. I made a dash forward, and took one leap from the trap-door to the ground-floor below. Being light, I came down safely. I found Mrs. Wilson with me very soon in the street. Once in the open street, these cowards did not dare to offer us violence. We went straight to our own hotel, and there we had a magnificent women's meeting. Such a revulsion of feeling came over the inhabitants of Pontefract when they heard of this disgraceful scene that they flocked to hear us, many of the women weeping. We were advised to turn the lights low, and close the windows, on account of the mob; but the hotel was literally crowded with women, and we scarcely needed to speak; events had spoken for us, and all honest hearts were won.

On the day before the voting day we held a serious consultation of friends in our hotel, and agreed to work all that day and night, and leave the town early in the morning, before the polling began; as after that we could be of no further use. We drew up a last appeal to the electors of Pontefract, and had it printed quickly. The appeal was short, and printed in large type. When night came, the gentlemen, about half a dozen in number, obtained a plan of the town, and mapped out their operations, each taking a certain district with the intention of going to every house,

AFTER THE ELECTION

and pushing this appeal under the doors, so that it might catch the eye of every householder first thing in the morning. It was already too late to secure its delivery in time by the post. The appeal was as follows:—

"ELECTORS OF PONTEFRACT.

"Pause, before you exercise your solemn trust, to consider whether the man can be worthy of your support who, for eight years, has been deeply implicated in the immoral, cruel, and treacherous policy embodied in the Acts we oppose, and in the Government Bill of 1872, which proposed to extend the principle of these Acts to the whole country.

"If you vote for Mr. Childers you endorse the sentiment that a holy life is impossible for unmarried men, and that women must be provided for them by the State, and sacrificed, both body and soul, to their lust—a sentiment which blasphemes God, insults manhood, and destroys both men and women, body and soul.

"As you will have to answer at God's judgment bar, will you uphold the man and the Government who would thus demoralise and ruin the nation?

"If you are Liberals, save your party by forcing the present Cabinet from their suicidal policy."

The night was fine and calm, and the moon shone down upon the quiet streets. The citizens seemed all to have retired early to rest after the heat and excitement of the day. I was sitting at my open window in the silence, and watched one after another of our scouts pass out of the hotel door and quietly glide away each to his respective district, carrying packets of our appeal to slip under the doors of the houses. When they had all disappeared, a solitary figure passed beneath my window, and a man paused, looking up. It was a member of the Town's Police. In a low but distinct voice he begged my pardon for addressing me, and then went on to express his sympathy and that of his fellow policemen in regard to the treatment we had received from the mob of assailants at our women's meeting and from the members of the Metropolitan Police. He spoke indignantly of the latter, and begged me to believe that had the Pontefract Police known of our situation they would have acted very differently towards us women, even if our cause had not been so just and good a cause. I felt grateful for these furtive words of kindness spoken in the silent night.

After several hours, and towards dawn, our friends began to return and quietly re-enter the hotel. Mr. Stuart had had some adventures. His district of action included an old Church and graveyard. The moon had set, and he, missing his way, wandered into this dark cemetery. After stumbling about for some time over the crowded graves, with difficulty he found an exit and regained the street.

We left the town betimes the next morning. The result of the voting was such as to prove to the Government that we Abolitionists were on the alert and determined, and the incidents of the Election contributed to open the eyes of Mr. Childers himself to the true nature of the question at issue, for he became later a convert to our principles.

The following letter was written to me after the Election by a working man of Leeds. He had gone over to Pontefract from Leeds after his day's work was done, solely for the pleasure of aiding our efforts by the distribution of papers and leaflets, though well aware that, in order to accomplish his purpose without failing in his duties on the following day, he would be obliged to perform the journey home (a distance of nearly twenty miles) on foot.

I say nothing of the self-sacrifice required to undertake such fatigue after the labours of the day. We were well used to such proofs of devotion on the part of our working-class supporters, and we knew that it brought with it its own reward:—

"MADAM,—I venture to give you a short outline of my proceedings. When passing down Bridge Street, Pontefract, with the bundles under my arm of papers which I got from

A WORKMAN'S REPORT

Mr. Edmondson, they were noticed by people in the streets, and more than one called after me, saying that if I went to Knottingley with them I should be thrown into the river. An incident occurred whereby I was on the brink of being torn to pieces. In distributing papers I spared neither distance nor persons—men or women—and after going the rounds of Ferrybridge and Knottingley, I called at an Inn. I got permission from the landlord to distribute in his house. I went round the room with the *white* papers first, and so far all was well; but I no sooner commenced with the red bills (Mr. Childers' colours) than the whole company rose up and surrounded me for the purpose of demolishing me and the few bills I had left. The uproar brought to my rescue the landlord and landlady, who remonstrated with their customers, saying, 'Fair play amongst Englishmen! one dog, one bone!' etc., during which I mounted upon a stool, and at the top of my voice shouted out that, with their permission, I would be glad to tell who and what I was, and would be happy to answer any question anyone liked to put to me at the close of my observations.

"In addition to this uproarious meeting, I held two open-air meetings, and have promised to send books and papers, etc., to certain addresses which I took down. My thoughts were now directed towards home. To say I was *tired*, to start with, is to give but a faint idea of my condition; it was a case of *must be*; therefore I cheerfully accepted the task, and, walking on through the night, I arrived home at 4.30 a.m., suffering more from want of food than the distance, for I could not get anything before I left, as everything was locked up. The road to Leeds I knew not; so, to get over the difficulty, when I came to finger-posts, I lighted matches and paper to read them by. The silence of my journey was only broken occasionally by the fluttering of game birds, or the sudden dart of a hare across my path. For a part of the time it was extremely foggy and dewy, so much so as to completely saturate my clothes, as though I had really been dipped in the river at Knottingley. I was a little drowsy during the forenoon, took a good sharp four-mile walk in the evening, and am now glad to say that I never was better in my life ; and, if necessary, I am fully prepared to accept the same amount of pleasure again in endeavouring to rid my country of these Satanic Acts."

In the winter of this year the annual meeting of the Trades Union Congress was held in Leeds. A Conference and a Public Meeting of our Associations were arranged to take place simultaneously. Prominent members of the Northern Counties League (Abolitionist) attended. My husband and I were there. We met in friendly conference, and by arrangement, the leaders of the working men, who were present in considerable numbers. There were Joseph Arch, Henry Broadhurst, George Howell, Mr. Pickard of Wigan, Mr. Banks of Newark, etc. ; several of these afterwards were elected members of Parliament, and their names are held in honour for their services rendered to the cause of labour. It is needless to say that their sympathies were wholly with us. At the public meeting in the evening the speeches made by some of these men were weighty and pathetic. I was most struck by that of Joseph Arch; he was followed by my husband, who expressed his own and my deep sympathy with the daughters of the working classes and the poor, from whose ranks so many of the victims of the social evil are drawn.

CHAPTER IV

" More than we hoped, in that dark time,
    When, faint with watching, few, and worn,
We saw no welcome day-star climb
    The cold, grey pathway of the morn.

" O weary hours! O night of years!
    What storms our darkling pathway swept,
Where, beating back our thronging fears,
    By faith alone our march we kept."

THE year 1874 was a period of great depression and discouragement for our cause, while in that same year were recorded, more openly than ever before, the bold and vast designs of our opponents, the Regulationists, throughout Europe. For them it was the year of the greatest hope, and of the apparent approaching triumph of all their schemes.

Mr. Gladstone's sudden resignation of office in the early part of the year, and the dissolution of Parliament, took the country by surprise and confused the reckonings of our Abolitionist party, who had for some years laboured, and with considerable success, to win the personal adhesion, one by one, of the members of the Parliament now dissolved. Our faithful Parliamentary leader, Mr. W. Fowler, lost his seat in the General Election which followed. Several of our best friends in the House also failed to secure their return to Parliament. But still more unfavourable for us was the excitement which prevailed during the spring and summer concerning several other political questions important for the people at large, causing our movement to take only a secondary place for the time, even in the minds of many who were truly convinced and in earnest about it. Our principles, indeed, seemed to be scarcely represented in the General Election. Those among us who understood the vital and far-reaching nature of those principles, and who had learned wherein our true strength lay, now held many grave and rather sorrowful consultations. It was at this time that one of our most solemn agreements was formed for united waiting upon God. An invitation was sent to our friends and allies throughout the United Kingdom to join, on a certain day, in groups in their own towns or neighbourhoods, in order definitely once more to place this sacred cause, and everything connected with it, in the hands of the Omnipotent Ruler of all.

It will be necessary to go back in order to trace the growth of the Regulation system in Europe, and the increasing audacity of the pretensions of certain medical and administrative cliques, culminating in a vast design, of which I am about to speak. This sketch shall be brief, for it is not my intention in these Reminiscences to enter into any of the medical and police details, which we were forced for many years to look into and judge. The aspects of the question on which these bear are set forth in other works, which are obtainable in England and on the Continent; for at the time of which I am now writing, a vast literature from the pens of the Regulationists had already been produced. I may mention the most important of the works on that side, namely: a ponderous volume by Dr. Jeannel, of Lyons; a large and, from the literary point of view, meritorious work by Dr. Mireur, of Marseilles; two books by M. Lecour, Prefect of the Morals' Police in Paris, and others in German and other languages.

Up to the times of the First Empire in France, all regulations and laws directed against the social vice in the different countries of Europe were simply repressive, sometimes ferociously repressive, and in general taking effect upon the physically weaker sex only. Vicious men or women, who were hopelessly smitten by the greatest physical evil result-

MEDICAL SCHEMES FOR REGULATION

ing from vice, were generally expelled or forcibly isolated. In some towns of France at one period such were hanged! I have already indicated that it was during the profound disorganisation and misery produced by the wars of the First Empire that the system of the Police des Mœurs was first discussed, and in some cases established throughout the different countries of the European Continent. Gradually the contagion in favour of this oppressive and delusive scheme spread, until a complete network of regulations was formed, the meshes of which were drawn more tightly year by year. At first, in some countries, respect for individual liberty and for the private life of the humbler citizens, opposed a feeble barrier against the wholesale adoption of this system; but ultimately the hygienic question (considered solely from the materialistic point of view) dominated all others, and medical cliques sprang up in every country, claiming to be the sole repositories of wisdom concerning this great question which involves principles of justice, good government, economy, liberty, and virtue. This new-born medical tyranny, once having found its feet, never paused in its onward march, and it was generally acknowledged that the professional dictum of the doctors on this subject must become of absolute and exclusive authority. *Salis populi suprema lex* was their boasted motto, applied in a very limited sense, however, and, because (of necessity) indissolubly linked with police and Governmental tyranny exercised over one sex alone, it became a falsehood and a mere cloak for the most selfish and cynical system ever devised by the materialistic egotist.

Having now grown bold, the defenders of this system began to feel that there was only one thing more needed to crown their success, one step further to be taken in order to complete this vast network. In 1825 the Belgian Society of Natural and Medical Science had thrown out a feeler in the direction of extending the system throughout the whole of Europe. Ten years afterwards, 1835, this question was again discussed in Brussels by the Medical Congress of Belgium. In 1841 the Council of Salubrity of Marseilles discussed the question, and resolved on the desirability of unity of action among all the different European administrations. In 1843 there again was held a deliberative meeting on the subject in the Belgian Academy of Medicine. In 1852 the "International Hygienic Congress" met in Brussels and discussed "the legislative and administrative measures necessary to impose upon all Communes the duty of carrying out the Regulations." Finally, upon the invitation of the Belgian Government, the Belgian Superior Council of Hygiene elaborated in 1855 and 1856 a project for this purpose for all the Communes of their own Kingdom.

I cannot help remarking here on the fact that, while the public authorities in Belgium seem to have been the first to adopt, and, I might almost say, to devour greedily these evil principles first promulgated under Napoleon I., and while, up to some twelve years ago, the Belgian regulations were looked upon with profound respect by the defenders of this system in all countries as being the most perfect, the ideal form of this system, and the one which it was desirable should be imitated everywhere, later Belgian authorities, on the other hand, have been the first in Europe to take the initiative in endeavouring to throw off the yoke of this detestable tyranny. I say the Belgian *authorities*. In every other country the authorities have been slowly and with difficulty moved by the persistent action of different classes of the people, and the pressure of public opinion continued year after year. Nowhere except in Belgium has there been witnessed the remarkable sight of a Prime Minister with the majority of his colleagues in the Government, men of weight, and of serious character, deciding to endeavour themselves to bring about this reform which we advocate, and openly coming forward to announce their agreement with the principles of the Abolitionists. It is true that these honest men had been previously influenced—I may say, quietly educated—on the whole question by the "Belgian Society of Public Morality," the prime mover in which was M. Jules Pagny, of Brussels, who afterwards had the powerful support of M.

PROPOSAL FOR INTERNATIONAL SCHEME 59

Emile de Laveleye, a Belgian himself. But till the year 1890, when we were invited to hold our International Congress in Brussels, and, indeed, up to the moment in which I am now writing, no Government of any country except that of Belgium has placed itself at the front of this movement, mastering the whole subject with an admirable humility and patience, and studying the best means of combating immorality, beginning with the abolition of this great public injustice and iniquity, State Regulation of vice.[1]

To return. It was the example of Brussels in 1856, probably, which influenced the doctors of Paris to promote a great demonstration by inviting the International Medical Congress to meet in that city in 1867. At that Congress the question of a universal application of the Police des Mœurs was considered. In order to give more *éclat* to the measures there proposed, the Congress voted by acclamation, before beginning to discuss the question, that a Commission should be nominated at the end of the discussion which should be charged to visit the Governments of all countries to urge them to adopt a uniform system of medical police government in order to stamp out throughout the world the scourge of the physical effects of men's vices. Among the numerous papers read on that occasion the most important was that of Dr. Jeannel, which entered minutely into all the international measures proposed to be adopted.

In 1869, the same year in which our organised opposition to the system arose in England, the question of international action in favour of regulated vice was discussed at a Conference at St. Petersburg. In the same year the well-known Dr. Crocq, of Brussels, and Dr. Rollet, of Lyons, presented at the Congress of Florence a report which they had been charged

---

[1] Unhappily a *Projet de loi* which has since been proposed in Brussels as a substitute for the actual system contains all the old evil principles in a more veiled form. The sincere men who had embraced the Abolitionists' views had more or less retired from public life, and the work of so-called reform fell under the influence of experts who are not sincere in their aim.

to draw up by the Congress at Paris. This report concluded with a petition from the Commission to the French Foreign Minister, praying him to further the appointment of an International Commission in order to "draw up a uniform regulation which should have the force of law in every country in the world."

In 1873 the question was again brought forward in Vienna by the International Medical Congress held in that city. It had been somewhat cautiously, in the meanwhile, brought up at a Medical Congress in Rome in 1871, and again in Bordeaux early in 1873. It was at this Congress of Vienna, however, that the boldest and most triumphant note was sounded which had ever been heard from the Regulationist camp. The Congress demanded the prompt enactment of an international law in order to carry out their vast designs. A majority of the speakers on this occasion warmly recommended that the regulations of Brussels should be adopted as the model, one of them asserting, amidst the approbation of the listeners, that "*from the moment when prostitution shall become a regular and recognised institution, admitted and regulated by the State, its perfect organisation will become possible.*"[1]

We have strong evidence that the placing upon the English Statute Book of the law 1866-69 for the regulation of vice had greatly contributed to raise the hopes of the promoters of the international system which was aimed at. They looked upon the action of the English Parliament as a most happy presage; and from the year 1867 they had begun to act, with increasing determination, to multiply their assaults everywhere, and to arrogate to themselves the powers of legislators by drawing up endless Bills (*Projets de loi*) which they believed they would ultimately be able to impose on every nation. Everything pointed to the fact that they were about to strike a blow which should bring all the Governments of the civilised world down upon their knees before the

[1] Dr. Schneider, Report of the Vienna Congress, p. 49.

DISCOURAGEMENT OF THE REGULATIONISTS 61

great god of so-called medical science, and force them to conform to its will.

At this moment, however, a little cloud began to be visible on the edge of their vast and brilliant horizon. The Organising Committees of the Medical Congress of Philadelphia in 1876, and of one which was proposed for Geneva in 1877, learned with astonishment that certain doctors who were to be present at these meetings were coming prepared to oppose not only the great ideal International Project which had been so laboriously built up, but the principle and essence of the system of the Police des Mœurs itself. It would not do, they thought, to meet this opposition unprepared, or in any way to be drawn into a compromise. The Committees of these two Congresses therefore deemed it prudent simply to cut the question entirely out of their programmes!

From that time forward the International Regulation System which had been so imperiously demanded from the different Governments has been but rarely and very timidly defended. One may judge of the decline of the courage of the Regulationists by the ever feebler and fainter echoes of that demand which have been heard in every succeeding Regulationist Conference on the question, concluding by the Congress recently held at Lyons (in 1894), where the system of the Police des Mœurs only found three defenders.

On the 25th of June, 1874—the year of discouragement of which I have spoken—a few friends of the Abolitionist cause met to confer together at York. Their conference was in many respects a remarkable one. It consisted of a mere handful of the most steadfast supporters of the cause, who had come, some of them, from long distances. All were filled with a profound sense of the solemnity of the purpose which had brought them together. It was a time, as I have said, of deep depression in the work. Those who were present fully recognised the powerful array of organised forces against which they had to contend; they were filled with a kind of awe in the contemplation of those forces and the magnitude of the difficulties with which they were called to grapple. At the same time, every one of that group seemed animated by a deep and certain conviction that the cause would triumph. The circumstances under which this conference took place were such as to call strongly for the exercise of that faith which alone can animate reformers to contend against a sudden increase of an evil at whose destruction they aim. The voice of the Abolitionists had for a time been partially stilled by the clash of parties in the general election. For a time even the most energetic workers were unable to see what steps for the continuance of the work could most effectively be taken. Having hitherto felt themselves engaged in a battle for the abolition of the State sanction of vice in Great Britain only, they had become aware that a large and powerful organization on the Continent was seeking to increase the efficacy of the vice regulations, and for that purpose was appealing confidently to England to take the lead in organising under all the Governments of Europe an international scheme for the application of these regulations to every country, and to every seaport throughout the world.

After a period of silence for united prayer, the Rev. C. S. Collingwood, Rector of Southwick, Sunderland, addressed the little group around him in words which have never been forgotten by those who passed through the trial of faith of that year,—words which were assuredly inspired by God, and were His message to us at that period of anxious suspense. He said:—

"Our ceasing to be heard in Parliament for a time, or in the Press, or by public meetings, means necessarily so much clear gain to the other side. We have a most solemn charge, and cannot even maintain our ground except on the condition of ceaseless warfare. Much of the hostile pressure comes from abroad, and we shall do well to consider the propriety of carrying the war into the enemy's country by establishing relations with leading and earnest opponents of the regulation of sin, say in France, Belgium, Prussia, Italy, etc.; and

A SMALL BUT STEADFAST BAND 63

stimulating opposition in these countries, and perhaps holding our own International Congress. There can be no doubt that in all the countries subjected to this degrading system, a few sparks would create a great fire of indignation and revolt against the immoral system.

"Observe the world-wide schemes of the enemy—they will not rest till the whole world is under their regulations; and they have hitherto got all they wanted, until they touched the sacred soil of England. From the moment when that desecration was known opposition commenced. North, South, East, West, the Regulationists have marched without let or hindrance, and they dream not yet of anything but further conquests. 'What,' we may imagine them saying 'what are trifling checks at the Cape of Good Hope, or in the United States, or in Bombay?[1] What is a temporary delay in England to a party whose plans embrace the whole wide world? There are plenty of other fields to occupy. Only keep up a steady fire upon England; she is the centre of the position; carry England and you are masters of the world.'

"We must not suppose that it is only the *Lancet*, or a Mr. Berkley Hill, or a Mr. Acton that we have to face. Behind them is a sort of International League of the doctors, supported by the institutions of Continental Europe. What (they ask) are a few women, a few noisy agitators, a few hundred thousand petitioners, a few superannuated prejudices? Yes, what are we,—only a few Christian Englishwomen and Englishmen—what are we against so-called science, and all the allies it invokes, against Kings and Prime Ministers, many-voiced over all the face of the earth? What, with International Medical Congresses, International Conferences, Governments looking on us with contempt and anger, newspapers stamping us out, the majority of a most influential profession smiling scorn on our protests, all kinds of figures arrayed against us, even the

[1] We had gained, up to this time, the abolition of the system in the Cape Colony, and in Bombay; also in St. Louis, U.S.A., a victory had been won.

figures of our own insignificant minority, against the voice of civilised Europe—What are we to think?—to do? Should we not rest content with the verdict[1] of May, 1873, and leave the field to the undisputed possession of supervised vice? *No! a thousand times no!* We will remember the victory over Amalek, 'the first of the nations,' by a feeble people sustained by prayer; we will think of the stripling David, how he defeated Goliath with a sling and a stone; we will mark the vanity of Sennacherib's 'great host' and how it melted away before the might of God, invoked by the faithful Hezekiah; and time would fail to multiply encouraging facts which abound in modern as well as ancient times, and command those who defend God's cause never to despair.

"Some of us must remember how hopeless we used to think the abolition of American slavery. The constitution of the United States, the political power of the South, the apathy of the North, the attitude of the religious bodies, all made it seem the wildest of hopes. But we have seen it abolished, and we will never despair in any struggle where we are sure God is on our side. It is the blessedness of history, both sacred and profane, that when all the force is spent, and the noise of the times is over, it tells us of the power of the pure, the just, the true, and the impuissance of whatever has arrayed itself against these angels of God. As 'principles are rained in blood,' so they have their dark hours, which daunt no true man nor woman, but drive them to God's footstool, there to receive faith and strength for fresh encounters and new efforts. The weapons of our warfare are not carnal; we believe, and therefore we speak and fight; and comparatively few though we may be, we measure not our prospects of success by numbers, or weight, or metal; we recall those former Heaven-blessed struggles, in which the King's soldiers were as few and as feeble as we, and we know that we shall succeed if we faint not.

[1] Alluding to the Bill proposed by the Home Secretary, Mr. Bruce, which would have been practically a repetition of the Regulations.

"When Granville Sharp, in 1772, obtained the famous decision that a slave is free as soon as he touches English territory, he did not think it one of the first steps towards the general abolition of the slave trade and of slavery everywhere; but it was so; and thus, when some noble ones among us raised a cry of horror and indignation on finding that supervised vice had presumed to desecrate our English soil, they little guessed how far their voices would reach, nor what the work was upon which they unwittingly were entering, nor what the victories which they were to achieve. But they have already been able to produce great effects in Africa, Australia, and the United States; and, though still unsuccessful at home, we and they believe that the opposition which has commenced in England will obtain its utmost success here, and that a force of public opinion and true sentiment is being slowly generated which will cross all lands and seas, and in its progress sweep away everywhere the monstrous organisation of vice, against which we lift our voices to-day."

These words found an echo in the breasts of all present, and from that conference all departed feeling that a new era was dawning upon the whole movement, which could only lead to the final triumph of the cause of justice and morality, far beyond the limits of our own country.

This conference at York marked the first step in that great expansion of the movement which has called forth a protest against legalised vice in so many countries, resulting in an organised international opposition to that modern slave system. The meeting at York passed a formal resolution, not embracing any large scheme, but merely accepting, with approbation, a proposition to open correspondence with opponents of the Regulation system abroad, and requesting the Ladies' National Association, who had already several foreign correspondents, to commence operations, with a view to stimulate public opinion in Continental countries.

This work of opening correspondence, in accordance with the resolution above mentioned, was, in its beginning, an apparently feeble, as it was, indeed, a laborious undertaking, carried on somewhat in the vague and in the dark. Having obtained a list of addresses of philanthropic workers in various countries in Europe, I posted a brief appeal to every address contained in it, in the hope of drawing forth some expression of sympathy in our objects.

One little incident may illustrate the manner in which, before and during that campaign, every effort seemed to be providentially guided.

In August of that year I picked up, by what we call chance, a little book containing the names and addresses of persons connected with some international benevolent organization. I addressed a few letters to some of these, making an appeal on this question. One of these was addressed to a Mr. Humbert, of Neuchâtel. It never reached its destination, and, had it done so, possibly might never have met with a response; but the Neuchâtel postman made a mistake, as postmen sometimes, though very seldom, do. In this case it was a happy mistake. He took the letter to another Mr. Humbert, Mr. Aimé Humbert, who opened it. He was no stranger to the question. He had for years said to himself, "When I am more free from other public work, I must turn to this terrible subject."

Shortly afterwards I received a letter from Mr. Aimé Humbert, acknowledging my appeal as providential. I had told him of my projected visit to the Continent that same winter, and in reference to that he said :—" You are about to confront not only the snows of winter, but the ice that binds so many hearts on the Continent. Bring among us, then, the fire of that faith which can remove mountains. The breath of the most High can break the icebergs in pieces, and kindle a mighty conflagration."

It was one of the most severe winters of this century (1874–1875), but the opposition of the elements seemed a little matter in comparison with that of the prejudice, blindness and passion which threatened at first to block the way to success in such an enterprise.

As Mr. Aimé Humbert occupied for so many years a very prominent position in our International Federation, I may here give a brief account of his career previous to our becoming acquainted with him.

He was born in 1819, in the Canton of Neuchâtel, educated at Lausanne and several of the German Universities, and married, in 1843, Marie Müller, daughter of the Secretary of the Royal Consistory of Wurtemburg. At the close of the revolution which severed Neuchâtel from the crown of Prussia, M. Humbert, who was one of the principal actors in securing the freedom of his Canton, was called to take a part in its Government, and filled for ten years the office of Minister of Public Instruction. Nominated at the same time a Member of the Federal Parliament, he occupied for one year the Post of President of the "Chambres des Etats Suisses." The Federal Council charged him, in 1858, to act with the Minister Plenipotentiary of Switzerland, M. Kearn, in concluding the treaty of Paris concerning Neuchâtel. In 1862 he was entrusted by the Federal Council with a Mission to Japan, as Envoy Extraordinary and Minister Plenipotentiary, to bring about a treaty of Commerce with Switzerland. His very excellent work on Japan, which has given him a status in Europe as a geographer, has been translated into English.

In his character as a scientific man he was also appointed a Member of the École Polytechnique of Zurich, Corresponding Member of the Geographical Society of Geneva, and a member of the Honorary Committee of the International Geographical Congress of Paris; besides being appointed President or Member of many other Literary and Scientific Societies.

But before I go on to speak of our first essay on the Continent, I must record an event at home which gave a great impulse to our cause.

The defeat of the Liberal party in this year (1874), freed Mr. Stansfeld from the restraints of office as a Minister of the Crown. In July Sir Harcourt Johnstone invited a number of Members of Parliament to his house to discuss the position of the Abolitionist question. Mr. Stansfeld went there with others, and proposed that Sir Harcourt himself should move in the House for leave to bring in a Bill for Repeal. This he did.

On the 15th October a great public meeting was held in the Colston Hall, Bristol, at which Mr. Stansfeld made his first public appearance as a champion of our cause. It was a notable occasion. He was surrounded on the platform by a number of the best and most devoted men and women, who had worked from the beginning, and who watched his entrance upon this field of battle with a very deep and solemn interest. It was the first time that an ex-Minister of the Crown, a distinguished and recognised leader of one of the great political parties, had appeared upon our platform. It would be difficult to exaggerate the value of such service to our cause; but Mr. Stansfeld brought to it not only his widely known name, but deep convictions, indomitable courage and great eloquence. This, his first speech for us, attracted the attention of the whole country, and led to a discussion of the question by the press of the country, which for a short time abandoned the "conspiracy of silence," resuming it again, however, some weeks later. The *Times* sincerely regretted " that a statesman of Mr. Stansfeld's eminence should identify himself with such an hysterical crusade, in which it is impossible to take part without herding with prurient and cynical fanatics." The *Saturday Review* said that "Governments with real responsibility upon them cannot regard life with this primitive straightforwardness, and must be content to trust that what is required for the health of a people is also the most in harmony with Christianity." Which was a supremely haughty way of saying that if the methods of Governments and Christianity did not agree, so much the worse for Christianity.[1]

After an address of extraordinary power, **full of lucid**

[1] Mr. Benjamin Scott's "A State Iniquity."

argument, Mr. Stansfeld concluded with the following words:—" Full of a sense of special responsibility, I have dived down into the very depths of this question, and have impressed myself with the profound conviction that this system is immoral and unconstitutional, and calculated to degrade and debase the manhood and the womanhood of the country. I have watched the insidious materialism creeping over the country and entangling in the meshes of its wide-sweeping net many good men and good women unconscious whither they were going, and deceived by appeals made to them in the name of benevolence, and for the sake of diminishing physical suffering. I have seen good men and women, brave men and braver women master the intense repugnance which a refined and sensitive person must feel on such a subject; I have seen women with all their exquisite sensitiveness coming before the public to plead the cause of virtue against that of legalised vice; and I have marked these women hounded down, hooted at with unseemly language, gestures, and even threats, and I know that, were not the spirit of the law of this country too strong, their lives and persons might have been exposed to danger and to outrage, as the lives and persons of the Abolitionists of America were at the hands of the man-stealers and slave-holders of the South. I have marked these things. I have put my hand to the plough; I have cast in my lot with those men and women (for ever reverenced be their names!) who hitherto have led a hope which too long has seemed a forlorn hope; and never will I desist, and never will they desist, from this sacred agitation until these degrading laws are blotted out from the statute book for ever."

Mr. Stansfeld made no vain boast on this occasion. He has kept his word. He has fulfilled his promise. In numberless meetings at home and abroad, on many important occasions, his powerful advocacy of our cause has been heard, and up to the present time, in spite of the pressure of other public duties, and of the encroaching disabilities of age, he has maintained the same attitude; he has lent his powerful aid to the great question of Abolition in India, and never fails in his interest and helpfulness in any part of the work in which we are engaged.[1]

I left England for the Continent in December, 1874, and reached Paris, accompanied by one of my sons, my husband and my other sons joining me ten days later.

I was armed with some good introductions, or rather affectionate recommendations from English friends to all and every one who might consent to hear my message. One of these was signed by Mr. William Shaen on behalf of our National Association, of which he was the able President for a long period of years. Another was from the Friends' Abolitionist Society, and was signed by leading men and women among the Quakers. This body of Christians had gained the hearts of our Continental neighbours in a remarkable degree by their devotion to the sufferers (of both nationalities engaged) during and after the Franco-German War. I found their name a ready passport on several occasions. Lord Derby, our Foreign Minister at the time, very willingly gave me a letter, written from the Foreign Office, stating briefly my aims, and his desire for my safety and success. This last was useful in Paris.

It was bitterly cold. The streets of Paris were filled with melting snow, and a depressing fog hung over the city. After making several calls on members of the Protestant community, I went to the headquarters of the monstrous police tyranny in Paris. I gave an account of this visit, in writing, to one of our leading friends at home. I reproduce the letter here, as impressions recorded at the time are more vivid than those which we may try to revive after many years.

"*December*, 1874.

"I spent a part of yesterday at the Prefécture of the Morals' Police; it was an exceedingly painful visit to me.

---

[1] These lines were written while our revered friend was still living and at the post of honour among us.

I was struck in the first place with the grandeur of the externals of the Prefect's office, and the evidence of the political and social power wielded by that man Lecour. The office is one of those handsome blocks of buildings on the banks of the Seine. It has great gateways, within which guards are pacing up and down; a broad stone staircase, where guards stand at intervals; a number of official-looking men passing to and fro with papers, or accompanying people desiring an audience. I reached the top of the stone stairs and the Prefect's outer door, over which in large gold letters were printed the words: '*Arrestations, Service des Mœurs.*' I was faint and out of breath, and an old guard stared at me with curiosity as I gazed at those mendacious words, 'Service of Morals.' I knew it all before, but here the fact came upon me, with peculiar and painful vividness, that man had made woman his degraded slave by a decree which is heralded in letters of gold, and by a tyranny of procedure which, if it were applied to men, would soon set all Paris in flames, and not merely a few of its buildings. That *Service des Mœurs* seemed a most impudent proclamation of the father of lies; it so clearly and palpably means the '*Service de Debauche.*' M. Lecour's whole conversation showed that it is debauchery and not morals that he is providing for and serving.

" I entered, and was kept waiting in an ante-room for half an hour, until the great man had dismissed certain business. At last a venerable servant, in livery covered with gold lace, directed me to follow him. He ushered me into Lecour's audience chamber, a well-furnished room. His appointments and surroundings are more imposing than the room of any Minister of State that I have yet seen in England. There were two men in the room whose business was not yet concluded; why Lecour admitted me then I do not know; perhaps he was nervous about seeing me alone. He might have guessed that I would take stock of all I saw and heard. He was standing behind an imposing desk, with his visitors in front of him. He waved his hand majestically, and bade me be seated, telling the venerable servant to give me a newspaper to read. I pretended to look at the newspaper, but kept my ears open to every word which was spoken, What occurred left on my mind the most mournful impression. What a tragedy there seemed to be implied in the scene which passed! The first man Lecour asked to state his case was a gentlemanly elderly man, fatherly-looking, grave and sad; he spoke in a low, hoarse voice, and appeared to be making a great effort to repress his feelings; his voice and words were those of a man full of wrath and sorrow. I thought there was a look of suppressed vengeance about him. He leaned on an umbrella, clutching the handle tightly with both hands; there was a long altercation; on Lecour's side flippancy, sentiment, many words, and an apparent desire to get rid of the man by a few promises while making out a case against a woman for whom this man had come to plead. Frequently the Prefect lowered his voice so that I could not catch his words, while, in the midst of his gesticulations and talk, the other man repeated three times in a voice which I can never forget: ' But you accused her! you accused her!' Then I heard Lecour detail in many and rapid words how the woman (she might have been the daughter of the elderly man; she was evidently some one dear to him) had at one time been guilty of 'levity.' He hinted something mysteriously about her antecedents having been questionable. I longed to fling back the charge and ask the Prefect of his own antecedents, and the present life of the men for whom he now provides shameful indulgence. Lecour then told of an interview he himself had had with the woman (this seemed fearfully to agitate the elderly man), in which he described how she wept and showed signs of deep distress. 'I told her,' said the Prefect, ' that if I saw signs of a real repentance persevered in, I should *forgive* her.' These last words were spoken in a tone of conscious power and pride. The man Lecour appears to me—and I tried to judge without prejudice—very shallow, vain, talkative; his arguments are of the weakest; he has a certain dramatic cleverness, and acts all he says with face, arms and legs. His countenance

THE PREFECT

is to me very repulsive, although his face, which is in the barber's block style, might be called handsome as to hair, eyes, eyelashes, etc. He has a fixed smile, that of the hypocrite, though certainly he is *not* exactly a hypocrite. He is simply a shallow actor, an acrobat, a clever stage-manager. Probably he persuades himself of what he is constantly saying to others; intoxicated with the sense of power, chattering and gesticulating like an ape, at the head of an office which is as powerful as that of the Roman Prefects of the City in the time of Rome's corruption. And such is the man who stands in the position of holding in his hand, so to speak, the keys of heaven and hell, the power of life and death, for the women of Paris!

"The elderly man was not in the least consoled by the assurance 'I would forgive her,' and only repeated his sullen 'but you accused her.' I think he was pleading to get her name taken off the register of shame. That he did not succeed, and turned and left the room in silence with no salutation to the Prefect, should show to our Englishmen what a tyranny for *themselves*, as men and fathers, this horrible system may become. M. Jules Favre tells me that the head of the Government in France can do nothing without the consent of the Prefects of Police, permanent officials, stronger than the Government itself, and that MacMahon sends for these men first thing every morning to take counsel with them. Is it not a good deal like that wretched time in Rome, when the Pretorian Guards elected, deposed, or dictated to the Emperor of the time, and became themselves the most oppressive of tyrants?

"The second man who had an audience was of a different kind. He was a young, stout, overfed-looking man, and his conversation with Lecour was of a friendly character. The Prefect called him near to him behind his great desk, and much of the conversation was in whispers. It seemed to be concerning the internal economy of some of the protected houses of debauchery. The young man asked about the literature allowed in these houses, and Lecour deprecated certain journals, which were too republican, and ought not to be read by women. Lecour regulates the reading in these houses, and he turned to a great bundle of papers to show the young man those papers which were allowed. Lecour professed affection and esteem for the young man, and there was a kindness in his manner which contrasted strongly with his conduct towards the elderly man.

"Having dismissed his young protégé, the great man was ready for me. By this time anger had made me bold. I stood up before him, declining to sit. I told him who I was, and why I had come to Paris. He said he knew very well who I was. His manner became rather excited and uneasy. I continued all the time to look very steadily, but not rudely, at him. I knew that I, at least, was utterly sincere, and I inwardly invoked the presence of Him who is the searcher of hearts, that He might be there, a witness between us two. Instinctively, therefore, I kept my eyes fixed on the man to see if there was any sincerity in him. He became more and more talkative, as if to drown me with words; in fact, I could scarcely get a word spoken. I therefore just put a distinct question or two in the few pauses allowed, as if desirous of information, and then he started off volubly with his answers. This was useful to me, for he surely said much more than was prudent. I asked him the latest statistical results. He hesitated, but when I pressed for it he opened a desk and gave me a little book, the last written by himself, which has some curious matter in it. I asked if vice and disease were diminished or increased the last five years in Paris. He answered promptly, 'Oh, increased, they go always increasing, continually increasing'; these were his words (in French, he does not speak a word of English). Then I tried to hold him to a point, and get him to tell me the causes of this increase. He attributed it solely to two things, which I think will surprise you, *i.e.*, to the temporary ascendency of the Commune, and the increasing 'coquetry' of women. I could not restrain an expression of contempt at his last remark, which he seemed to think quite a satisfactory and exhaustive answer. I then made an onslaught, and said (looking up at a speck of blue sky, which I saw through the window, and holding on to it, as it were) that I —we—consider the whole system which he represents as an absurdity, because of its inequality of application; that men are immoral, and liable to the physical scourge of vice as well as women, while the system only attacks women; and that any theory of health, based on injustice and a supposed necessity for vice, must end in not only ridiculous and total failure, but in increased confusion and vice. He listened impatiently, still with his fixed smile. I purposely avoided speaking of morality or religion, and tried to nail him to the logical view of necessary failure through injustice and one-sidedness of application. Off he went again, denouncing women and their seductions. I interrupted him rather abruptly by reminding him that in this crime which he was denouncing, namely, prostitution, there were two parties implicated. I asked him if he had been so long at the Prefecture without its occurring to him that the men for whose health he labours, and for whom he enslaves women, are guilty in the same sense as women. This challenge as to the equality of guilt, and, perhaps, a little irony in my tone, roused him, and he became agitated and excited. He left his retreat, and came out into the room and paced up and down. He then acted, in the most disagreeable manner, an imaginary scene between a poor woman, a temptress, and a young man. He seemed to think that I was an ignoramus, and that this would convert me. He described in the old, hackneyed, sentimental manner with which we are familiar, an 'honourable young man' dining out, partaking *un peu généreusement* of wine; a girl meets him, marks his unsteady gait—and then he acted how she would place her arm in his and tempt him. There was no comparison, he said, between the two: the man was simply careless; the woman was a deliberate, determined corrupter. 'With what motive?' I asked, 'tell me, is it not often the case that the woman is poor, for I know that in Paris work is scarcely to be found just now; or else she is a slave in one of your permitted houses, and is sent out by her employers on what is their, rather than her, business?' He smilingly denied this and said, 'Oh, no, no, it was not poverty, it was simply coquetry.' Then he said in a pompous and would-be impressive manner, 'Madame, remember this, that women continually injure *honest* men, but no man ever injures an honest woman.' Then he stood as one who had cast down a challenge which could not be taken up. 'Excuse me,' I said, 'you, yourself, have written otherwise in your book. Here you speak of "wives and honest girls injured by immoral and depraved men."' Then he changed his tone and replied, 'Ah, yes, but all that belongs to the region of romance; I am only speaking of what can be recognised and forbidden by the police. The police cannot touch the region of romance; nor can the State. You would not desire that it should, would you?' I replied that I desired justice, but that I could not expect justice in this matter at the hands of the police. Then he suddenly assumed a solemn expression and changed his line of argument. He said, 'Madame, écoutez! moi, je suis religieux; I am as religious as yourself.' Then he said, as a religious man, he must admire the punishment of vice (in women only), and that when you could not punish you must regulate; that among all the plans the world has ever tried, which is of any avail, and the thing of which I would myself become eventually the advocate, when I had had more experience, was his own system, the system of arrests, constant arrests of women. He kept reiterating that he was as religious as myself, and I said rather sharply, 'That may be, sir; I did not come here, however, to speak to you about religion, but about justice.' To me they are one. The religion he spoke of was merely a bit of sentiment unworthy of the name. I brought him back to the failure, hygienically, of his system, on account of its injustice. He shrugged his shoulders and said, 'But who hopes to see perfect justice established? Who hopes for great hygienic results?' 'Those,' I replied, 'belong, I suppose, to the region of romance.' I thanked him for his information, and asked him to be so good as to give me a letter which would admit me to the whole of the St. Lazare. (The St. Lazare was then entirely at the Prefect's service, an immense prison, hospital, and general depôt for all the unhappy women of Paris, both for the vicious and those accused only of *vagabondage*, or who were seeking work and had no friends.) He summoned a secretary, and in a commanding way, directed him to write a letter giving me *carte blanche* to see everything. When the man brought it back, Lecour sat down and wrote a postscript, in which he requested 'that every facility should be given to the very honourable lady from England.' Then he signed it largely and stamped it with the stamp of the Prefect. So now I can go about under his benign protection. I smiled as he wrote, thinking of the shadowy fears which some of my friends felt when I was leaving England, lest I should be seriously annoyed by the police. How wonderfully Providence turns things upside down! Here was the very head of the much-hated Morals' Police himself sanctioning all I might wish to do with a great flourish, and full of vanity in the performance.

"I could now enter even any of the dreadful houses which are under his superintendence; his letter would be all-powerful. At the door, I suddenly remembered the case of an innocent Swiss girl I had found, whom his police are tormenting. I stated her case, assuming that he would at once give orders for her to be let alone. At this his smiling character suddenly changed for a moment. Almost spitting like a cat, he said, with sudden irritation, 'Mais quelles bêtises vous ont-elles dit!' and a strange expression came over his face. But he quickly recovered himself. He evidently was making an effort to produce a good impression, and to part friends. I felt very sad as I left his place."

CHAPTER V

"The curse which thro' long years of crime,
Is gathering, drop by drop, its flood."

THERE was a whole world of misery contained within the walls of the St. Lazare. As I reached the stone portico leading out of the street to the large gates of the prison, a huge prison-van rolled in under the arch, drawn by stout horses with clattering hoofs, and followed by *gens-d'armes*, also on stout horses, and armed. The van was on high wheels, and had apparently no window at all; strongly secured, and dismal to look at, like an immense hearse. People fell back as if awed, and the great iron gates rolled open; the *cortège* rattled in, and the gates rolled back again. I tried to make my way through the gates in the wake of the prison-van, but there was no time, they closed so quickly and looked so inexorable when shut. What powerful ruffians, what dangerous, strong-sinewed criminals were they conveying with all this show of armed force into the prison? The van contained only a few poor, weak, helpless *girls*, guilty of the crime of not ministering to impurity in accordance with official rules. I could not help exclaiming to myself in my bitterness of soul: O, manly, courageous Frenchmen! ever athirst for "glory," how well it looks to see you exercising your brave military spirit against the womanhood of your own country! You cannot govern your own passions, but you can at least govern by physical force the poor women of your streets, and swagger to your hearts' content in your hour of triumph, as you proudly enter the prison gates with your trembling caged linnets. But no! miserable men, you cannot even do this; you are beaten by your own women. They cannot meet you on stout horses, with helmets and military swagger and police tyranny, but they beat you with other and more deadly weapons. We speak much of women, under the vicious system we oppose, being the slaves of men, and we realise all the tyranny and oppression which has reduced women to so abject a state; but when I went to Paris I began to see the picture reversed in a strange and awful way, and to understand how the men who had rivetted the slavery of women for such degrading ends had become, in a generation or two, themselves the greater slaves; not only the slaves of their own enfeebled and corrupted natures, but of the women whom they have maddened, hardened, and stamped under foot. Bowing down before the unrestrained dictates of their own lusts, they now bow down also before the tortured and fiendish womanhood which *they have created.* Till now I had never fully realised Nemesis in this form. The degenerates of to-day plot and plan and scheme in vain for their own physical safety. Possessed at times with a sort of stampede of terror, they rush to International Congresses, and forge together more chains for the dreaded wild beast they have so carefully trained, and in their pitiful panic build up fresh barricades between themselves and that womanhood, the *femme vengeresse*, which they proclaim to be a "permanent source of sanitary danger." M. Lecour, in his last book which he gave me, appeared to regard every woman who is not under the immediate rule of some man as he would a volcano ready to burst forth under his feet; his terror had driven him to contrive a scheme by which all the single women of Paris, the virtuous as well as vicious, shall be netted by the police and held fast!

When a man abuses the good gifts of nature to brutalise himself by excess in wine, that passive agent, in itself unconscious and incapable of motive for good or evil, becomes to him a fiery scourge, his tyrant, and he its slave; "in·the end it biteth like a serpent." Much more, and in a far more awful sense, does abused womanhood become the fiery scourge, the torment, and the tyrant of the men who systematically outrage, in her, God's best gift. Just so far as the soul of a woman is above all inanimate things which are susceptible of abuse, so far is the punishment of the man who outrages it increased. It is true he does not become the slave of the woman, but merely of the *female*. Yet, inasmuch as she is not a mere inanimate thing, like intoxicating drink, nor a mere animal, but is endowed with intellect, affections, will, responsibility, an immortal spirit, and inasmuch as men have turned *all this to poison*, so is the vengeance suffered by those men in exact proportion. The men who are guilty of the deliberate and calculating crime of organising and regulating the ruin of women prepare for themselves an enslavement, an overmastering terror and tyranny, compared with which the miseries and enslavements brought about by other vices, terrible as these are, are but as the foreshadowing of a reality. Already they cringe, the abject slaves of the tyrant they have created; they are ruled, cajoled, outwitted, mocked and scourged by her. They rave at and curse her, as a wretched dipsomaniac curses his intoxicating drink, madly grasping it all the time, and in the end she slays them.

A couple of surly-looking guards at the gateway of St. Lazare did not vouchsafe me any answer when I asked how I was to get in; as I persisted, however, one said "Vous pouvez battre," jerking his head over his shoulder towards a smaller and heavily iron-barred door. Yes! I could "beat" no doubt, but my hand made no sound or impression at all against that heavy iron door. I thought it rather typical of our whole work on the Continent, beating at the outside of a strong Bastille of misery and horror. Then the words came to me—"I have set before thee an open door, and no man can shut it." I went into the street and took up a stone, and tried beating with that. It succeeded; a solemn old man in livery opened; I gave him M. Lecour's

THE PRISONERS OF ST. LAZARE

letter, desiring that they would show me the whole place; and after looking at it narrowly, he passed me on to the care of a nun, the second in charge. . . . I visited every part of the building; it took a long time. . . . In the central court of the prison, where a few square yards of blue sky are allowed to look down upon the scene, troops of young girls were taking their hour of prescribed "recreation," namely, walking in twos and threes round the sloppy and gloomy yard, where half-melted snow was turning into mud. It was a sight to wring the heart of a woman, a mother! Most of them were very young, and some of them so comely, so frank, so erect and graceful, in spite of the ugly prison dress. Well might Alexandre Dumas exclaim, " O besotted nation, to turn all these lovely women, who should be our companions in life's work, wives, and mothers, into ministers to vice!" They were not all Parisian; they were from all the Provinces, and some from Switzerland, Germany, Italy, and England. I was not allowed to speak to them. Never in my life did I so much long to speak; and I fancied *they* wished it too, for their steps slackened as they came round, and they paused when they got near me, with looks of kindness, or gentle curiosity. One knows enough of the heartless, artificial, or hardened women of Paris, but my memory recalls *these* who were the raw material, fresh from nature's hand, out of which Babylon manufactures her soulless wild beasts who become a terror to their manufacturers.

After the other members of my family, with Professor Stuart, had joined me from England, we accepted several invitations to hold meetings in the salons of leading persons of the Protestant community of Paris. One of the first who offered his aid was Pastor de Coppet, who suggested a Conference at the house of a friendly member of the Chambers, where, he said, " we shall all speak out what we have kept down in our hearts so long." Pastor Lepoids also strongly aided us in our efforts, and soon after we gained the efficient co-operation of M. de Pressensé, M. Theodore Monod, the venerable Dr. Monod (a physician), M. George Appia, of

G

the Church of the Augsburg Confession, M. Frederic Passy, Mme. André Walther, and others; Madame Jules Simon and M. Victor Schoelcher, Senator, gave their adhesion and advice. I received letters of sympathy and approval of our efforts from M. Jules Simon, at that time President of the Chambers, and from M. Louis Blanc. I had an interview by appointment with M. Jules Favre, in his own house. My readers of the present day may not perhaps know the position then held in France by M. Jules Favre (who died not long after I saw him), nor the high character of his utterances as an Advocate and politician. His words to me on this subject were impressive. He spoke sadly and doubtfully of the probabilities of realising so great a moral reform in his own country, but yet resolutely as to the necessity of taking immediate steps to create an improved public opinion on the subject; he expressed full concurrence in our view of the absolute equality of moral responsibility for both sexes. He gave me introductions to some Catholic gentlemen, urging upon me the importance of appealing to all religious denominations. He admitted that he had no faith in governmental help in this matter, reminding me that " governments had never looked the question fairly in the face, but when interfering at all, had almost invariably done so in order to elevate the social vice into ' an institution,' by which means they had increased and given permanence to the evil." He said: " Regard for the public health is their sole excuse. But even the worst that could befall the public health is nothing to the corruption of morals and national life engendered, propagated, and prolonged by the system of official surveillance. It is utterly inexcusable, and an act of supreme folly, to give a legal sanction to the licentiousness of one sex and the enslavement of the other." He further spoke emphatically of the necessity of women being heard on this subject. As he was curious to know by what methods the French system had been introduced into free England, I gave him an account of the tactics pursued, at which he appeared profoundly astonished.

Madame Jules Simon invited me to attend the annual meeting of the committee of management of the Professional Schools established by Madame Lemonnier. She said to me (though speaking sympathetically) that my mission would not have any success in France, " because it was too high and holy to be understood." She said, and I feared there was truth in this, that "all men, even the best men, in France had been from their childhood so accustomed to look upon this shameful evil as a legal institution that it would require a very long process of patient educating to get them even to acknowledge that it is not honourable for governments to create and maintain such an institution." Madame Simon, however, having read, ten months later, " A Voice in the Wilderness," wrote to me: "You are not under any illusion, for your voice is indeed at present but a voice in the wilderness; but you have no grounds for any discouragement; for those who do not understand you to-day *will understand you to-morrow.*"

My sister wrote to me from Naples on New Year's Eve, 1874-75:—

"*Midnight.*

"Beloved of my Soul. I want to spend this solemn hour with you. My heart is overflowing with gratitude to Him whose cross you bear. This passing year, which began with so much discouragement, has finished gloriously with the carrying of the standard of the fiery cross over the sea and into another land; and you—God surrounds you with His shield. Everyone out of England to whom I told your mission said you would be insulted and outraged in Paris, and could not do any good. Even people who believe in your mission told me of the way in which irreverent Frenchmen ridicule anything spoken with a foreign accent, spoke of the dangers you would incur, and the impossibility of your making any impression. When they talked thus, I smiled and said, ' Wait and see ! this is of God, and He will justify His handmaid ! ' I felt so surely that God gave it you to do, and whatever the world may think, God knows what He is

about. He is not an idealised Joss who lives in churches. He is present among us. He can manage even the Paris police! How He laid your enemies under your feet!
"Your mission is too high and holy to be understood, they tell you! Is it not strange how people persevere in thinking it lovelily humble and sweetly meritorious to go on picking off an evil-smelling leaf here and there from the upas tree, instead of taking the sword of God and striking at the root— nipping here and there the results of its growth, instead of cutting off the source of its life? The long chain of prejudice, habit, and received opinion twists itself, coil after coil, around men's minds. It is the virtuous and religious whom I mean who are so chained, not by vice, but by faithlessness and timidity. It is not to all that it is given to break the chains of others, but there seems to me little excuse for those who do not allow their own chains to be broken."

We went on to Lyons, Marseilles and Genoa, at each place gathering individual adherents, men and women of real worth of character. Thence we went to Rome.

In Rome we first met one of the most ardent apostles of our cause whom we have known in any country, Signor Giuseppe Nathan. His mother was a distinguished Roman lady, and his family were friends of Mazzini. I had been told of the recent overwhelming sorrow which seemed for a time to have broken short the promise of Giuseppe Nathan's noble young life, and which had had so serious an effect upon his health as to alarm his family. He had married a young English lady, who died very suddenly, after a few months of an ideally happy marriage. He was a young man of great ability and earnestness of soul. It was thought by some of his friends that if some vital work were to be put before him at this time he might recognise it as an authoritative call to action, and that it might be to him a revival of interest in life, and a motive for living, after all life's sunshine, for him, was gone. The rapid progress made by our principles in Italy after this first visit to Rome was almost wholly due to the untiring energy and apostolic zeal of Giuseppe Nathan He had been known before to his countrymen as a friend of Mazzini, and had, in fact, like most of that group, suffered for his principles. His personal influence was great for one so young, especially among the working populations, whom later he succeeded in arousing throughout the length and breadth of Italy, travelling himself to every place, engaging the best men and women in the work, and winning the hearts of all to our cause. I recall my first interview with him. He looked sad and absent, and was very weak in health. He had the appearance of a man who had had a shock which might prove to be his death-blow; and, in fact, he died only six years later, the end probably accelerated by his arduous labours in our cause telling upon a sensitive frame already shaken by his domestic sorrow. His loss was a very serious one to our cause in Italy. There was no one of like character who could entirely take his place, although his brother, Signor Ernesto Nathan, has worked indefatigably for the cause up to recent times.

The following quotations from letters which I received from Giuseppe Nathan after my return from Italy to England will throw some light on the gentle, chivalrous, and, I might say, almost inspired character of the man. In addition to his arduous propagandist work, he laboured to save individual victims of the curse against which he continually protested, and had planned a work of rescue on simple, kindly and humane principles. It was in regard to this effort that he wrote to me as follows:—

"I wish you were here to teach me how to act in this case. I would ten thousand times sooner face the mouths of twenty guns than a poor girl who feels that she has lost all right to respect; though not in *my* eyes. No! God is my witness that I judge *no* woman unworthy of respect; her womanhood outraged is in itself more than sufficient claim for the respect of every man. Had not one of *my* sex robbed her of her peace, withered in its bloom all happiness, all that made life a blessing to her, she might now have been happy and making others happy. Her poor betrayed soul, her robbed innocence, her misery and suffering, call loudly in God's name for the respect which all men owe to grief and suffering.

"It is impossible for me to tell you how much I long to be of some slight comfort to these poor fellow-creatures of ours, whom cowardly man has taught even to despair of the salvation of their souls. Could my remaining years bring but one of them to hope in God's everlasting mercy; could I make but one of them feel that the possibility of redemption is eternal as the everlasting soul with which God animated their bodies; could I but awaken in one city the true, deep, fervid faith, that without purity and morality no nation can possibly advance; could I teach effectually in even one place the lesson, that because woman is our *first* teacher, her lessons can only bear good fruit on condition that we hold sacred and *do not despise* our teacher—then I could understand why God has dealt so sternly with me, and I could patiently wait till I should be able to prove to my lost angel through my actions that *together* she and I have accomplished on earth the task appointed us."

Later he wrote:—" I have received a paper from England relating to the *Social Purity League.* I not only sympathise with the aim of the League, but I consider its aim noblest among the noble. To talk of purity is well, to lead a pure life is better, but it is best of all to oppose impurity with all the powers of heart and intellect bestowed on us by God, under whatever form it presents itself to our eyes, and by whomsoever it may be promoted. Destroy purity, admit the necessity of prostitution, and materialism and profligacy will have full sway; but then efface from the English language the words *Mother, Home,* and *Heaven.*"

Under Mr. Nathan's guidance we visited the Italian Parliament, where, as in London, one may request an audience of any member of the Chambers. Our guide knew very well upon whom in the Chambers he could depend for sympathy in this matter, and we had several memorable conversations in the Lobbies.

Signor Asproni, an old man, formerly a monk, but who had found it impossible to continue in that character, had been, when we saw him, for some years a hard-working Deputy. He was known as a most honest man, attached to principle rather than party. He expressed great sympathy with our movement. Several others, men of weight and character, took up the question; and from these elements Mr. Nathan was enabled soon after to form a Committee in Rome for active work.

I must go back a little to describe briefly the introduction of this system into Italy, and the opposition which it had already met with.

In 1860 Count Cavour proclaimed the Regulation originally invented and imposed on the French people by Napoleon I. Cavour seems to have deemed it an admirable measure. An explanation of its professed benefits was appended to a subsequent issue of it by the Minister Lanza in 1871. Public opinion was at once aroused against this regulation, its meaning having been thus explained. The Liberal party in the Chambers have been at different times accused of party-spirited motives, in having from the first protested against the Regulations of Cavour. It is not true that the Radical party alone revolted against this system. Italian Radicals assured us that from the first a protest had arisen from every part of the Chambers. From Dr. Bertani, who sat on the extreme left, to De Renzis on the left-centre, and Vittorio Giudici on the extreme right, all took part in the revolt against what the Italian conscience instinctively felt to be a measure degrading to women and to manhood. Outside Parliament it was the same; "Men of all parties," said a well-known Deputy, "rebelled against the idea of this judicial oppression of women, which no possible argument was found to justify." This awakening of the public conscience continued through all classes of society until it reached Pope Pius IX. The Venerable Pontiff, shortly after the Regulations were introduced in Rome, wrote a letter with his own hand to King Victor Emmanuel, protesting against the iniquity which had just been perpetrated, and solemnly adjured him to forbid that a "patented merchandise of human flesh" should be established in the Holy City.

So early as 1862 (only two years after Cavour's publication of the Regulation) the revolt against it was such that Rattazzi, then Minister of the Interior, and President of the Council, was driven to appoint a Commission to modify or alter it.

But little came of this. Attempted modifications of an essential evil always fail.

After the impulse given by the exertions of Giuseppe Nathan, and when he had successfully convinced and moved some of the most earnest public men of Italy, the cause in that country went through the usual Parliamentary course of Reports called for from experts, Commissions of Enquiry, Parliamentary Debates, partial reforms and attempted substitutes; and up to the present day it cannot be said to have got much beyond that stage.

To return. I was counselled to see Senator Musio and his wife. I first saw her alone. She was in her bedroom surrounded by a number of ladies who had formed a Committee for aiding the needy families of working men. I gave her a little Italian paper setting forth the objects of my mission. She read it slowly and carefully to the very last word, and then said "Good! Musio must see this." She had grasped the whole question simply and clearly at once. She was very aged and "old-fashioned," but full of intelligence. She then tapped her snuff-box and conversed with us in a low and feeble voice, but in a manner that showed no feebleness of judgment. In the evening we called again, and were quite as much pleased with her venerable husband as with herself. He was a very distinguished jurist, and was then working at some important legal reforms. I must not omit to mention Signor Maurizio Quadrio, one of the old Mazzinians, a true patriot, who had suffered much and long for his principles. He encouraged us much in our work. It is needless to say that I found very hearty sympathy among

THE MINISTER OF *IN*JUSTICE IN ROME

the Protestants (Evangelici) then working in Rome, Signor Ribetti, for example, Mr. Wall, and others.

Of a very different kind was a visit I paid to the Minister of Justice and Police, Signor Vigliani. I had been advised to appeal to him concerning our mission; but when I announced to Mr. Nathan my intention of doing so, he smiled and remained silent. I said, "Do you not advise me to go?" He replied, "Oh, yes, go, but——"; and he smiled again. I went alone. The reception Vigliani gave me was cold and scarcely courteous. Few things are more chilling than the atmosphere of the audience-chamber of a great Government official, who has no sympathy with your errand. It was clear to me from the first moment that nothing was to be gained here; but I remained a little longer, just to get the Minister to express his own opinions on the subject, which were curious enough, though not new to me. He seemed immensely amused at the idea of abolishing legal prostitution; spoke of the enslaved as *not human* at all, and of the errors of men as something to be regretted, but inevitable, and to be taken into account, *i.e.*, provided for. He said: "A woman who has once lost chastity has lost every good quality. She has from that moment '*all the vices.*'" And so pleased did he seem with this theory that he smiled and repeated it, "Once unchaste, she has *every vice.*" He asked, "Who have you got to help you in the Italian Parliament?" and seemed to wait eagerly for the answer, which he did not get! As I went down the broad marble stairs and through the gateway over which the beautiful title of his office is inscribed, I thought, "You are ill-named, Office of Grace and Justice!"

Then I understood why Giuseppe Nathan smiled.

From Rome I went on alone for a week to my sister Madame Meuricoffre, at Naples. We had there one or two quiet meetings. The medical men offered some opposition at one of them, but, on the other hand, we had then, and for some years after, the strong adhesion of Dr. Palasciano (who became publicly an opponent of the Regulations) and of another distinguished medical man of Naples. The tender sympathy of my sister, Madame Meuricoffre, and her deep understanding of our motives, I need scarcely say, were from that time, and have been all along, among my most constant consolations and sources of strength. I cannot refrain from giving the substance here of a letter which she wrote to me shortly after my visit to Naples; for it expresses what comparatively few even now understand—the hold which this question takes upon some thoughtful and tender natures, and the reasons why it makes this impression:—

NAPLES, *January*, 1875.

"I told my friends here that when you were sent to us I had asked to meet you those whom I thought likely to wish to hear you, in order to see if God would choose any of them to come forward to the rescue of those most pitiful and most unpitied of Christ's little ones. He who looked for some to have pity on Him, but there was no man, neither found He any to comfort Him, called *us* to have pity on *these*. But none of those to whom I refer have been led into *that* work. Still, I must not for this reason judge that they are not His servants. I have faith that they are, and are working in some other way, for in His army there are many kinds of soldiers,—sappers and miners to open up roads, artillery to attack forts, troops who have an easy victory, and 'forlorn hopes' who will never see victory, but make a bridge of their dead bodies for their comrades to march over. There are, I doubt not, many who have been elected to this work who, when God first took them by the hand, shrank back. It was the last thing they would have chosen for themselves, but He kept them to it till they accepted it, and then taught them the sweetness of the dedication, by letting them feel how close it brought them to Himself. There is a great deal in ordinary society, even where there is nothing bad, which imperceptibly hardens, or gradually establishes in the mind slightly false standards; and I wish to tell you how strikingly I felt that entering into and interesting oneself in your work brought one back, every time one touched it, into realising the Living God, His nearness to us and our dependence on Him, and forced one to measure all one's thoughts, acts, and feelings by the standard of His purity, instead of lowering oneself to the convenient and conventional standard of the world. A person whose conscience has never been wounded about this question, whose heart has never burned and bled with pity for the woes of the helpless, devoted to destruction, might wonder, and ask, ' Why should *this* subject, above all others, produce this effect?' Well, I cannot quite tell; perhaps because *in it* culminates the awful contrast between the results of man's devices when he forgets God and the unspeakable tenderness and pity of Christ for the most forsaken and lost. He stooped to take upon Himself our nature, and to minister to us. How much less is the interval between the best man or woman and the most fallen! and how He pitied them, and how awfully solemn are His warnings, not only not to offend one of the little ones, the weak and young, but not to pass them by with the cold, worldly doctrine that ' it must be so.' Such doctrine rouses in me a passion of grief and indignation that some of us should be so honoured, while others, born with like capabilities for virtue and sweet family life and happiness, should be sold to men's lusts, and then held down by a network of laws and regulations; *held down in hell.* You and your fellow-workers will understand well what I mean when I speak of a vital interest in this question becoming a sifting power and a purifying fire in one's own soul; I tremble for those who are obliged, or think they are obliged, to crush it out. Pray for them."

On our return journey we visited Florence. Several persons here told me that the system of Regulation was, for the moment, practically at an end. This was, in part, the result of the opposition of the country people of Tuscany, who resist the registration of their daughters on the roll of shame. The character of the Tuscan peasant is simple, honest, home loving. Mr. McDougall, a Scotch clergyman, who had resided many years in Florence, said to me: "In character they stand as high as the peasantry of my own Scotland." Some sad tragedies had occurred. A peasant girl escaped from one of the Government houses of infamy and fled to her parents' cottage. She was followed by the police, who endeavour to "reclaim," that is, *bring back to bondage*, every girl who escapes. The parents barricaded their house; a struggle followed, and blood was shed. This and other incidents which I might relate, illustrating the tyranny of the system, had become public; the Florentine people have hearts; their sympathies had been roused for the homes and daughters of the poor; the State regulation of vice had become unpopular, and was then very languidly carried out in Florence.

In Milan we had again the advantage of the presence and organising ability of Giuseppe Nathan, who joined us there. We had a large conference in that city. There were present some ex-Deputies and well-known doctors. Some of these latter were strongly opposed to us, especially Dr. Pini, who spoke at some length. He was seconded in his views by an advocate of Milan, and Signor Brusco Onnis replied to him. The address of the latter made a great impression on those present. A useful discussion followed. Dr. Pini made a kind of recantation towards the close, and a resolution in our favour was passed almost unanimously. *La Gazetta di Milano* of January 28, 1875, reported the meeting, and remarked favourably on our aims. It gave also the resolution, and a brief address to the group of citizens who had supported us, which was printed and circulated the next day.

The address was as follows:—

"Gentlemen! the expression of sympathy with the cause which I advocate, conveyed to me through you from the city of Milan, is deeply gratifying to me; and in the name of all who co-operate with me in this holy crusade, I tender you my heartfelt thanks. For pioneers the path is always arduous and difficult, especially when before building up they have to destroy an evil which for a long period has been corrupting the moral sense of the most civilised populations. Such is our own case. I will not, at the present time, dwell upon the fact of man having gone so far as to convert that which is in itself supremely a question of morality into one of opportunity and facility for the satisfaction of his physical instincts, simply as instincts, and of his having, in order to attain this end, perpetrated the most flagrant violation of right and justice by crushing one of two persons equally guilty, in order to render more easy the commission of sin for the other.

"The question for us resolves itself entirely into a moral question—a question of justice. Even if it were the fact, which is not the case, that statistics seemed to prove that by means of the existing system it is possible to diminish the maladies attendant on prostitution, our cry would be precisely what it is to-day—war, war to the death against all which tends to deaden the moral sense in man, and which, ultimately, must of necessity enervate the race. We believe that the aim of all legislation should be the gradual moral progress of the governed, and that the labours of science should be directed to the furtherance of that aim.

"In order to obtain pure laws, and a higher morality, we will lend all the force of our intellect and will.

" Will you, gentlemen, give us your aid, and do what you can to form throughout the whole of Italy, committees which will put themselves in relation with our associations in England? "JOSEPHINE E. BUTLER."

I must not detain my readers too long on this journey through Italy.

After a brief visit to Turin, we crossed the Alps to Geneva. It was at a meeting at Geneva on this question at which one of the hardest and longest portions of our conflict was inaugurated. Up to the present time Geneva clings to the odious system which was on that occasion—twenty-one years ago—first publicly arraigned, in spite of reiterated protests from her best and noblest citizens, and blows aimed from many sides. But the doom of the system is approaching, in spite of its apparent vitality.

Everything looked very dark for my first meeting beforehand. The opposition threatened was of a different kind to that which we generally met, which had been mainly materialistic. Here, in Geneva, there was a good deal of sentimentality, much talk about the police being good Christian men, and about reclamations effected by them. It was requested by a friend that the legal aspect of the matter should be especially dealt with. Professor Hornung was with us in sympathy from the first. He was Professor of Jurisprudence in the University of Geneva, and a very able and distinguished man. My spirits fell, however, when a note came in the afternoon to say that the Professor had been taken suddenly ill and could not come to the meeting. The room was crowded at the hour announced, and at the last moment Mr. Hornung entered, wrapped in shawls and looking very pale. He took the presidency. Towards the end, when a pause was given for objections to be brought forward, behold, there were no objectors! but one after another stood up and gave in his adhesion to our cause. Père Hyacinthe spoke very eloquently for us. He also wrote a kind letter to me the following day, in which he said, "One feels, dear Madame, that God is with you in your heroic crusade against what you have so well called 'the typical crime, the gigantic iniquity' of our race. God is with you, Madame; it is necessary that men should be with you also. I beg that you will count entirely upon my weak but sincere services."

I cannot easily forget the impression of that first visit to Geneva, a city of glorious traditions, and formerly the stern upholder of liberty of conscience.

Geneva! still full of activity and life and educational movements, whose glory is chiefly of the past, but in whose midst there is still high profession of religion and spirituality, and at the same time desperate social evils and Governmental iniquities which many of your best men and women find too horrible to speak of; what, I asked myself, will be *your* judgment at the last?

Before the meeting many proofs had come to me of sinister influences exercised to prevent my being heard, and to discourage people from coming. Some of the professing Christians of Geneva seemed to be the most deeply in love with the system of legalised vice. At one time the anxiety was almost greater than I could bear, and I felt the pressure of the responsibility all the more because at that time my husband had been compelled to return to his duties at the Liverpool College, leaving me to complete my immediate mission on the Continent without his comforting and strengthening presence. My heart was burdened with all the shameful things I had heard concerning the slave system in Geneva, the buying and selling of young girls, and the corruption of young men, students, school boys, and whole families. The good and venerable Pastor Borel had told me of his experiences, and a tradesman of the town, M. W.——, who had worked hard to try to save a few victims, called to see me. The latter was an old, hard-sinewed man, apparently with little sentimentalism about him; but during his recital he was so moved that he burst into tears.

When the hour came, however, for the encounter, pity and sorrow were stronger than the anger I had felt; and as I spoke I could see that the people were moved. I happened to stand with my back to the light, which fell fully upon the audience, and I was much struck by the rows of old, grey heads and venerable faces. It was like an assembly of Elders, not only of the Church, but Elders in science and in learning. I thanked God when I saw that many of the Elders wept! Those tears made me glad. In some sense no doubt this was a fruitful initiation of our Abolitionist work; but of results we saw little or nothing for many years, in spite of Geneva having become, two years later, the seat of our first great and important International Congress.

On the morning following this meeting it was that I became first acquainted with Madame de Gingins, whose name is so well known as one of our most constant friends on the Continent. She was then emerging from the shadow of a great sorrow, and felt that the call to this work would be to her a revival of life and hope.

From Geneva I went on to Neuchâtel, where the tone was very different. It was here that I first made the personal acquaintance of our beloved friends and fellow workers for so many years, M. and Mme. Aimé Humbert, and their family. M. Humbert speedily called together a Conference, and it was on this occasion that I first gained a knowledge of his breadth of view and intellectual grasp. His long experience of political life and of men had endowed him with a readiness and tact and power of controlling and guiding an assembly even of the most discordant elements such as I have scarcely seen in any other man. I must give some extracts from M. Humbert's address at this first meeting.

"What response," he asked, "shall we make to the appeal which has been made to us?"

"We are not, it is true, in the same situation as the associations which have been mentioned. The reformist agitation in England aims at effecting the repeal of laws protective of immorality. In the first place, no *Federal law* analogous to these exists in Switzerland. Legislation relating to public morals is within the province of the several cantons. Then, again, in the canton of Neuchâtel, the criminal code takes cognisance of vice, and visits it with correctional or criminal penalties, as the case may be, without consideration of person or sex. We have, then, a legislation protective of morality, and which admits neither exception nor reservation. I may add that in general it is respected, especially in our chief city of Berne, which is, perhaps, of all Switzerland, the town the most exempt from the scourge of prostitution. On the other hand, in our principal industrial centre, at Chaux-de-Fonds, immoral houses were established some years since, as in Geneva. The fact is public and notorious, and it has already called forth the remonstrances of the Synod of the National Church of Neuchâtel, which have been without result. Consequently our situation is this:—We have, I repeat, a legislation protective of morality, but this legislation is openly violated in a portion of our territory. Thus, instead of seeking, as in England, the repeal of a law the enactment of which constituted an innovation, we have to demand the strict observance of the existing law. If we do not do this, we sanction by our silence a state of things worse than in England. There, at least, there is no longer any *legal hypocrisy*! the law declares openly what it intends to tolerate. Here, on the contrary, the prohibition of vice is held to be complete; it is officially proclaimed, and, nevertheless, in one portion of our territory, all the crimes and misdemeanours which fall under the ban of the penal code are daily committed with the full knowledge of every citizen.

" Without respect for the laws, there is no true Republic. If a good law becomes a lie, it tends to deaden the national conscience and to deprave the people, just as much as a bad law could do. Let us, then, have the courage of our opinions! If our law is good, let us compel its observance ; if, on the contrary, we judge that we ought to substitute for it the toleration of immorality, let us boldly legalise vice ! I am persuaded that this will not be done. A law of tolerance is an impossibility in our canton. Neither our present Grand Council, nor any Grand Conncil of Neuchâtel, will ever sanction it. Could an institution exist in our Republic of Neuchâtel which braves the legislative power, and subsists iu spite of public opinion ? Such a thing would be the commencement of the downfall of our Republic. And what description of institution is it, for which we should have to introduce a *régime* of privilege incompatible with our constitutional guarantees ? An institution which is, in itself, a flagrant violation of individual liberty, and of the equality of all the inhabitants of the country, whether men or women, before the law. The inauguration of legal prostitution is

H

nothing else than the triumph of brute force, the consecration of police despotism over the weaker sex—the protection of a white slave-trade—in a word, the organisation of female slavery.

"But hygienic considerations are invoked. We are told that certain diseases would thus become rarer or less pernicious. Well, let us admit for an instant—what I consider by no means proved—that this assertion is incontestable. I will tell you of another disease, which, wherever this system obtains, becomes ever more deadly and less rare. It does not, indeed, attack any single organ of the human frame, but it withers all that is human—mind, body, soul. It strikes our youth at that unhappy moment when first they cross the threshold of the abodes of State-regulated vice; and when they recross that threshold to the purer air, oh God! what fatal deed has not been done! For them the spring of life has no more flowers; the very friendships of their youth are polluted; they become strangers to all the honourable relations of a pure life; and thus it is that more and more in these days we see stretching wider and wider around us the circle of this mocking, faded, worn out, sceptical youth, without poetry, without love, without enthusiasm, without faith, and without joy. And yet this is the generation on which the hopes of our country rest!

"There is something truly mysterious in the way in which a social scourge makes its way and propagates itself; but what is still more astonishing, or rather more admirable, is the means by which Providence puts an end to it.

"For some time past have Jules Simon, in his work, *L'Ouvrière*; Victor Hugo, in *Les Misérables*, John Stuart Mill, Acollas, Hornung, and many other writers denounced the crime of female slavery, and declared it the duty of democracy to provide for the extinction of prostitution. Many applauded; but the thing would have ended there had not the advocates of legal prostitution in Great Britain themselves solicited and obtained from Parliament an official sanction of this system of slavery. Then—not till then—this system was unveiled in the full light of publicity, and publicity is fatal to it; for on the one hand vice cannot bear the light in a country where the Press is free, and on the other hand no *law* of Parliament can, in the mind of the British nation, over-ride the *Charter* of its ancient liberties, it having been one of the first among the great nations of Europe to formulate the guarantee of personal rights. The Charter of our little country of Neuchâtel is of still more ancient date (1213). The first Compact of alliance of our Confederation belongs to the close of the same century (1291). *Individual Liberty* founded alike the greatness of England and the happiness of Switzerland. We cannot, any more than the English, permit slavery upon our Republican soil. It may not be allowed an entrance there, whether official or secret. Let us all mutually unite to protect liberty and justice from the evil which threatens them in common. Mrs. Butler's mission will prove to be for us a providential event, the opportunity which we must quickly seize, in order to act upon our canton and upon Switzerland, and to associate ourselves with the great reformatory struggle which is coming upon Europe, and, sooner or later, upon the whole world."

In company with Madame Humbert, I visited the largest industrial town of the Jura, La Chaux-de-Fonds. There was much moral evil there, but also many sternly just and good people. I was fully rewarded for the visit there by the adhesion of persons who have remained constant to our cause, and whose work was crowned by complete success in 1892 by the final abolition of the infamous institution in that city, and in the entire canton of Neuchâtel.

The town stands high on the Jura. I was warned that the cold would be many degrees greater than at Neuchâtel; and, indeed, I found it so. Even the extraordinary beauty of the vast expanses of snow, the black forests of enormous pine trees, with their weights of heavy clinging snow, the glimpses of the distant Alps, stretching from Mont Blanc to the Wetterhorn and Wellhorn, scarcely gave me courage enough to hold out against the cold as we ascended. Madame Humbert kindly accompanied me. As we came near the town, however, I found I had not come among cold hearts. Several venerable men met us a little way from the town, with fur wrappings about them, and faces full of kindly welcome, and stood with heads uncovered until the sledge started again for the town. The deep snow made everything very silent; no rattle of wheels, only the soft, sweeping sound of the sledges flying swiftly about, and the musical ringing of the horses' bells. We had excellent meetings there.

From Neuchâtel I visited Berne and Lausanne, finding warm friends in each place. Thence I returned to Paris. It was on this second visit to Paris that I made the acquaintance of Madame de Morsier, whose name is endeared to many of us with whom she has worked on the Continent ever since. M. Humbert joined me in Paris, having determined, after grave consultation with his wise and gentle wife, to throw himself into the cause, although it might involve for him some sacrifice from a material point of view. "*God wills it*," he said. "This was the cry of the old Crusaders, and still more do I feel that it is the motto of those who are being drawn into this great movement."

I will not dwell upon the rather bitter experiences of the first part of this my second visit to Paris, arising from the opposition and cynicism which we met with. "It is a hard crusade," exclaimed M. Humbert one day, as he returned from a long and fruitless controversy with M. Mettetal, ex-Prefect of the Morals' Police, the predecessor of Lecour. M. Mettetal was a Protestant, and esteemed a religious man, but on the subject of justice, equality and legality, *he was stone blind*.

It is pleasanter to recollect the kindness, which never failed, of certain warm friends, and the readiness to accept our message which we found among the humbler classes of the people. Several interesting meetings were held, promoted by M. Ed. de Pressensé and other distinguished men of the Protestant community, and others by leaders among the working men and women of Paris. At one large meeting, at which there was a crowd of women present, an advocate opposed us. He proceeded to say all the untrue and cowardly things which men generally say when defending the enslavement of women, for they use the same arguments all over the world. Before he had gone far, however, he seemed rather taken aback, and I must say I was pleasantly surprised by the furious burst of scorn and anger which proceeded from all the women, and almost all the men, present. He endeavoured to go on, but the women hissed, and moaned, and protested so energetically that his voice was drowned. It gladdened my heart to see this furious protest from these poor Frenchwomen. The advocate became somewhat excited and tried to fling back the scorn of the women, getting, however, more and more into the mud, and floundering hopelessly. When he declared that the unhappy women for whose civil and natural rights we had pleaded, were the vilest of creatures, scarcely human, and justly expelled from and scorned by society, the women present sprang to their feet, and almost with one voice demanded, "But the men! What about the men? Are they not equally guilty, base and despicable?" I thanked God in my heart for this storm of righteous indignation. But there was sadness, too, in it. It had a maledictory sound which reminded me of the deep and deadly wounds which had been inflicted upon the population of Paris, and spoke of still further tribulation which might be in store for her.

Dr. Armand Deprés, a physician of the Lourcine Hospital, a man of great statistical knowledge on this question, gave me valuable help during this visit. He attended with me another large meeting, chiefly of the working class, and addressed them with a wonderful tenderness, giving also at the same time, clearly and delicately, the results which only a medical expert like himself could furnish.

Many proofs of sympathy reached us from other parts of

France. One of the most touching of these was a letter from Mr. Charles de Bourbonne, a magistrate of Rheims, who had pronounced a severe, just, and eloquent judgment in a case which had occurred in carrying out the regulations in his own city. On account of that judgment, which is a masterpiece of clearly-stated principle *versus* opportunism, and would well deserve to be quoted in full, he was degraded from the magistracy. He wrote to me:—

"Madam,—Yours is a work of lofty aims and noble purposes. Your voice will not sound in the desert. You will be able at length to create that phalanx of workers so much needed, which shall constitute an indissoluble alliance, an alliance indispensable to the cause which you defend. England is a privileged country, since liberty of discussion prevails there. It is not so in France. It is as a martyr in the great Cause which I dared to defend, that I address you to-night. I have committed the wrong of being in the right, and, after nineteen years of arduous labours in the Magistracy, I am degraded for having dared to oppose abuses which I considered infamous, and am now compelled at an advanced age to seek some retired business which shall permit me to live honestly. You ask me to become an honorary member of the International Congress to take place next year. I accept it with all my heart, and I am proud to do so.

"C. DE BOURBONNE,
"*Ex-Justice of the Peace.*"

This Magistrate had said, in his published judgment, "I have discovered, and have proofs, that it is the police itself which is one of the main causes of the depravity and demoralisation of our great cities. Without much education, of a morality at least doubtful, and in possession of an arbitrary power which is beyond any possible control, the agents of the Morals' Police are believed upon their simple word, and their reports obtain credence."

AWAKENING IN FRANCE

The close of this year was marked by a vigorous correspondence in the French Press on the subject of the Police des Mœurs, which bore much fruit, bringing many hideous things to light, and arousing slumbering consciences in the matter.

CHAPTER VI

"Thy will was in the builder's thought;
Thy hand unseen amidst us wrought;
Through mortal motive, scheme and plan,
Thy wise eternal purpose ran."

BEFORE I go further with the recital of the events in connection with our crusade which stand out most prominently in my memory, I must pause to speak briefly of some of the persons with whom I was most closely allied in the early years of our work.

They rise before me now—those faces and those groups of faces of dear friends and companions in labour, of all classes and conditions, and of different lands and races. Many have passed away; but their memory lives in the hearts of thos with whom they were associated for a time in work and prayer and hope.

First among the many groups comes that of the earliest and most active leaders in the Ladies' National Association. One of these, the Bristol group, still continues to be full of life and energy. I refer especially to the sisters Priestman and Margaret Tanner, with Miss Estlin and others closely associated with them, who have been to me, personally, through this long struggle, from the first years till now, a kind of body-guard, a *corps d'élite* on whose prompt aid, singleness of purpose, prudence, and unwearying industry I could and can rely at all times, and the knowledge of whose existence and loyalty alone, even when parted from them for long periods, is a continued source of comfort and strength. The utter absence in them of any desire for recognition, of any vestige of egotism in any form, is worthy of remark. In the purity of their motives they shine out " clear as crystal."

The mere mention of their names, and those of a host of others, is but a cold and poor tribute. Nevertheless, I cannot pass on without a brief allusion to others. Mrs. Kenway, of Birmingham, was another of my strongest friends; her house was always my home in passing through and working in that busy centre, a home in which I was always lovingly received by herself, her husband, and all her family. I must mention her sister also, Mrs. Henry Richardson, of York. Other names which crowd upon me are those of Mrs. Edward Walker, of Leeds, of Mr. and Mrs. Clark, of Newcastle, Mr. and Mrs. Spence Watson and the Richardson family, of the same town; of Mrs. Pease Nichol, Miss Wigham, and Mrs. Bright McLaren, of Edinburgh; of Mrs. Lucas, Mrs. Maclaren and other ladies of Glasgow, and Miss Isabella Tod, of Belfast, one of the ablest, and certainly the most eloquent, of our women workers of those times. Miss Lucy Wilson, whose loss to our cause through death some years ago was a serious one, might be numbered as one of the legal helpers of our cause. She had a remarkably keen intelligence and extraordinary capacity for sifting evidence, unravelling tortuous argument, and dividing the true from the false. She was often employed by our Parliamentary friends to examine and pronounce upon doubtful proposals, emanating from the Government or elsewhere. Her verdict was generally found to be just. Her character and feelings as a woman, at the same time, were true and tender.

There are many more names revered and honourable which I might bring in, but I do not know how to enumerate them. I am forced, like the Apostle who gives us the record of the heroes of faith, to sum up with the words, " And what shall I say more? for the time would fail me to tell " of this and that standard-bearer of righteousness. Their record is in heaven; they do not need my poor homage; they never coveted earthly praise.

The lofty and perilous position to which the first women

workers in this cause were called, was indicated by Dr. Guthrie, one of the venerable leaders of the Scottish Free Church, in a letter which was published in 1872, as follows:—

"There is a picture in the old Dutch town of Leyden which I have looked on with the deepest emotions. Its object is the brave, and, by God's blessing, successful defence of that city when besieged by the forces of those two fierce persecutors, Philip II. and the Duke of Alva. And what there most moved my heart was the sight of women, in whom the fear of outrage from the brutal soldiery had swallowed up the fear of death, standing beside their fathers, brothers, and husbands on the crests of the crowded ramparts. No place for women, that, it may be said. But turn the light of history on the scene; read in Motley's pages the unutterable horrors to which both maidens and mothers were exposed, and you will look through tears of sympathy on the beautiful woman, pale with loss of blood, whom they are bearing off to die in a quiet chamber, and on those of her sex who, undaunted by her fall, stand boldly by the guns and, with hands used to gentler work, point the muzzle and fire on the assailant. Circumstances, as they say, alter cases. They did so there: they did so when, in lack of men, Grace Darling hastened to the rescue, put her own young life in peril, and pulled for the sinking wreck. They did so in Jerusalem also, when women, casting aside the ordinary restraints of their age, openly followed our Lord to Calvary, and, in the face of His raging enemies, bewailed and lamented Him.

"Such honour as I give to these I give to those ladies who have stepped out of their ordinary sphere to publicly expose the vice-regulating laws, and to become leaders of men,—to inspire the hesitating with firmness and cowards with courage. A good while ago different persons urged me to take pen in hand and address the mothers of our country, the guardians of its homes and household virtues, on the jeopardy into which both were brought by the authors and advocates of these foul laws. Fear of being thought presumptuous made me, while I acknowledged the honour, decline—at least delay—the task. But when these ladies, braving in this crisis the scoffs of profligates, rising above all fear of misunderstanding and misrepresentation by their public appearance on such a subject, offered up a sacrifice on the altar of virtue that only the delicate and pure and high-minded can fully appreciate, I were a coward to hang back. They have thrown themselves into the breach, and I cannot but follow."

The position which the women took was also well described by our venerable Christian statesman, the Right Honourable J. W. Henley, when from his seat in Parliament he uttered these words: "It is objected that this agitation is the work of women; but it is impossible not to see that it is women who are above all others affected by this law. We men do not know what they suffer. These women have set their feet upon the Rock of Ages, and nothing will drive them from that position. They have taken up the cross, despising the shame, and they will not shrink or turn back."

These words were uttered in the House of Commons, in which were many cynics, in the midst of an awed and reverential silence. The character and age of the speaker himself contributed to this feeling of respect.

If in the course of my imperfect narrative I have omitted to mention some of those who are worthy of mention and honour, I ask that I may be pardoned for that omission. We were many. As the years went on, we gathered adherents from all parts of the civilised world; we came to be a host which it would be difficult to number. There were in the front many distinguished men,—men of European and world-wide reputation, economists, philosophers, statesmen, writers, patriots, leaders of men; and at the same time there were countless helpers whose contribution to the great awakening and onward movement was a hidden one, resembling the vitalising influence of a stream or fountain flowing underneath the soil, whose presence is only known by the verdure and freshness of the pastures around. How many victories have been won for us by the silent prayers of these, while we were in the midst of the battle, will only be known when the secrets of all hearts shall be revealed.

Among the men who stood foremost in those early years, I have already spoken of some. Emeritus Professor Francis Newman, brother of the late Cardinal Newman, gave us strong help by his powerful pen and unflinching rebukes of those in authority who had conspired to bring this trouble upon our country. An anonymous friend won the gratitude of the Ladies' National Association in its infancy, when its resources were meagre, by a gift of £100. This friend proved to be the father of Mr. John Thomasson, of Bolton. His son, in the same spirit, has never failed to stand our friend up to the present day; his gentleness of character and manner, combined with great firmness of principle, has made him to be beloved by us all. Mr. R. F. Martineau, of Birmingham, was ever a firm and clear-headed upholder of our principles, and was the inspirer of the work, during many years, of his own creation,—the Midland Electoral Union. He had strong supporters in Mr. Morgan, the Rev. J. G. Brown and others at Birmingham. Mr. Joseph Edmondson, of Halifax, aided us powerfully by his pen as well as by active labours. The tortuous methods, arguments and subterfuges of our opponents, when they began to take refuge from approaching defeat in manifold "substitutes," were exposed by him in a masterly manner in his pamphlet "The Regulationists and their Policy."

Mr. Henry J. Wilson was from the first, and is now, one of our strongest champions.

I have already mentioned Mr. Edward Backhouse, who supported us munificently year by year by his generous donations as well as by his commanding presence on many public occasions. When his death was announced it was said with truth, "A prince has fallen this day in Israel." His name again recalls those of many other pillars of the Society of Friends, two of Birmingham, Mr. Albright and

Mr. J. E. Wilson, and more especially of those two pure and saintly men George Gillett and Frederick Wheeler. A year or two after our first attack on the vice-regulating laws, there appeared, equipped for the battle, and powerful, though young, another member of that Society, Alfred Dyer, whose action and influence in India, and their important results, are well known to my readers.

For legal advice and help all through, we were greatly indebted to Mr. William Shaen and Professor Sheldon Amos. Mr. Shaen held a prominent position for many years as President of the National Association. I first became acquainted with him in 1870, and retained his friendship till his death. He was a man of great firmness of character, who on first acquaintance appeared cold; yet his nature was one of great gentleness, and his counsel was always kind. One could go to him for advice in the most tragic and criminal cases, sure of his sympathy. Some allusion was once made at a Conference to persons who might be called the *refuse of society*. Mr. Shaen remarked: "For me, there is no refuse of society." Very valuable work was done by him for the British and Continental Federation. He drew up several weighty documents on the legal side of our question, which stated clearly the lines upon which the legislation of the future, connected with the subject of our work, should be based.

Of the National Committee which sat at Westminster, and worked especially with a view to influencing Members of Parliament, the two Mr. Mallesons were pillars of strength, Mrs. W. Malleson contributing by her refined and able pen to our literature. Mr. Banks was from first to last the able and laborious secretary of that Committee. As members of the same Committee I must not fail to mention Mrs. Venturi, a friend of Mazzini, and Mrs. Steward. To the latter was assigned an arduous task in visiting Belgium in aid of the inquiry into the criminal "white slave trade," which was carried on between that country and our own. This mission was promoted by the Abolitionist Committee of the City of

London, headed by our late venerable friend, Mr. Benjamin Scott, for many years Chamberlain of the City of London.

Since the year 1880 a host of younger workers has gathered into our ranks, of whom, while thinking of them with loving regard, I will not attempt here to give even such an imperfect notice as the above.

I have named, after all, only a portion of those who deserve all honour for the sacrifices they made and the good work they did. Our Parliamentary friends, as well as certain leaders of Churches and Denominations who were prominent in our work, are noticed in the course of my narrative. Our principal Continental, American, and other friends come in the same way into the story itself.

Most certainly we have had strong consolation and high privileges in the midst of much obloquy, and some painful experiences. Among the former advantages stands first the fact that the question we dealt with has brought forward at all times, and in all countries, the best men and women of those times and countries, welding them and us into a great league of solid friendships and common aims. Those who have gathered round the Abolitionist standard from the first till now have indeed been of "the salt of the earth."

Personally, it has been to me an indescribable blessing and strength to have been surrounded all along by tenderly loyal adherents and supporters in the persons of my own family, and of those dearest to me. Few, perhaps, have been so highly favoured in this respect. My husband's character and his position in the work are known. My sons, following in his steps, always gave me loving sympathy, and, as they advanced to manhood, practical help, for which I here record my affectionate acknowledgments. My five sisters were, at different times, more or less associated in the work, and were always and strongly in sympathy with it. One of them was for many years an active member of the Executive Committee of the Ladies' National Association, and at her death was succeeded in that position by another sister. Another though frail and in failing health, laboured closely with me

MARTYRS OF THE REGULATION SYSTEM 111

for several years, especially in promoting petitions and memorials from Churches.

The year 1875 has few clear recollections for me, personally, in direct connection with our cause. Six years of work, and more especially the winter months spent in very difficult work on the Continent, had over-taxed my strength. My health gave way, and was only restored by several months of rest, during which I heard only the distant echoes of the conflict, while I remained at home.

Some of those echoes were of a mournful nature. The *Gazetta di Milano* recorded early in that year several cases of girls who had committed suicide to avoid the agony of being placed on the Government register of shame, and of another who had been deliberately and cleverly entrapped into the "service," and who had locked herself into her room, and attempted suicide by breathing the fumes of charcoal. She was found in the morning, stretched on her bed quite insensible, with a crucifix clasped in her arms. The immodest pictures, and other objects suggestive of evil, with which her apartment had been furnished, were found all broken to pieces by her hands, and lay strewed about the room. Happier had it been for her if that sleep had been her last; but life was not extinct, and she was restored to consciousness, to her own bitter grief.

In the month of March, Mrs. Percy, of Aldershot, a widow, who had for some years during her husband's illness maintained her children honestly, drowned herself in order to escape from police persecution, by which, if she had yielded, she would have been driven to be registered on the Government roll of shame. Before taking the fatal resolve she had written a letter to the *Daily Telegraph*. It was a wild appeal of terror and indignation, relieved by a faint hope that some heart would be touched, and her case would be taken up. No answer, however, coming at once to her cry of anguish, she sought refuge from dishonour in death. The National Association instituted a strict inquiry into all the circumstances, which were found to be as Mrs. Percy and he young daughter had stated. That Association also charged itself with the care of the little orphan sons of Mrs. Percy, while her daughter was committed to my husband's care and mine, and was sent to our home in Liverpool. Much indignation was aroused in the country; the Government agent who had hunted this poor woman to death, however, retained his position, possibly receiving a mild warning from the Secretary for War to be more careful in future in the selection of his victims.

An Indignation Meeting was held in St. James's Hall, London, at which our Parliamentary leaders spoke out plainly on this matter. My husband read to that meeting an informal deposition made to him by the young girl soon after she came under our care.

"The statement," he said, "which I am about to read to you was drawn from little Jane Percy in the confidence of a quiet Sunday chat after she had been a fortnight in our house, and it was written down immediately. We asked her to tell us exactly all she could recollect, if it was not too painful to her. She replied, 'I will tell you exactly what I saw and remember'; and then, speaking for the first time of the bitter trial to which she had been subjected, she said: 'They called the police and ordered my mother to go up to the Metropolitan Police Office and bring me with her. Mamma and I went. We there saw Inspector G——. He was in his room, and mamma was first called in alone. I cannot, therefore, tell what passed between mamma and the Inspector, because I was not there. I can only tell you this, that mamma was never the same person again after that hour. She told me that she assured Inspector G—— that she would rather sign her death-warrant than the paper he gave her to sign. I was then called in. I shall never forget the moment when I stood before Inspector G—— and he accused me. He said, "Do you know, girl, why you are here?" I replied, "No, sir, I do not." He said, "You are here because you are no better than you should be. You know what that means, I suppose?" I said, "No, sir, I do not." He laughed in a horrible way when I said this. I continued to deny that I knew what he meant; for, indeed, I did not. I knew what a bad character was: there are plenty in Aldershot; but I could not understand that he meant to accuse me and my mamma of being bad characters. He asked me if we had a "pass" into the camp. I answered " Yes, we always had one : for we had engagements to sing while papa was lying ill." He then shouted to some one, " See that these two women have their passes taken away from them ; we will put a stop to all that!" You see, mamma could not earn a living after this. It hurt me so when he called mamma and me " these two women !" Mamma said to me when we came out, " Jenny, this will be the death of me." She never looked cheerful any more. She was watched by the police wherever she went. Then she wrote that last letter to the *Daily Telegraph.* Soon after that we went away to try and get an engagement elsewhere, but could not succeed. Mamma was always crying, and we began to feel what a loss father was ; for though he was so ill that he was not able to earn a penny for two years, he was a good friend. We used to tell him every trouble, and he would talk it over and advise us kindly. Nobody but myself knows what mamma suffered. She could never rest at night ; for she said Inspector G——'s face was always before her, as she saw it when he accused her. If she fell asleep, she would wake up sobbing and in a fright. I consider that man has been the death of my mamma. He said to her at the end, " I will not let you alone." Well, a friend came from Aldershot to ask mamma to go back there. We went back. Friends used to say to her, " Cheer up! you will be all the more respected when this is cleared up and the truth is known." She again said she would choose death rather than do as Inspector G—— wished her to do !'

" Jenny spoke all this in a low, quiet voice, not at all excitedly. Her visit to the police station seemed to haunt her even more than her mother's death. She is proud of her mother, and this pride helps her to bear the loss. She said at last: 'What a law this is! I never could believe there was such a law. Since this law was made it is not considered respectable to speak to a soldier, nor have one in your house; but I can tell you that, though I have lived among soldiers ever since I was born, I never had a rough word or an insult from one in my life, and they were always respectful to my mamma. I think you will find that all those who knew her spoke well of her.'"

In May of this year a very important series of conferences was held in London on the occasion of the visit of several well-known Continental members of the Federation whom we had invited to meet us. Among these was M. Edmond de Pressensé. This distinguished man has been described as "one of the most eloquent scholars and scholarly divines of the French Reformed Church." He had an intellectual countenance and a rich and pleasant voice; but his success as a preacher was chiefly secured by the solidity of his attainments and the depth of his religious convictions. He published many solid works, among which are "Lectures on Christianity in its Application to Social Questions," "A History of the First Three Centuries of the Christian Era," and his "Life of Christ," which was published in 1866. He was a member of the National Assembly, and was nominated by it as Chairman of a Committee for investigating the Penitentiary Laws, and was later the principal actor on a Commission on the prison of St. Lazare. He was created a Chevalier of the Legion of Honour for his devotion in relieving the poor during the Franco-German War, and was finally elected a member of the Senate.

M. George Appia, an Italian by birth, was well known as an ardent apostle of the ancient Waldensian Church in Italy. He had been called to Paris as a Pastor of the Church of the Augsburg Confession; a man of genius and of a highly spiritual nature.

Two of our other visitors on this occasion have already been introduced to the reader, viz., M. Aimé Humbert and M. Giuseppe Nathan. Père Hyacinthe also was among the

CONFERENCES IN LONDON

invited, but took ill after arriving in London, and was prevented attending these Conferences. He addressed a meeting some weeks later in St. James's Hall on behalf of the Federation.

A Conversazione was held in the Westminster Palace Hotel on the evening before the Conference, when one or two informal addresses were given by the Continental visitors. M. Humbert, speaking in French, said: "I must tell you that the work of reform which you have taken up is not entirely an innovation in our Continental history. As far back as twenty years ago Pastor Borel undertook singlehanded in Geneva the stupendous task of bringing the question before the public, and of combating for the abolition of these laws. But he was alone in the work; alone in signing a petition to the Grand Council. He sent his petition. It was acknowledged and sent back to be examined by the Council of State, and no more was heard of it. The following year he made another charge, with no more success than the first. He continued to labour on, and by great tact and effort succeeded in securing the escape of several of the victims from the tolerated houses. The track had been opened, and pioneers came in. Two years ago the newspapers of Geneva acquainted the public with the startling fact that an English lady had come for the special purpose of holding Conferences on the question raised by Pastor Borel. Every one said, 'Ah, a very English proceeding, indeed!' The matter was treated with more or less of levity until the Genevese learnt that a British and Continental Federation had been formed to deal with the matter, and that the seat of the Federation was London. This news stirred them. A Federation with its headquarters in London must be something worth notice. . . . I believe that henceforward both sides of the Channel will advance hand-in-hand in this great question of justice."

A very large and representative Conference was held the following afternoon. A crowd of delegates came from all parts of the United Kingdom. Mr. Stansfeld presided

Canon Butler read several letters, one from Père Hyacinthe regretting his enforced absence, a second from Professor Emile de Laveleye, whose attention had only recently been drawn to this question, and who now sent us the expression of his complete adhesion to our principles and work. Another letter was from Pastor Theodore Monod, who was prevented joining us by the obligation to attend a series of Conferences in the South of France. He wrote:—

"We are with you in spirit; we are providing ourselves with ammunition; we shall make use of your guns on the battle-field. Surely it is high time that every Christian should rouse himself to more earnest prayer, more steadfast trust and more whole-hearted devotion, and, as a necessary consequence, march forward in the Saviour's might against these citadels of iniquity."

M. de Pressensé's speech on this occasion was one of the most remarkable we had ever heard. Mr. Stansfeld spoke of it as follows: "I knew that M. de Pressensé was a politician with a great and well-deserved reputation in his own country. I knew that he was an orator and a well-known divine; but I did not expect the privilege which was in store for us in the discourse to which we have just listened, a discourse displaying merits which are very rarely to be found combined in the speech of one man. It was the speech of a philosopher who has alike the instinct and training of a statesman. It contained the clearest statement of principle, and it was full of the divine sentiment of love which should fill the hearts of those who preach the Gospel. It was delivered with an energy and antithesis of eloquence of which, I fear, few Englishmen are capable."

Every word of this speech is worthy of reproduction, but I only give here an extract or two.

"I entreat you to observe," M. de Pressensé said, "that the State can only defend rights conformably with right, and with respect for individual liberty. Now in the case we are considering, not only does it pursue the opposite of right, but the means by which it acts are a flagrant violation of right. It withdraws the individual liberties of thousands of human beings from the guardianship of law and of justice, and delivers them over to the caprice of the administration; by this act all those laws and rules made to prevent injustice being done, and to prohibit imprisonment except under formally determined conditions, are abrogated; they are replaced by the *régime* of arbitrary will.

"I will consent, however, to come down to the lower ground of consequences, of results, although, in advance, I assert I am convinced that there can be no real conflict between principles and results, and that evil must always bring forth evil. You, who are the partisans of these sanitary laws, speak of the public safety. Well, I will confine myself to this question—Who do you save? We will not speak of the woman; she is the necessary victim of the system—the living material, which has to be mangled and torn by the iron teeth and wheels of this pitiless mechanism. We will speak of her later; for the present I leave her out of account. I repeat my question, Who do you save? (putting out of account the woman, doomed to irremediable perdition.) Is it the *man* whom you save? I deny it! Placing myself even at your own materialistic standpoint, I deny it. You speak only of the man's body; you speak not of his soul, and you are right. But you do not save his body. This is certain, even from the documents furnished by the partisans of the system themselves. A competent writer,[1] who has deeply studied this subject, has uttered these words (speaking of Paris): 'Prostitution engenders prostitution. That which lights a fire at one point propagates it everywhere.' So true is this, that this sincere writer records the fact that prostitution, outside of the sanitary laws, increases from day to day in a most frightful degree.

"Statistics are peremptory in their condemnation of these laws. For one victim who comes under sanitary observation hundreds escape you, and your measures of protection are

[1] See the book of Lecour, "La Prostitution à Paris et à Londres." 1782–1872.

useless. How could it be otherwise? You wish to regulate vice, but it is of the essence of vice to refuse to be regulated. Vice violates moral law, and you may expect it to transgress human rules. It is like a torrent which has overflowed its banks; you cannot say, 'Thus far shalt thou lawfully go, and no further.' It mocks all your regulations. You will never succeed in making disorderly passions universally well ordered in their gratification.

"You do not save the body! And the soul, the moral nature!—does not the State contribute towards its perversion in sanctioning the idea that debauchery at a certain age is a natural law, before which the young man must bow— a law which the State recognises? And thus the State facilitates the first steps to immorality, and becomes the tempter of the young man. In facilitating these first steps, it favours public immorality; for the patented evil has its recognised place in human legislation. You speak of the harm which prostitution does to the body. You would preserve the body, and you begin by poisoning the soul. Ah, you have forgotten that *trifling thing*, the immortal soul! You have forgotten the soul of youth, the soul of your country. You have forgotten that this profligacy which you facilitate contributes to the corruption of the youth of the nation, and sends it back to the domestic hearth blighted, corrupted, prematurely aged, when it is not separated for ever from the domestic hearth, as is the case now in certain countries, where the complaint is made of the diminution of marriages, and (as in the decline of the Roman Empire) rewards are held out to those who will marry and bring up children. You have withered the purity, the vigour, the moral energy of those young hearts. The Proverbs of Solomon tell us that the house of debauchery (officially regulated or not) is an open sepulchre—that it rests upon the tomb; and it is true. And you wish that the State should hold the key to that chamber of death—that the State should be the door-keeper to admit to it our youthful citizens! You will not hinder, by your sanitary laws, the realisation of the terrible genealogy of sin recorded by St. James: 'When lust has conceived, it bringeth forth sin; and sin, when it is finished, bringeth forth death.' Yes, prostitution kills the soul, even when it does not kill the body. This is the dialectic of evil, which follows its own inexorable course.

"The partisans of this system say to us, however:— 'Society has a right to defend itself against physical evils which destroy it; it has a right to resort to any means when it has to deal not only with debauchery, but with debauchery which is a commerce; and these regulations, after all, only apply to the infamous creatures who sell themselves, and have put themselves beyond the pale of the law and of society: they are but the dirt of the street.' Now I do not under-rate the abomination of paid debauchery. Yes, the vice which sells itself is abominable; what, then, shall we say of those who buy it? But there are distinctions to be made among those who sell. Let us look a little closer at the situation of the woman whom Governments have submitted to a regulation which is a complete and abject slavery. She deserves nothing but contempt you tell us! She is invariably as morally perverse as you tell us she is! I ask, how many of these girls are thrust upon the streets by abandonment after seduction, or dragged down by want into the infamy from which they cannot escape? What is your part in the matter? You engulf them further; you thrust them down lower; you throw on them the last shovelful of earth to hurl them to the abyss; you roll upon them the stone which cannot be removed except by a supernatural effort. 'Ah! you have fallen, unfortunate creature,' you say; 'well, we will complete the work, we will consummate your degradation: that which is already soiled shall be made still more vile.' This is logic; but it is the logic of demons!

"I have supposed the case—so frequently occurring—of the misfortunes which precipitate into public vice a young girl, a weak being, a mere child, perhaps, of fifteen or sixteen years, the victim of infamous seduction. Let us go further, and passing beyond all the various shades of difference, let us take the worst cases of degradation. I have admitted, I admit, that the woman who sells herself is a shameful being; but what, I have asked, and ask again, shall we say of those who buy? Is the stronger sex, being the purchaser, worthy of greater respect than the weaker sex which is purchased? You desire that the State shall sacrifice to the supposed public security thousands of female victims doomed to perdition, and you forget that the profligate man is equally a peril to public health with the impure woman. When I look at this extremity of degradation which is set before us in order to justify measures so terrible as those we oppose, I remember that I belong to a religion of divine pity, and that no Christian can dare to say that even these most degraded beings are beyond hope. I remember that there is a love which seeks the lost soul, the lost treasure, in the very dust of the road, and that that love is faithful and powerful and hopeful. A noble Christian has said: 'The world will believe in God when it sees that the disciples of Christ believe in the human soul'; or, rather, that they believe in that immense charity which descends into the lowest abyss to seek that which is lost. In the face, then, even of the profoundest debasement, we have no right to say, 'All is over! we may now treat this being as vile matter which may receive the official stamp at the custom-house of human merchandise.'

"Here is a poor sinner who has heard of Jesus of Nazareth; her heart beats with a new hope; she curses her abominable life; she feels an impulse to go forward and throw herself weeping at His feet. But the State policeman steps in and says, 'Stop! you cannot pass; you must wait for our authorisation; you must wait till your name is removed from the register: you belong to us, and we will not give you up until you have been long tested.' She turns away and waits, and while she waits her tears dry up, her heart again hardens, and she returns to infamy. Thus the poor drowning creature is plunged once more into the waves of impurity, and when she would seize hold of the plank of

A SOLEMN WARNING

salvation it is dashed away from her trembling hands. Such is your system! and there are *Christians who approve it!* I know that there was an age when pagan temples were devoted to the worship of Venus, and where there were priestesses who were also the victims of horrible vice; but I had believed that, eighteen centuries ago, Eternal Love had appeared upon the earth!

"I do not hide from myself the horror and the peril of the prostitution which exists where there are not these laws— the horror and danger of prostitution under every aspect, independently of the moral guilt of governments which guarantee it. We must enter upon a grand crusade, not only against legal prostitution, but against profligacy itself; we must form an indomitable league. . . . We must pursue vice up to its source; we must follow it in all its forms and in all its hiding-places; we must attack the unholy literature, the impure art, and the debased drama which are connected with it. Above all, we must combat the disastrous delusion, so fixed in many minds, that vice is an inevitable fatality; we must hold up before our youth the ideal of purity and of domestic worth.

"One word more: contemporary Christianity has done much for the furtherance of the Christian faith, and we are profoundly moved at the sight of its noble works. This is the month in which religious societies hold meetings and record their labours. Nothing better! but let us take care that, in giving ourselves to these good works, we do not forget the wrongs which lie at our door; that in the midst of this activity, so rich, so varied, carried to the very ends of the earth, we do not overlook the perdition in which are plunged the victims of our civilisation. Let us take heed, lest the Master say to us, 'Yes, you have served Me; you have adorned My sanctuaries to receive Me with honour; you have shown great zeal in the propagation of your religion; but the Pharisaism of old did the same; yet I rejected it because it rejected the poor lost woman. He who truly **loves, loves** that which is lost; but you, O Christian who bearest My name, what have you done for her that is lost? what have you *allowed* to be done to her? You have suffered her to be taken and devoted to infamy for the security of your sons. Therefore I say to you, I cannot endure your solemn feasts.' May we be spared this condemnation!"

During the meeting a letter was received bearing the Paris postmark, and handed to the Chairman, who pronounced it to be important. It was an address expressing the fullest sympathy with the aims of the Federation, and was signed by a long list of divines and laymen, Protestant leaders throughout France.

Professor Sheldon Amos made a very weighty speech on this occasion, full of close reasoning, and supported by legal arguments. He was followed by Sir Harcourt Johnstone, the Rev. James Martineau, the Right Honourable G. Shaw Lefevre, and others.

In April of this year Mr. Gledstone and Mr. H. J. Wilson started on a mission to the United States as delegates from the Federation. I asked Mr. Gledstone to write for me briefly his recollections of the chief events of that important mission. He consented to do so, and the following is his account:—

"It was, I remember, a cold stormy Thursday in April, 1876, when you persisted in accompanying Mr. Wilson and me to the river, to see us on board the *Adriatic*. The anti-regulation struggle has seen some uncommon things; I think so now, as I recall your slender form seeking shelter from the keen wind that swept through the little tug that conveyed us to the huge steamer lying in the middle of the Mersey—two strong men sent out on their mission and cheered to it by one woman! Snow was on the tops of the Welsh hills as we got into the Channel. The next day—Good Friday—was spent in Cork; then came a cold enough voyage.

"Bearing, as we did, letters of introduction to several of the leaders of the old anti-slavery party, we thought of beginning our mission to the American people at Boston, and using that as a centre for our propaganda. Providence had arranged it otherwise; we began at New York and ended at Boston, thus reversing our plan.

"First of all we tried, simultaneously with our missionary efforts, to learn exactly the state of opinion on the system of State regulation of vice, and what had been done to keep it out of the country. We found that attempts had been made at many centres, in different ways, to get the system a footing. Doctors and sanitary specialists were its apostles. Some of the medical journals had, at odd times, for some years past, been doing what they could to commend it to the notice and favour of the profession. Although we never came upon any sign of the existence of an organised pro-regulation party, we saw abundant evidence of the existence, all over the States, of men, chiefly doctors, who were resolutely bent upon having the regulation established in some form or another. *The Medical Gazette* of New York had been very zealous in 1870-71 in that direction.

"In New York, in Chicago, in California, in Baltimore, in the district of Columbia, in Cincinnati, in Pennsylvania, unsuccessful attempts had been made to get State or municipal regulation. In California the Bill which was introduced into the Legislature became known to a quick-witted woman, the wife of one of the members, who immediately had another Bill drafted, exactly the same as the first, save one word—for *woman* she substituted *man*. She then got several members of the Legislature to promise that they would bring her Bill forward if any further progress was made with the other. The mere sight of hers drove the other into oblivion! She played a bold and risky game, for had her Bill been accepted along with the other, it would have lain a dead letter, whereas the police would have worked the other with vigour. She saw, so far, only the injustice of the proposed Bill, inasmuch as it touched women and exempted men; but did not see that it was also immoral to apply regulation even to men and women alike.

"On three occasions attempts had been made in the

district of Columbia, for the sake, of course, of including Washington. One of them was defeated by the energy and resolution of Miss Edson. Learning late one evening that a proposal was to be brought before Congress the next day, she instantly left her home, and spent almost the whole night in visiting newspaper offices, interviewing editors, and ringing Congress men out of their beds to inform them of the character of the Bill, and to implore them to oppose it. By this means time was gained, and with the assistance of others she continued an opposition which was ultimately successful. Her effort cost her her life; she soon fell ill from over-exertion and died.

"In every case the women seemed to have been particularly vigilant and resolute, and from them we got some of our most effective help. The women doctors, who were just as capable as the men doctors of understanding the question in its physical bearings, were entirely with us; at least, I cannot remember one who was not.

"As an example of the service that may be rendered by one intelligent and resolute man, I think I ought to name Mr. Francis King, of Baltimore, a member of the Society of Friends, who, when the Chairman of the Grand Jury broached the system of regulation, gave it his firm resistance. Mr. King had studied the subject in Europe.

"One place, St. Louis, had been afflicted with regulation from 1870 to 1874. It had been introduced with a craft quite worthy of the 'father of lies,' a clause of the City Charter which dealt with the suppression of houses of ill-repute being modified by the introduction of two words, 'or regulate'; the Charter was thus altered—'to suppress *or regulate* houses of ill-fame.' Rev. Dr. Eliot, of Washington University, led the opposition to it; 4,000 women petitioned for its repeal; and it was removed by a unanimous vote of the Senate of the State of Missouri.

"There was evidently work to be done; more than the Federation which had sent us knew of, much more than the American friends of purity for a moment suspected. They were mostly living in happy ignorance of this plotting against the rights of all the women of the States, and against the morals of the whole Republic. If our mission did nothing else, we have the satisfaction of knowing that it effectually broke up that self-confidence.

"In New York, where we landed on April 24th, we found that preparations had been made by Mr. Aaron M. Powell and Mrs. Gibbons for the holding of a conference the next day. This was only a small gathering at Mrs. Gibbons' house of some twelve or fifteen ladies and gentlemen, to whom we explained the object of our coming, and from whom we received suggestions as to the best course for us to pursue. During the ten weeks of our stay in America, we held six conferences in New York, each of them interesting in its own peculiar way; one of them, in the New York Infirmary, specially so, owing to the number of young women present who were studying medicine.

"In Dr. Cuyler, of Brooklyn, we found a warm and influential friend; he took me with him to the house of Mr. Dodge, where I had the opportunity of addressing some twenty-five of the most noted Presbyterian, Dutch Reformed, and Congregational clergymen of the city. The same privilege was extended to me by the Baptist ministers, of whom a hundred were present at the meeting. I believe that by means of these ministerial associations I succeeded in addressing almost the whole of the ministers in all the great cities of the East. They were, of course, busy in every case with their own local concerns, and could not find time to discuss the theme brought before them; but there is ground for believing that interest was excited and sympathy gained.

"Among the more striking incidents of our tour was the presentment, while we were in New York, to the 'Court of General Sessions of the Peace for the City and County of New York,' of its own Grand Jury in favour of dealing with the social evil by means of regulation. The presentment closed with a resolution earnestly requesting the Legislature of the State of New York to adopt some system of laws calculated to confine houses of ill-fame in large cities to certain specified localities, and to subject them at all times to the careful and vigilant supervision of the Boards of Health and Police. This presentment appeared in the *Evening Post* of June 2nd (Friday), 1876; and before we slept that night we had penned a protest against it in the name of the Federation, taking up each point and answering it in the light of our English and European experience. The next day we spent in interviewing editors, and on Monday the *Herald* published our protest; three other papers also had articles on the presentment, either condemning it as immoral, or making light of it as a suggestion made too late in the day for acceptance.

"I cannot leave the subject of New York without saying a word about the kind and devoted friends we met. Mr. and Mrs. Aaron M. Powell gave us a cordial welcome and unstinted help, and have carried on, ever since our return, the work of meeting and resisting all attempt to legalise vice. Mr. Powell had formerly been editor of the *Anti-Slavery Standard*, and, like all the surviving members of the great anti-slavery movement, seemed to have an intuitive knowledge of the great moral principles for which we were contending. Mrs. Gibbons was another of our good friends, and in the rooms of the Isaac T. Hopper Home (a benevolent home named in honour of her brave, unselfish father) we had one or more of our conferences. Mrs. Gay, of Staten Island, another Quaker and Abolitionist, gave us excellent help, and has continued in the good work till now. Mrs. Hussey aided us much among medical practitioners.

"As one result of our visit, a Vigilance Committee was formed, which has kept a sleepless eye on the movements of the enemy, and has defeated many insidious plans to introduce regulation through sanitary arrangements, or municipal laws, or State enactments. It has also created a literature, modest indeed in size, but appealing to all that is best and purest in the nation. Ten years ago the *Philanthropist*, a monthly journal, was started, to be the organ of the purity party, and has done good service. I cannot but believe that in New

York alone our work was a quiet introduction to the energetic White Cross Crusade, and to the daring attacks of Dr. Parkhurst upon the corrupt police and municipal authorities. The friends who had co-operated with us have, for almost nineteen years, not only kept up a protest against every form of legalising vice, but have also thrown themselves into every available form of service for the promotion of a sound public opinion on the relation of the sexes.

"By the time we reached Washington a Bill had been framed by the Board of Health and introduced into the House of Representatives, which, on its face, looked innocent enough, but which really contained clauses of a very dangerous character. Professing to be only a sanitary measure, it, in fact, gave ample powers for working a system of inspection and license. At one of our conferences we had the presence of the Rev. J. L. Townsend, Chaplain of the House of Representatives, who, hearing of what was being proposed, said he should confer with the Chaplain of the Senate, so that together they might co-operate against the objectionable measure. Mr. H. J. Wilson also had an interview with Mr. Willard, who had introduced the Bill into the Legislature, but who frankly declared that he had no intention to support the regulating system; he said the phraseology of the Bill, which was evidently open to a bad interpretation and use, must be altered.

"One of our best friends in this city was Mrs. Dr. Winslow; she was one of the first women in America who took a medical degree, and in consequence she suffered a good deal of domestic and social persecution. The people who had smelt the fire of trouble for conscientious convictions seemed to fall to our side by a kind of instinct; they grasped the moral principles we set forth, and understood their bearing at once.

"At Baltimore the General Conference of the Methodist Episcopal Church was sitting. Dr. Rigg and the Rev. W. B. Pope, who were attending it as delegates from the Wesleyan Methodist Conference in England, having been entrusted with an address to it from the Wesleyan Society for the repeal of the English Acts, the former gentleman carried out this commission. A special Committee which was appointed to draw up a reply, heard evidence from Dr. Rigg and myself as to the nature and futility of our English Acts, and as to the great uprising of opinion on the Continent of Europe against licensed vice. In their reply they expressed themselves as being utterly opposed to regulation; and I believe I am right in saying that both in America and by its missionaries in India this powerful Church has always and consistently gone against regulation in any form.

"It is pleasant to recall the kindnesses and aid of single persons and of groups of persons; Dr. Thomas, a Quaker physician, was the friend who specially aided us at Baltimore.

"We had quite a remarkable experience at Philadelphia, both in the way of assailing our opponents and in making for our cause new and influential friends all over the States. At the time of our visit the doctors of Pennsylvania were holding the annual meeting of their Society, and gave our work aid which was as unexpected as it was unwilling. They had been told by one of their journals that a 'vehement effort' ought to be made by them to get prostitution legalised; it was their 'duty' to do it. Of any intention to do their 'duty' they gave no sign; but at the last moment, just as we were on the point of leaving for Boston, two anti-regulation doctors, of whom the city had a goodly number, informed us that on the following day a determined effort was to be made to commit the Society to an active regulationist policy. Thereupon we got Mrs. Franciscus, the President of the Women's Christian Association, and Mrs. French, President of the Moral Education Society, to send a letter to all the doctors known to be opposed to regulation, asking them to attend every meeting of the Medical Society, and resist any such attempt. At the meeting of the W.C.A., the hundred women who were present rose to their feet to signify their approval of the letter; a feeling of intense indignation was aroused, and a regulationist doctor would have had determined opposition from the women of the capital city of the State.

How it came to pass we never could learn, but it is certain that the 'vehement effort' never was made. As we came across many friends in Philadelphia who saw no need for doing anything—the subject being 'unpleasant,' 'not before the public,' and 'not fit for discussion before men and women' —we had the doctors to thank for effectually scattering all these objections, and sending a shock of much needed energy into our work. So the way of men was over-ruled by the higher way of God.

"Let me recall the friendly faces and names of those who aided us—the Rev. Andrew Longacre, the Rev. Joseph May, Mr. and Mrs. Enoch Lewis, Bishop Simpson, Mr. Rowland (of the Y.M.C.A.), Dr. Herman Thomas, Mr. and Mrs. Ingraham, Mrs. Harriet French, Miss Anthony, and that brave old lady, Mrs. Lucretia Mott. To some of your readers, dear Mrs. Butler, these names will mean nothing; but please let them stand on the pages of your book of reminiscences, for they mean much to others, and deserve a record.

"Our good friends Mr. and Mrs. Powell, of New York, were present during part of the time of our visits to Philadelphia, attending the meetings of the International Temperance Convention, and they kindly arranged a meeting of Temperance friends from all parts of the States for us to address. It was a choice opportunity, of which we made the most. Mrs. Powell sent you home an account, in which she spoke of the meeting as 'a very impressive meeting,' in which the power of the Spirit of God was present, and where many of the audience, men and women, were in tears. Yes; I remember it from a long distance of time as a season of help and blessing.

"The city of Boston, which we had at first counted upon as sure to be the most responsive and most easily worked, proved to be one of the most difficult, until we obtained the countenance and co-operation of Mr. William Lloyd Garrison. Even the women, usually the quickest to come to the aid of our cause, were cautious and doubtful. That Massachusetts should ever legalise immorality seemed to them to be as remote as the end of the world. New York was a dissolute city, under the control of foreigners, and might do anything bad; but Boston had some regard for the moral law. Our arguments were met with simple incredulity and indifference. Since then our warnings have only been too abundantly justified.

"When Mr. Garrison, to whom we had the best of introductions, heard our case and the difficulties which had been thrown in our way, he said:—

"'Do not listen to the dissuasions from going on with your work, and speaking the message you are entrusted with. I do not agree with those who affirm that it is inexpedient to speak the truth here on this question. Speak it; it will do good. But do not hold a public meeting. Get those to hear you who will influence public opinion in the day of need. My name is at your service for any circular you may issue, calling such a conference as I have indicated.'

"This was the plan of operations we had followed all the way through, and as soon as the great Abolitionist's name was put upon our circular, it was adopted by the leading reformers of the city. Never before had I seen so great a change wrought by the word of one man; his judgment was evidently regarded as a final court of appeal. With that splendid loyalty to his old chief which always distinguished Mr. Wendell Phillips, the great orator of the Abolition cause, he immediately gave us his aid, and consented to preside at our Conference. About a hundred and fifty of the most active of the reformers of the city came together in the rooms of the Y.M.C.A. (that institution always had an open door for us), and a most enthusiastic meeting was held. My colleague, Mr. Wilson, had gallantly offered to do the hardest part of the work, viz., answering any question that might be asked, but after more than an hour of severe catechising he was tired out, and I had to come to his aid. You may know a subject very well, but when you have been tested by the inquisitiveness of a Boston audience you may feel pretty comfortable anywhere else.

" Our meeting was favoured with short speeches by our Chairman, by Mrs. Livermore, and by Mrs. Stone.

"I cannot leave Boston without mentioning the inspiration which Mr. Garrison's words and influence were to every good work; he started me on the study of the great Abolition movement, a cause which, indirectly has done much for our own. Then, again, I remember with a tender heart the modest kindness of Mr. Wendell Phillips in taking us to see some of the sights of Boston, and in calling with us on some newspaper editors. I remember his snug, quaint little house, which might have been taken from one of the ancient streets of York or Chester; I see now the bust of John Brown's magnificent head, just arrived from the sculptor's, standing on the sill of the staircase window; and I still hear the soft tones in which he said, as I parted from him—'Don't forget an old man.' I can never forget him; his speeches have become to me the noblest models of Christian moral teaching; I know nothing like them in the whole range of English oratory, either for substance or for style.

" One strong desire which we felt at the termination of our work was for the American people to make common cause with the English and with Continental friends against legalised immorality; and this they have done. The American Committee joined the Federation, and have frequently sent Mr. Powell to attend its meetings; they realise that in this sacred cause the nations are one. If we were permitted to render any service to the great Republic, the debt has been more than repaid by the priceless work of Mrs. Andrew and Dr. Kate Bushnell on behalf of India. Bonds of love and sympathy have been woven which nothing can break."

CHAPTER VII

> " Who serves to-day upon the list
> Beside the served shall stand ;
> Alike the brown and wrinkled fist,
> The gloved and dainty hand!
>
> The rich is level with the poor,
> The weak is strong to-day,
> And sleekest broadcloth counts no more
> Than homespun frock of grey."

I WENT with my husband to Switzerland in the month of June of 1876 to see the friends who were then preparing for the Congress of the following year, and to seek among the mountains the calm of spirit which we wished to possess, and to be able in a measure to impart in the midst of the increasing conflict. We first visited Neuchâtel in order to confer on the arrangements for the Congress with that master organizer, M. Humbert, who accompanied us to a beautiful rural retreat on the Jura for a short time of rest. A week or two later other representatives of the Federation arrived in Switzerland, Giuseppe Nathan from Italy, and Professor Stuart and one of my sons from England. My sister, Madame Meuricoffre, and her family also came to their Swiss summer home. A meeting was held at Berne, in July, for the purpose of forming a working Committee to arrange for the Congress. The meeting and the Committee were presided over by a distinguished Swiss gentleman, the Federal Colonel Othon von Büren, whose memory lives in the hearts of his countrymen. It was he who, in the disastrous Franco-German War, went to Strasburg and drew out from that beleaguered city and other parts of Alsatia a vast host of aged and feebled persons, women, and children, and led them to Switzerland, to be received and nourished and protected by that hospitable nation, which added in that year one more page of heroic and pathetic beauty to the many noble pages of its past history. Colonel von Büren performed this service with a patience, firmness, military orderliness, and fatherly tenderness which endeared him to every one. This service, added to his reputation as a soldier, and the consistency of his Christian character, has made his name deservedly renowned. He and two other well-known Swiss soldiers became from this time staunch adherents of the Federation. Those others were Colonel Steiger and Colonel de Perrot, the latter a Neuchâtelois. We were joined later by another officer of high rank and noble character from Eastern Switzerland, Colonel Kaiser, of Zug, who had, before our acquaintance with him, written and published some excellent brochures on the work of the Federation, "Letters to the Athenians," addressed to the people of Zurich, which was sometimes called the Modern Athens.

It was an overpoweringly hot day when we held this meeting at Berne in the Hall of the Abbaye des Bouchers. It was in the afternoon, and nothing less than the great interest of the approaching events about which we were taking counsel together could have sufficed to keep us awake! M. Humbert made a clear statement of plans and operations, M. Nathan spoke with deep feeling concerning his own country, and my husband explained the prominent position taken by women in this cause with a force and gentleness which deeply impressed the ladies present, and won many to leave their retirement and join our ranks. Our good allies, Madame de Gingins, the two young Mesdames de Watteville, and others, had already become leaders in the movement in their own country.

Once more my husband was obliged to leave me, being recalled, in the month of August, by his imperative duties at the Liverpool College. I went to stay with my sister, Madame Meuricoffre, at her home in the Canton de Vaud. While there an unexpected invitation was sent to me to address, the following day, a mass meeting of the working people of Geneva in the Electoral Hall in that city. I had not yet addressed any great popular assembly in French, and felt unable to do so at such short notice. In my first tour in 1874-5 I had spoken in French and Italian, but always with time for careful preparation. But as the invitation was urgent I accepted it, on the condition that my sister, who was perfectly at home in the French language, should accompany me, stand near me, prompt me, and, if necessary, interpret for me. On the morning of the day when the meeting was to take place I went to her room to confer with and be strengthened by her concerning it, when I found to my dismay that she was completely prostrated by an attack of faintness and severe pain in the head. It was too late, however, to change my decision, and the afternoon was a time to me of a good deal of anxiety.

Towards evening I went to say farewell to her before starting on the short journey to Geneva. Her room was darkened, her eyes were closed, and she spoke with difficulty on account of pain. I stooped to kiss her, and she whispered to me, in a calm tone of conviction, the words, "*they spake with other tongues, as the Spirit gave them utterance.*" It was a revelation to me, and I went in the strength of those words to the dreaded meeting.

I was met in Geneva by M. Humbert, M. Sautter de Blonay, of the Canton de Vaud, Professor Stuart, and others. An eye-witness wrote to friends in England of the meeting as follows: "We arrived punctually at the hour, and soon perceived what sort of a meeting we were about to have by the fact that hundreds of people, chiefly working men, were coming away from the hall saying, 'no use, not a place to be had, even to stand'; while not only the hall itself, but a long outside gallery surrounding it, and open to the air, was crowded. The crowd was so dense that Mrs. Butler and her friends could with difficulty press in. Even such persons as the President of the Grand Council of Geneva, and Père Hyacinthe Loyson, were obliged to stand, not finding a seat unoccupied. It was a hot and brilliant moonlight night, and from the body of the hall might be seen outside the doors and windows a sea of faces of persons standing patiently the whole time to catch what they could of the words spoken, while groups of men sat on the ledges of the open windows, or hung on where they could."

It was affecting to observe, even in Geneva, where the consciences of the working population were said to be, in a measure, falsified by the influence of the system of Regulation, that the sentiments which were responded to with the most evidence of feeling were those which expressed pity and sympathy for the fallen, and indignation concerning the principles of justice and equality outraged by the system we oppose. M. Sautter de Blonay and M. Humbert spoke eloquently, and I was able, by God's grace, to deliver my message with comparative ease to that large assembly. At one moment there was a movement in the lower part of the hall, and evidence of some sinister presence and influence; an attempt to utter coarse words of opposition and insult, which was immediately quelled by the working men surrounding the person who had risen, and who was finally carried off bodily by them and placed in the open street. We found, afterwards, that this was the keeper of one of the notorious houses of debauchery in the town under the protection of the Government of Geneva—a person holding an official authorisation, in fact, who felt he had a right to be heard; a man with a most hideous expression of countenance resembling a vulture greedily scouring the face of the earth for prey.

I had not at this time visited any German town in the interests of our cause; I therefore accepted a proposal to travel homewards by the Rhine. I stayed some days in Frankfort-s.M., and was there encouraged, by the sympathy of several leading citizens, above all by that of Dr. André, a medical man, and a philosophical writer, whose convictions on this subject were very deep, and supported by a very considerable experience as a doctor. M. Gerard, a pastor of

Swiss origin, called a meeting in his own house, in which I was very kindly received.

I went next to Cologne and Elberfeld. In the latter town I found a very considerable group of ministers and ladies, who showed an intelligent sympathy with our motives and work. Returning from Elberfeld, I visited Liège and Brussels. M. Emile de Laveleye was absent at that time from Liège, but some little initiatory work was done in that city, through the kind help and zeal of Pastors Durand and Nicolet. The latter was a strong and active adherent from that time forward. It was during this visit to Belgium that I made my first acquaintance with the awful crimes and cruelties resulting from the system of regulation long established there, and which were brought fully to light, later, by the action of the City of London Committee, and the investigations so courageously undertaken by George Gillett and Alfred Dyer. In Brussels our chief friends were, in those early days, Pastor Anet and Mr. Cor van der Maaren, the famous champion of Free Trade principles in Belgium, who in the early days of his political career was stoned in the streets of Brussels, and who, after his death, when his principles had triumphed, was honoured by having a statue erected of him in one of the public squares. He at once took up our cause, and gave me an introduction to M. Couvreu, a Member of Parliament. Madame Behrends also helped us, and became one of our correspondents for some years.

In the late autumn of this year a "newspaper war" on this subject broke out suddenly in France. It was probably kindled by numerous cases of Police brutality, and frequent arrests both of men and women for resisting, or even speaking against, the *Police des Mœurs*. But a deeper source of resistance was the growing force of public opinion against that immoral system. So systematic did this Press conflict become that every week the *Droits de l'homme* had an article summing up its results, and pronouncing upon the attitude of the different journals, not only in Paris, but in

A NEWSPAPER WAR IN FRANCE

the provinces. The journals which demanded the instant and complete abolition of the Regulations were the *Droits de l'homme*, *La Révolution* and *La France*. Others which attacked it, but without demanding its total abolition, were the *Tribune*, the *Siècle*, the *Rappel*, the *Ralliement*, the *Nation*, the *Estafette*, and the *Gaulois*. Beside these papers, which wrote on the question continuously for several weeks, the following had single articles in favour of abolition :—The *Republicain*, of St. Etienne ; the *Bien public*, Paris ; *La Liberté*, Paris ; *La Gironde*, Bordeaux ; the *Tribune des Travailleurs*, Lyons ; the *Petit Lyonnais*, Lyons ; and the *Critique Philosophique*, Paris.

A meeting of citizens was held in Paris to draw up a petition to the Government. It was a weighty and noble petition. Private letters were poured in upon members of the Senate and the Chambers praying for the redress of this great wrong so long endured in France. This extraordinary awakening was compared by M. Aimé Humbert to the bursting of a mine under our feet. Five or six respectable citizens were sent to prison for various terms for taking the part of helpless women in the streets. Many of the highest Municipal authorities ranged themselves on the side of the Abolitionists. The conflict became more bitter every week, and we looked on in wonder, almost in awe. A writer in one of the Paris journals on November 13th said that M. Lecour "deigns not to answer nor to argue; he only arrests. But his hour is come. It is written up against him, 'thou art weighed in the balances, and art found wanting.'" Literary men, such as Pillon, Assolant, Tacussel, etc., wrote nobly on the subject. Even the opponents of our movement, represented chiefly by the Imperialistic journals, gave daily well-attested cases of honourable women who were arrested by the Morals' Police.

The Municipal Council of Paris now began to move with vigour. Two of its members, M. Yves Guyot and M. Lacroix, brought before the council towards the close of November a charge against the Police of Morals, and made at the same time a proposal that the money which the Municipal Council had always been called upon to provide for the expenses of the Morals' Police should be stopped. There followed soon after this a prosecution by the Prefect of Police of M. Yves Guyot, of which I shall presently speak. That that prosecution did not take place until after M. Guyot had brought forward this resolution in the Municipal Council suggested that it was an act of revenge, an attempt to terrify M. Guyot into silence. One of the first steps taken by the Council was the appointment of a special Committee to report on the matter. The report of that Committee was to this effect:—That it was unendurable that such an arbitrary power should exist in Paris as that exercised by the *Police des Mœurs*; and that this same *Police des Mœurs* had no legal foundation for its existence. After a long discussion on the subject, M. Thulié, the President of the Council, rose and said, "I do not think this matter will be finally settled either by stopping the supplies, as proposed by M. Lacroix, or by referring the matter to the Chambers. We must first have a Commission appointed by the Municipal Council to inquire into the whole question, with the view of having this system completely abolished." This proposition being carried, MM. Guyot and Lacroix withdrew for the time their proposal to stop the supplies.

We learned later that the prosecution of M. Guyot had been instituted by M. Voisin, the Prefect of the Correctional Police, at the instigation of his personal friend the powerful and haughty Prefect of the Morals' Police, M. Lecour. The report of the trial was full of interest. The charge against M. Guyot was that of "Publishing false news," he having recorded the assault by the police on a well-known actress of good character and reputation, Mlle. Rousseil, by an agent of the Morals' Police. Mlle. Rousseil, made strong by the force of her just indignation, had flung the man who attempted to arrest her with such violence from her that he measured his length on the pavement. A crowd gathered round, and as the young actress was a popular favourite, the news of the scene spread rapidly. M. Lecour afterwards asserted that the man who made this arrest was a private individual who had pretended to be one of his agents. This was never believed by the public. M. Guyot's sole fault, then, was that he had said "an agent of the Morals' Police," instead of "a person calling himself an agent." For this he was condemned to six months' imprisonment and a fine. It was never proved that the man was not an agent of police. The outcry in the Press had alarmed M. Lecour, who gave orders to his police to appear at once to be engaged in an energetic search for the false agent. The man was found and tried. He came into Court frankly confessing— rather too frankly, indeed—that he was merely a silly fellow who had done this for amusement. He accepted a very brief imprisonment without more ado. Meanwhile the courageous Town Councillor, M. Guyot, accepted his sentence cheerfully, assuring us in England that it would do good to the persecuted cause. Three times during these events did M. Lecour stand before the Municipal Council of Paris and plead passionately and with tears in favour of the honour and purity of his own motives and those of his women-hunters (men who were recruited from the very scum of society in all countries).

A Commission of Enquiry was appointed by the Municipal Council, the following being the text of its appointment:—

"(1) Considering that the Municipal Council cannot avoid being concerned with the question of the *Police des Mœurs*, which is a question of great importance to the security of the Parisian population;

"(2) Considering that it has the right to control the services for which it pays, and to study the ameliorations which they may require;

"(3) Considering that the acts of the *Police des Mœurs* are not authorised by any laws, and that they lead to the perpetration of crimes punishable by the penal code;

"(4) Considering that at present it being difficult to propose to the Municipal Council to refuse the money required for the *Police des Mœurs*, a Commission of twelve members be nominated to study the service of the *Police des Mœurs*, and to propose either its entire suppression or such reforms as it requires."

The Prefect of Police objected that the Municipal Council had no jurisdiction in the matter of the Police des Mœurs and signified his intention to appeal to the Minister of the Interior ; and, in effect, at the next meeting of the Municipal Council, he laid on the table an order signed by Marshal MacMahon annulling the appointment of the Commission because of the direct imputations on the conduct of the police which the resolutions contained. M. Lecour therefore had "energetically defended the Police des Mœurs, he had condemned a Municipal Councillor to prison, and had secured the annulling of the Council's Decree." The Municipal Council, however, were not to be beaten, and three days later they passed a resolution in place of that annulled simply providing for the nomination of a Commission, without giving any reasons for its nomination, and at once elected twelve of their members to act upon it. Mr. Herrison, who had become President of the Municipal Council, was elected President of the Commission.

That Commission invited a certain number of persons from different countries, who had studied the question, to give evidence before it. From Switzerland came M. Sautter de Blonay and M. Humbert; from Italy, M. Nathan; from Belgium, M. Nicolet; and from England, Messrs. Stansfeld, Stuart, my husband and myself. The Commission sat day by day in a large room of the old Palace of the Luxembourg ; their labours were very conscientious and prolonged. When summoned there we were struck by the old-fashioned stateliness of the ancient royal residence, now used as Government offices, but still more were we impressed by the kind and courteous reception which we met with. It was a true pleasure to me to appear as a witness there, contrasting strongly with the effect produced on me by the ordeal which I, with others, had passed through in 1871, when giving evidence before the Royal Commission in our House of Lords. All the foreign witnesses here sat round a large table, at the upper part of which were the twelve Commissioners. We felt at once that there was *here* (though we were in Paris) no cynicism, no wish to perplex or entrap the witnesses, no motive, in fact, except the desire to elicit the truth, and to profit by the experience of other countries, in order that the Commission might do the best possible for their own country, by returning, in this matter, to the principles of just law, in place of the arbitrary and illegal police rule which was, they felt, destroying the foundations of liberty. The members of the Commission were not wholly of one mind on all points, and it was rather a severe exercise of brain and memory to meet and satisfy the various questions of a company of quick-witted, logical Frenchmen. It was an exercise, however, which left one feeling stronger and happier, because of the sincerity of motive which we felt animated the questioners.

Some days after giving our evidence at the Palais du Luxembourg, a great meeting was held (on the 21st January) in the Salle des Écoles, Rue d'Arras. No public meeting could at that time be held in Paris without the authorisation of the Government, which would not have been granted for a meeting on the subject of the Police des Mœurs. It was, therefore, styled a "private meeting," to attend which several thousands of invitations were sent out. These were fully responded to, and the hall was densely crowded. The meeting had been arranged chiefly by M. Yves Guyot and M. Lacroix. There was a considerable proportion of "blue blouses," working men from the St. Antoine and Belleville quarters, students from the Latin Quarter, and some members of the Chambers and of the Senate, besides Municipal Councillors. There was also a good attendance of women. M. Laurent Pichat (*Senateur Inamovible*) presided. M. Yves Guyot introduced the strangers of different nationalities to the audience with a few words explaining the object of their visit to Paris and of this meeting.

The several addresses given were listened to with extra ordinary attention and interest, and in a quietness which was remarkable, considering the mercurial and excitable nature o a portion of that audience. So keen was the sympathy (hav ing its roots deep in bitter experience) of the poorer part of the audience, especially the working men, that it was necessary ir some degree to restrain all that it might have been in our hearts to say on the injustice and cruelty of the system o which the victims were drawn so largely from their own ranks

On our return to England we found that a bitter attack had been made in the *Standard* and other journals on my husband's action in accepting the invitation of the Municipa Council in Paris, and speaking at the Salle des Écoles. "A clergyman of the Church of England," the writers asserted "had no business to be addressing Republican mobs ir Paris." My husband's weighty and dignified reply is giver in the Recollections of him, which I have published.[1] It was our rule not to reply to attacks of a purely persona nature, but in this case the censures were directed against him in his character as the Principal of a great College, and he thought it due to the parents of the boys entrusted to his charge to place the matter in its true light. We have seen how varied a gathering it was in Paris, and as to its being a "Republican mob," my husband reminded his traducers that "France being a Republic, it was natural that any audience there should be a Republican audience!"

Several other meetings were held before we left Paris. One of those was in the Salle de la Redoute, which was crowded with respectable working women of Paris. There were also a few ladies of the highest social position. M. Charles Lemonnier presided. M. Auguste Desmoulins, an ardent friend of our cause, spoke in a most beautiful manner to the working people present. A very affecting address was given also by Mlle. Raoult, a working woman of power- ful understanding and a loving heart, and the chief organiser

[1] "Recollections of George Butler." Arrowsmith, Bristol.

of a league of working women for their own protection. I give a few sentences from her address:—
"It is at the *root* that we must strike. Is the moment opportune? I believe so. It is time to act; for our generation, corrupted by many years of a nameless *régime*, presents deep wounds which must be healed." After describing the network of unhappy circumstances which causes the fall of so many girls into evil, she continued: " But while so many people make light of their morality, there are to be found in Paris young girls who are faithful to the lessons learned from their mothers, and to the memory of their homes, and who work and suffer without complaining. To be known, they must be seen in their wretched garrets, fabricating the most beautiful toilettes for the ladies of the high Society, working from morning till night, and *dying without a murmur, rather than yield.* These are indeed virtuous! It is an exact acquaintance with all these sufferings which has constrained me to depict them to you. No, lady, it is not in the wilderness that your voice has sounded, but rather in the conscience of every man of feeling those especially of the working class, who are invaded in their dignity, and in their most cherished affections, by this horrible plague which we are endeavouring to combat."

Adhémard Le Clerc, a leading working man, confirmed in the most terrible manner the facts given by Mlle. Raoult. He said: "Society with us has come to a dead-lock, because of the condition of our women. It is an accepted axiom in Paris that *a woman can no longer live by the work of her own hands.* The great social evil lies in the miserable wages granted to the work of women. This in itself, I say without hesitation, is debauchery justified, necessary, inevitable. There are some workwomen in Paris who have a father or husband, in which case the poor woman's 10 or 20 sous a day help a little towards the *ménage*; but there are thousands of single women in Paris who have no creature on earth to look to for support. Marriage has long been on the decrease. Many of these poor girls do not know their origin. As Dr. Després has said, 'the population is bastardised to such an extent that thousands of poor girls know not of any relationship which they have ever possessed.' They come handicapped into the world, bastards, orphans, and outcasts. Their life, if virtuous, is one terrible struggle from the cradle to the grave; but by far the greater number of them are drilled from childhood by exploiters and the police in the public service of debauchery. Ten thousand women every year go through the prison of St. Lazare. Every one of these, though she may have been imprisoned only for being homeless and wandering in the streets, or for begging, leaves the St. Lazare with the indelible mark upon her of shame and outlawry, which that word—St. Lazare—conveys to all. Her character is gone; and thus are the ranks of prostitutes recruited by the high hand of the Administration itself. The cry now, as formerly, of our women in Paris is for *bread*: they must have bread; they are ready to work for it, but when work cannot be found they will sell themselves to have it. Society is responsible for this misery and sin, for Society is *solidaire*, and must one day pay the debt it owes to outraged and maddened womanhood. Our ruined monuments are themselves prophetic of this. It will be again as it has been before. The handiwork of ruined women is visible in the blasted walls of the Tuileries. Their history is written in black smoke on the crumbling walls of our palaces in flames. There is no need of a Daniel here to decipher the handwriting on the wall. All the world can read, plainly written there, the words, *La femme déchue*—the ruined woman."

With this picture in my mind, and the memory of all I had seen and heard in Paris of the condition of the honest working woman, hunted from street to street and from room to room by the police, and looking at the troubled and earnest faces all turned towards me, I could not refrain from uttering these words: "The foxes have holes, and the birds of the air have their nests; but the honest workwoman of Paris has not where to lay her head." Many burst into tears, or hid their faces in their hands. In coming out from the meeting several poor girls came to me, their faces swollen with weeping, and said: " Ah, Madam, how true those words were about the foxes!"

The " Union Chrétienne," a Protestant Society of Paris, invited us to hold a meeting in their own hall. This meeting was interrupted and closed by the police. Towards the conclusion of my brief address, during which were present several police officers of high rank, I alluded to what had been asserted by one of Lecour's agents shortly before, *i.e.*, that parents of young girls sometimes came themselves to the Prefecture and requested to have their daughter's name placed on the register, and how, he asked, could the Prefect refuse in such a case? I found it difficult to believe that this was anything but a very rare occurrence; but I asserted that in such a case the Prefecture was none the less morally responsible. " Let us suppose," I said, " that a father came to the Prefect and said, 'Cut my daughter's throat for me'; if he consented to do so, would not the Administration by such an act render itself the accomplice of assassins?" The officials present, it seems, did not like this; the order was given, the gas was turned out, and in a few moments every seat was empty. The same officers reported to M. Lecour that I had said he was an assassin! The next morning the President of the Association was summoned to the Prefecture, and a verbatim report of what I had said was demanded. Three days later several members of the " Union Chrétienne " were again summoned to the Prefecture and questioned. Eventually they had to pay a small fine, and their hall was closed for a time; but they were in no way dejected by this result. The same could not have been said of the *Police des Mœur* itself. Several persons who had been present during M. Lecour's consultations with his agents reported to us that he had said " that the actual *régime*" was lost, and that certain changes or ameliorations of an external kind would have to be introduced, in order to calm the present agitation.

A final meeting during this visit to Paris was held in the large Protestant Chapel in the Rue Roquepine. It was presided over by Dr. Gustave Monod, and addresses were given by M. de Pressensé and M. Theodore Monod. The speakers denounced freely the system we opposed; but the police did not interfere with this meeting, the Protestant community of Paris being too formidable a body, and too highly respected to have one of their principal places of worship, and the words spoken in it, interfered with even by so insolent a tyranny as that of the Prefecture.

M. Yves Guyot's sentence of imprisonment was not immediately carried into practice. He was allowed to postpone its execution for a few weeks. He employed the interval of freedom by continued assiduous work on the Commission of the Council, and in other ways, for the exposure and condemnation of the *Police des Mœurs*. A number of Parisians were examined on the subject by the Commission —among them Drs. Déprès, Fournier and Mauriac, whose evidence threw some useful and curious light on the hygienic inefficacy of the system. Dr. Cléve, head physician of the Prefecture, was called; but the Prefect forbade him to give any information to the Commission. "This is a proof," said one of the Liberal journals, "that many things take place at the Prefecture which it is necessary to hide." Another official of the Prefecture, being called upon to appear, said furiously to the President, "Ah! if you think we will give you information, you are mistaken; you shan't have any at all." The Prefecture regards itself as an irresponsible Pashalik, which, though it has a right to receive money from the Municipal Council, is not bound to render any account thereof.

The following is a portion of a letter which I addressed to friends at home at this time :—

"PARIS, *February*, 1877.

"I think I told you how many poor working men and women appeal to us after our meetings, some of them very shabby and ill-dressed, but with much shrewdness and aspiration. Among these is Adhémard le Clerc, a working man, whose powerful verdict on the state of Paris I will send you. Among the waifs and strays who always follow us, the outcasts, the diamonds hidden away among the dust, who come to join in our train, are several of whom I should like to give you a sketch as an indication of the varied character of those who gather to this work:—

"1. A tall medical student, of modest, gentlemanly manner, looking rather delicate and absent, and not happy. You know, perhaps, what the medical students of Paris are as a rule; but among them we have many adherents of a character much raised above the rest. Indeed, many of the young men of France are rebelling against the odious teaching of their elders concerning the 'necessity of vice.' It seems to me that a deep melancholy and disgust with life has taken possession of some of these boys of eighteen or twenty; while together with this there is often a readiness to grasp at some higher aim if it is set before them. The student I speak of came shyly to our hotel to ask if we would think him too bold were he to try to get up a meeting of students and workmen to hear our message. We encouraged him to gather a meeting of these students, which was held a little later.

2. "A poor and elderly woman, very wretchedly dressed, whom the master of the Hotel where I stayed might have hesitated to admit had I not counselled him never to turn away poor people, or oddities of any class whatever. She had the appearance of having suffered years of hunger. Her large eyes were sunk in their bony sockets, but had in them a look of self-forgetfulness. To show me what she was she drew from her pocket a very old, soiled prospectus of her school. She had started, fifteen years before, a little school for girls in a very poor quarter of Paris, to teach them small handicrafts which she herself had learned, and to watch over them and to keep them from temptation. Her labour of love still lives, in spite of police persecutions, her own

poverty, the war, and the revolution. She is put down as one of the 'dangerous class.' She spoke very little of herself, but I heard of her from others, who said her life was one long act of self-denial and secret heroism. At one time, through want of food, her mind had given way, and she was taken for a short time to an asylum. Some of her friends, seeing her fainting on her walks through the streets on errands of mercy and helpful love, would ask her if she had had any food that day. Sometimes she had a dry crust in her pocket, which had to serve for to-morrow as well as to-day. To all such I speak, as well as I can, words of courage. Sometimes, like this woman, they would stand holding my hand silently, with tears rolling down their poor faces. They seemed to have a vague idea that a day of deliverance was at hand.

"We all know something of the wickedness of Paris; we do not yet know the sorrows of the poor of this city—of those who are the least guilty. A saying I commonly hear from them is, 'The people have suffered more than they can bear.'

"3. A Radical leader, Citizen ——, a 'dangerous man,' came evening after evening to see us, alone, sometimes in the dusk before our seven o'clock meal, sometimes later. His face is fixed in my memory as he sat at one side of the little table in our receiving parlour, shading his keen thoughtful eyes from the lamp with both his thin hands, and eagerly looking, as it were, into one's soul for an answer to his questions. Supposed to be an atheist, yet he spoke of God and of Jesus of Nazareth, not as men talk so often, but as if his life depended on the existence of a Divine Saviour. He spoke low, almost in a whisper. He is a true patriot, and his heart is almost broken for his country's woes. He asked us what hope we had for his 'beloved poor France.' He lingered on, and said he would come again if we would allow him. There was a deep pathos in his words and tones. His hair was almost white. He said, 'I am older than most of my radical confrères, and perhaps I have fewer prejudices and illusions; but I think that France will accept your great idea. Yes, the day will come when she will accept it, and not fear to argue it out. She will, moreover, put it in the purest formulæ and dress it in the most beautiful language. She will see it clearly and announce it clearly. All your people will be indebted to her for this. Yes, I think my poor France will bring forth this beautiful idea, and in bringing it forth she will die.' He uttered these words very slowly and mournfully, repeating the last words, —'elle mourira.' I do not quite know what he meant.

"4. Victorine S——, a washerwoman, tall and gaunt, with bright red hair and a small, shabby, black velvet hat on her red head, with a very old feather in it, a feather which has a look of misery, as if it had been plucked from a very indigent bird. I love and revere her. You are impressed in talking with her by her calm, womanly strength and good sense. And slowly you see also her profound pity for her unfortunate fellow women. Though big and bony, she has a remarkably soft and gentle voice; she does not gesticulate, but holds her arms stiffly and ungracefully by her side. Her hands, seamed with wash-tub operations, do not fit well into her poor, brown cotton gloves. She made a speech at a Working-man's Congress. It was a masterly speech, filled with statistics and facts illustrating the misery of Paris workwomen. She will do: one trusts her.

"5. The Marquis de B—— came and sat down on a bench beside me in the Tuileries Gardens. He is young, with yellow hair starting back from a fair face which wears a very innocent expression. He always has the most exquisite lavender kid gloves and shining boots, and belongs to an old aristocratic family. I asked him—'Where do you live? and with whom?'

"'Alone,' he replied.

"'Have you no father or mother?'

"'No; both dead.'

"'Brothers or sisters, uncles or cousins?'

"'No, not one.'

"'Are you rich?'

"'I have some money.'

"'Have you finished your education?'

"'Oh yes,' looking rather proud, 'long ago. I am twenty-eight years of age.'

"'Ah, that is good,' I said. 'Now what do you intend to do?'

"'I wish,' he replied, blushing a good deal, 'to be a servant of your cause. Ah! if I might, I should like to be one of the teachers in it.'

"A lady who knew him said to me one day, 'he is a good youth. Make him run messages or be useful in any way. He will do whatever you bid him.'

"Some time afterwards I was touched to see him addressing a group of poor men and a few porters and students and odds and ends of humanity. They were laying their heads together to think what they could do. 'We can at least,' they said, 'collect a little money from house to house, and sign petitions, and perhaps we could even save a few of our poor sisters.' They spoke together with much humility and deep earnestness of the small beginnings of what they could do. God will bless them. On this occasion the young Marquis had taken off his lavender kid gloves and put them in his pocket, and had become simply Citizen B——.

"6. A poor actor in a very inferior theatre; a man about thirty-five. His life had been a failure. His voice was not good, and he had to take the place of a kind of supernumerary. His life was a continual struggle for existence, shouting and acting night after night, and returning home to an attic with a very miserable bed in it. His poor soul took fire concerning our cause. He did not put himself forward at all, but we found he had been working really hard for us. He tells us he has now but one aim in life; he must still sing for a living, but he can give his days to our work. In conversation with him I could see that that poor man had been pining for some work of redress, and grieving over the sin and woe around him. He sees the whole of our objects with a clearness which not one in a hundred of our English Members of Parliament do, I fear; and his soul is filled with zeal for justice. He will pass on the burning torch he carries to other hands, and increase his own fire in doing so. I often think how sweet must be the sudden sense of companionship in a good cause to such a solitary being. He does not mind now the very feeble applause given to his poor singing on the stage, for he has found an interest and treasure of which the audience know nothing.

"I could go on multiplying these pictures, but these are enough to indicate to you the very varied character of the people who flock to our standard. My husband's tender feelings are very much drawn out towards the working women who call on me."

CHAPTER VIII.

" The violation of one law may sometimes be the fulfilment of a higher; and there are laws, which to obey is infamy."—Words of Lacordaire when tried for contempt of the law.

NOTWITHSTANDING the apparent diminution of the agitation in favour of Repeal in England, which somewhat discouraged our supporters during the early part of the year 1877, a careful retrospect of the progress made proved that year to have been one of the most auspicious since the movement began. The year in which the first International Congress took place upon a question involving neither territorial aggrandisement, dynastic ambition, nor commercial development, but something higher and greater than all these— national morality—was a year destined to remain memorable in the history, not merely of our movement, but of the world. It will never be forgotten that in the year 1877 the equal rights and responsibilities of the weaker half of humanity, whose voice had hitherto been unheard in the councils of nations, were solemnly and publicly acknowledged in an assembly of over 500 male and female delegates representing the most advanced minds of Europe and the United States. "This public recognition of the equal rights of all human souls was the logical outcome of the grand truth proclaimed by Christianity—of the worship of God, not as the Deity of a single people or race, but as the Father of humanity. For the first time since the days of the early Christians the children of the Heavenly Father stood side by side, without distinction of sex or race, to preach God's law of purity, and many of the women there present, and many of their sisters, who, with beating hearts, watched their action from afar, recognised that that Congress was for them the first step towards the realization of the magnificent promise—' the Truth shall make you free.' The first timid, imperfect recognition by mankind of a portion of the heavenly law decreed the extinction of the slavery of colour; a fuller, higher comprehension of its divine justice has decreed the extinction of the slavery of sex."[1]

In the early part of this year, as if to prepare the moral atmosphere of Switzerland for the great Congress to be held at Geneva, a bitter conflict arose in the Canton of Neuchâtel between the supporters of the opposing principles on this question. The story of it is briefly this. Several infamous houses had been established at la Chaux-de-Fonds, a great industrial centre in the Jura, and had been authorised, or licensed, not by the Government of the Canton of Neuchâtel, but in some irresponsible manner by the Magistrates of the town. M. Humbert and his friends made an attack upon this system, and a request was formulated by himself and other persons of weight in the town of Neuchâtel that these houses should be closed. Thereupon the municipality of Chaux-de-Fonds, who appear to have been largely in favour of the system, in order to secure its continued existence, held a meeting with closed doors, in which they voted by a considerable majority not only to maintain the houses, but to use their authority to license them after the manner of Paris. Thus the municipality of Chaux-de-Fonds, in the Canton of Neuchâtel, took upon themselves the responsibility of more firmly establishing this evil system in that canton, which had hitherto been free from any such public recognition of vice. The conflict was made the more painful to M. Humbert because a number of the members of that municipality had been his former friends and school and college companions. M. Humbert wrote to me, " I hope we shall succeed in making the people understand that we are threatened with a dreadful innovation, and

[1] *Shield*, 1877.

that unless we resist it with all our power, official profligacy will become an accomplished fact in the Canton of Neuchâtel. Locle, a town of between 10,000 and 11,000 inhabitants, distant one league from La Chaux-de-Fonds, is the most directly interested. I was invited to hold two meetings there. I held the first of these on the 5th March, at the German Temple, where I was the sole speaker for over an hour to a numerous and attentive audience. The second meeting was equally well attended. I have been told that the people of Locle are very strongly impressed, and have decided in favour of supporting us. I spent the morning of Wednesday at La Chaux-de-Fonds, returning in a sledge. There were two feet of snow, and I was reminded of your campaign of February, 1875, in our watch-making Siberia."

The Neuchâtel Committee of the Federation met soon after, and drew up a full declaration and protest to the municipality of Chaux-de-Fonds. On the 22nd March, a mass meeting was held at this town. The large Temple was completely filled; the political atmosphere of the town was very stormy. "We were assured," wrote M. Humbert, "that there would be great excitement at the meetings, and some of us received threatening letters. The President's speech was made amid considerable noise. As soon, however, as M. Sautter de Blonay began to speak there was silence. He treated the subject in a most masterly manner, and although it is not the custom to applaud in a church he was loudly applauded at the end of his speech. Other speakers having followed, it was now nine o'clock, and there still remained to me the difficult and delicate task of treating the question in its local character, and of speaking of the vote of the Municipal Council and the results which were sure to follow."

Scarcely had M. Humbert commenced his address, exposing what had taken place in the Municipality, than a cry arose from a chorus of voices in the gallery, where a number of upholders of the regulation system were seated, among whom were three Municipal Councillors. At the moment when M. Humbert uttered the words " with regard to the Munici-

A STORMY MEETING

pal vote," this group cried out, "The Municipal Council did well, they did well!" M. Humbert replied, "You are free to express your opinions; as for me, I will finish my speech." He then drew a striking picture of the difference between the present state of morality in the town and its ancient state. He himself had been a member of the Council in 1849, when the first house of ill-fame was secretly established there without any official recognition at all. He then in his address attacked the institution itself, giving a number of facts, and demolishing, stroke after stroke, the arguments of his opponents.

When M. Humbert had finished his masterly speech and come down from the tribune, and the President had risen to close the meeting, it seemed as if a victory had been gained for us, and the crowd was beginning to move towards the doors, when M. Robert, Municipal Councillor, got up, and in the midst of great excitement in the meeting, cried out that if this institution were closed they would be taking the bread out of the mouths of women! At these words there arose such a tumult of indignant protests that the President was obliged to beg in a loud voice that they would allow M. Robert to speak. Nevertheless M. Robert was unable to say anything more, except that he protested against the morality of the town being supposed to be worse than it had been. This was in allusion to a portion of M. Humbert's speech in which he quoted the beautiful description which Jean Jacques Rousseau gives of the moral life of the Neuchâtel mountaineers in his letter to d'Alembert, in connection with which M. Humbert had recalled many honourable names of mechanicians, engravers, painters, etc., speaking of them as the moral nobility of the Jura, whose memory ought to be an inspiration to us in the great work we have now to accomplish. The partisans of legalized vice had now gone down from the gallery, and were yelling around M. Robert, while M. Humbert's adherents were shouting in their turn. It was thought better not to prolong the meeting. The Municipal Councillors could not fail to see that M. Humbert had used the utmost possible delicacy in speaking of them; indeed, they confessed this, while they saw also that the impression on the people was most unfavourable to them. One of them said to M. Humbert, "You ought to have attacked the Council of State, who have caused us to fall into this wolf-trap." The majority of the people of Chaux-de-Fonds were gained, though our adversaries were very bitter. The women worked well.

The next event of importance that followed was a very bitter personal attack made on M. Humbert, who was selected as the scape-goat of the angry and defeated Municipal Councillors. This attack was printed and largely circulated before the date fixed for the meeting of the Grand Council of Neuchâtel. All the journals of the Canton began to be occupied with the subject, and our opponents, in fact, aided our cause by themselves obtaining for us the thing they most fear—complete publicity.

To this public accusation M. Humbert wrote a most dignified reply. I do not give it here, as it is lengthy. It is pathetic in its dignity. About the same time M. Humbert wrote me, "You will only receive this on the last day of your mission week on behalf of the cause. But you do not require it as an assurance that our hearts have been with our fellow-workers in England during that time. The past two or three weeks number among the most sorrowful and painful of my life. You can understand what I have gone through. It is necessary to have grappled face to face with the powers of darkness, in order to learn what there may be of sadness even in a victory gained, even in the congratulations one receives."

The Shield remarked, "M. Humbert has fought the good fight in so uncompromising and resolute a manner, that one is apt to forget the great personal sacrifice involved in a struggle maintained, as his struggle with the Municipal Council of La Chaux-de-Fonds has been, against fellow-citizens and former friends. How dearly the moral victory has been won can only be appreciated by those who have themselves undergone this species of social martyrdom, and their sympathy, admiration and gratitude is for ever assured to M. Humbert."

On April 25th I wrote as follows to M. Humbert :—

"DEAR FRIEND,—

"Your letter concerning the storm of feeling raging in your Canton reached me to-day. My first impulse was to kneel down and give thanks, so plainly do I see the footsteps of Jehovah in the storm. Did I not tell you long ago that you in Switzerland would have to go through the same fires that we went through five and six years ago? This persecution is the divine seal set upon your mission; let us rejoice and be glad, for it shows that the battle of the Lord is set in array against those principalities and powers which are leagued with the spirit of darkness. You ought not to regret that this struggle in your own country occupies so much of your time. Your country is to be the scene of our first great International Congress, and it is well that the country in which that event is to take place should be well prepared. If it were not so, Switzerland would not be so fitted to be the central battlefield of our International conflict. We will do our best to keep up correspondence with France and other countries, in order to leave you more free.

"I see in the conflict around you the same features which we have observed elsewhere—the same secrecy of procedure on the part of our adversaries, the same tactics when forced to act publicly, the same weakness in their own camp. If you yourself have to bear the brunt of the opposition, you will win adherents far more rapidly on account of this. If those in authority, if the Federal Government itself, were to pronounce against your principles, and its agents were to calumniate you, it will not do you any real harm, and will only be temporary. Wherefore let us 'stand fast in the Lord.' We have had already for seven years the whole authority of our Imperial Government against us, and our names have been blackened in public and in Parliamentary debate. In some cases incomes have been lessened and times made very hard for us, but the cause gains daily in strength and is consecrated by the sufferings of its advocates.

"Tell dear Madame Humbert that now is the time for *women* to be strong: women have never shrunk from martyrdom; they must not do so now.

"We have had a week of prayer for our cause, beginning on the 17th. We were glad to think that you and your family were with us in spirit. I told the tale of your Swiss conflict and we prayed for you all. The women who promoted this union for prayer are brave, instructed women who are not afraid of the reproach of being 'political women,' who have, in fact, made the 'last sacrifice,' by giving their names to public scorn for the Lord's sake who gave Himself to public scorn for their sakes. I trust that the dear Swiss ladies will be ready even to become politicians in order to deliver their sisters from slavery!

"My only regret concerning that splendid meeting which was held at La Chaux-de-Fonds is that there was no woman strong enough in the strength of the Lord to enter that meeting alone and uninvited, and cry aloud to the men there, the good and the bad alike, 'You men have no right to discuss the question, shall you or shall you not maintain female slavery in the interests of vice; the question is already judged, the verdict is already given, for I tell you in the name of all women that you shall *not* maintain female slavery in the interests of vice; and it is the voice of God which now declares that you shall not.' Such a proclamation, coming from the woman's side, strikes a kind of terror into the hearts of our adversaries, such as even the noblest man's voice does not inspire. Why? Because it is the voice of the slave herself; and the oppressor, with the abettor of oppression, fears, saying to himself, like Herod, 'It is John the Baptist whom I beheaded; he is risen from the dead!' The only thing yet wanting, dear friends, in your noble campaign is the resurrection of the slave in the person of some devoted woman or women who will tell the tyrant in the woman's voice, gently but terribly, 'You shall not do this thing.' Perhaps your ladies will be moved by the guidance of the Holy Spirit to put forth a united protest of this kind —gentle, solemn, but firm and powerful. Now is the moment to do it. It will shake the adversary in his inmost soul and will strengthen our noble masculine champions."

In quoting these words, written so long ago, I cannot help taking a brief mental retrospect, and tracing the wonderful and steady progress of the women of Switzerland in this matter. The fear of "meddling with politics" oppressed them at first. An important group of them now interest themselves actively in every social and political question which bears directly or indirectly on the interests of women; they have brought strong personal influence to bear on their Cantonal and Federal Governments, an influence which the late M. Ruchonnet, as President of the Federal Council, acknowledged to have been of the most salutary kind. Their labours are taken account of in the new Project for the Reform and Unification of the Penal Code; and under the skilful guidance of Professor Louis Bridel, they have already witnessed the achievement in certain cantons of a reform in the Civil Code, similar to our "Married Woman's Property Act," by which a woman's earnings and property are secured to herself. They are proceeding to follow this up by further reforms.

On the very day—the 22nd of March—when those men of the two Councils, the Municipal Council and Council of State, of Chaux-de-Fonds, the friends of M. Humbert's youth, furious with him, were recording their accusation against him of calumniating his native city, the corpses of two young working women of Chaux-de-Fonds were being dragged out of the River Doubs at Brenets, on the Jura. One was a young widow of twenty-three, and the other a girl of eighteen. They had fled from one of the strongholds of debauchery at Chaux-de-Fonds, had run as far as Locle, and then to Brenets. Friendless and poor, and fearing to return to the town or to say whence they had fled, having been enticed only lately into this slavery, and horrified at their lives therein, they saw no way of escape, they knew not of any human deliverance, and so they tied themselves together by an arm of each with their shawls and plunged into the water together. The corpses were dragged out after three days, silent witnesses of the justice of M. Humbert's denunciation of this vile slave system, for which he was now suffering bitter wounds even in the house of his friends.

About the same time another of those incidents occurred in Geneva which are the natural fruits of a system of organised vice. A young girl contrived to make her escape from one of the regulated houses there, and fled through the streets. She was pursued by the keepers of the house. One of the Police des Mœurs came to the aid, not of the victim, but of the pursuers, and by the strong hand of an authority which has no legal existence, the girl was forced back into the den from whence she had escaped, in spite of her agonised cries in the open streets. A gentleman of Geneva, a jurist, who had studied this question of modern slavery, observed, *apropos* of this event, that " we have, in fact, returned to the permitted practices of the slave-holders of America, and logically we might now also set up the practice of keeping bloodhounds to trace and hunt down the fugitives."

The conflict in the Canton of Neuchâtel was successfully concluded in September, about the time of the Geneva Congress, by a declaration on the part of the Prefect of La Chaux-de-Fonds that the municipality had withdrawn its official protection of the houses of evil repute, and that this withdrawal had been confirmed by the Prefect himself.

To return to events in France. During this time fresh fuel was added to the rising indignation of the people of Paris against the Police of Morals by the arrest of Mlle. Marie Ligeron, a gentle girl of irreproachable character, who was insulted and arrested by one of Lecour's hunters while walking with her fiancé, to whom she was shortly to be

THE TRAGEDY OF MARIE LIGERON

married. The police discovered their mistake only after she had gone through all the misery and shame of being taken to the Depôt and questioned, and detained in the prison of St. Lazare until sufficient influence was brought to bear to secure her release. Her case was taken up by our friends on the Municipal Council, and at their instigation a prosecution of the Prefect was instituted by the fiancé of the girl, whose sufferings were scarcely less than her own. That one of the people should have dared to prosecute the man who had hitherto been a practically irresponsible tyrant over all the poor women of Paris was a proof of the growth of public opinion there.

But Marie Ligeron was only released from the St. Lazare by death. That cruelly injured woman never recovered from the shock of the mental and physical horrors she was forced to endure in that depôt of shame, and sank under the illness to which it gave rise. She died. She was twenty years of age. Her death made a deep impression in France. It afterwards transpired that her cowardly medical inquisitors themselves had pronounced her to be a pure virgin, and that they had detained her in that horrible place, the St. Lazare, after this verdict as a kind of "curiosity." Some of the newspapers asked, "Could even the Turks have devised a more cruel method of slow murder?" The *Marseillaise* concluded a long and pathetic article on her fate with the words, " We will no longer endure this Police Inquisition which slaughters women. Every human being has a right to Law. If this is your civilisation, know that it is the civilisation of assassins! Sleep, poor dead girl! *you* have pardoned them, perhaps. We will not pardon them."

During the preparations for the Geneva Congress, a controversy arose in Switzerland concerning the part to be taken by women in the Congress. Certain gentlemen there, though friends of our cause, insisted that ladies should be excluded from special sections. Some of the ladies were inclined to yield on this point, and it was hoped that our English Parliamentary leaders would give the word as to the advisability

M

of ladies absenting themselves from certain meetings, and that this word would be authoritative. Mme. Humbert having fully explained the situation to me, I replied in the following letter, which I am induced to reproduce here, seeing that the same question, in one form or another, still occasionally arises, and that it may be useful to the coming generation to know the reasons for the firm stand which the pioneer women took in the matter.

"DEAR FRIEND,—

"I cannot disguise from you that the subject of your letter has been a cause of anxiety to me and my friends. We are to hold a private conference on the subject. Meanwhile, I give you my personal answer to the ladies of Switzerland. Here it is.

"Ladies! you have appealed to me to use my influence to cause to be authoritatively closed against women a portion of the sections and public meetings of the Congress. It is not I who rule the Congress. I have some influence, but if I were to make use of that influence with our men of England, who are allied with M. Humbert in the organisation of the Congress, in order to obtain this exclusion of women, they would not grant my request, and would be amazed at such a request coming from me. In fact, I believe there is not a man among them who would attend the Congress if a public announcement should be made of the exclusion of women from any part of the deliberations. Our gentlemen here would look upon such a public act as an abandonment of principle. It is precisely this peremptory exclusion of women by statesmen and others from all participation in council and in debate on such vital questions which has led to the present terrible wrong to Society by the passing of these oppressive and God-defying laws. Eight years of conflict and experience have convinced a portion of the Christian manhood of England that this has been at the root of many of the most fatal errors of legislators. I have sent your letter on to the gentlemen members of our Committee. I know their feeling will be on reading it, 'We have laboured hard all these years in the cause of womanhood, and, in doing so, we have learned the absolute necessity of the co-operation and the advice of women; and here there are women themselves who, bowing to the authority of certain men, ask us to bid them stand apart!'

"Do not imagine, dear friend, that I do not feel much sympathy with your ladies on the subject of being present in the Hygienic Section. Tell them I understand their feeling, and that so far as their having a tacit understanding in any group of themselves that they will not attend the Hygienic meetings, I have no objection to make. This can be quietly done. No one can find fault with any of the Swiss ladies for absenting themselves individually. None of us could wish any woman to attend who feels that the sacrifice is more than she could bear. It is perfectly legitimate for you to adopt your own plans in this respect, and this involves no abandonment of principle. You see the immense difference between such action and the public announcement on the part of men that no women are to be admitted.

"It is utterly useless for you to ask Mr. Stansfeld to promote such a public act of exclusion. He will not do it. You might as well ask him to strike you or thrust you out of the room. I think you hardly know what our best Englishmen are. They will be true to women now, even in spite of those women themselves.

"I hope, dear friends, I have made the matter clear. I would not do anything to shock public opinion so as to do harm. On the other hand, I will never, God helping me, bow down to public opinion when that public opinion is so far from being just and pure as it is now. Did our Lord ever bow down before public opinion? Would this Crusade ever have been begun at all if some English women had not openly defied public opinion? Believe me, when this Congress is over, you will be astonished to find how easy and useful it is for men and women to work and consult together, and how wonderfully the cynics have been silenced. Yes, I know very well some of the cynical and indelicate medical men you speak of. There will be few of such among us; but granted that there will be some, I do not fear their influence. They will be overpowered by the dignity, gravity, and determination of our abolitionist medical men.

"I believe, dear ladies, you will act for the best under the guidance of God, who will not fail us, and who will silence the enemy."

I take from a number of my own letters to M. Humbert, written at this time, which he returned to me, the following, which recalls some of the circumstances of the year of our first Congress :—

To M. HUMBERT.   *April* 30, 1877.

" We have much correspondence just now concerning the visit of members of the Paris Municipal Council to London. M. Yves Guyot was to have been one of the number; he was to come as representing the Commission on the Police des Mœurs, while the other visitors represented other Commissions. The Lord Mayor of London sent them an invitation to a banquet at the Mansion House, and we were making preparations for a Conference with M. Guyot and the other Paris Councillors who are in sympathy with us in the interests of abolition all over the world. But the Prefect of Paris was unwilling to allow Guyot to come to England, and has insisted on his taking his imprisonment now at once. The Minister of Justice refused a formal request from the President of the Paris Municipal Council to give Guyot a week's reprieve in order that he might fulfil his important mission to London. M. Desmoulins writes that M. Guyot went to the prison of Ste. Pelagie last Friday evening, the 27th, regretting much to bid farewell to the spring and summer.

" Our earnest fellow-worker, Mr. Collingwood, of Sunderland, is now in Paris doing good service for our cause. He is a man of great faith, and is endeavouring to persuade our Protestant friends in France that they ought to take political action at once, and not merely pray and make speeches. He tells me that they have begun to petition the Chambers, as M. Caise's group has been doing.

"I thank you for your *compte-rendu* of the Conference of the presidents of the five sections of our approaching Congress. In return I send you a little news from England. Our position is peculiar; for we have no Repeal Bill before Parliament this Session. Our chief Parliamentary leaders believe it would be quite useless to bring the question before the present Parliament. The news that there is to be no debate on abolition this year has been received throughout the country with deep regret. There never was a period in which so much activity and life was manifested in our work as now throughout the country. The Working Men's League and all the other Associations throughout Scotland and Ireland as well as England are in an attitude of suspense waiting for the word of command in order to renew the conflict with more determination than ever. But as it is, memorializing, petitioning, and deputations to the Government would be unfruitful. The question with us now is, to what point shall we direct the energies of our Abolitionist population? An international object does not afford an immediate scope for the activities of our working class abolitionists, though it has their earnest sympathy. We have thought of promoting formal delegations to the Congress from our working men's societies, and I should be glad if you could send me addresses of some working men's societies in Switzerland who might be put into communication with our working men's Abolitionist Committees in Edinburgh, Birmingham, Glasgow, etc.

"We have lately had some exciting Parliamentary elections, resulting in victories for our cause. At Oldham there was a hard-fought contest, which resulted in the election of Mr. Hibbert by a majority of 2,000 votes. Mr. Hibbert has been for many years a strong adherent of our cause. It is thus that in England we win slowly, step by step, our Parliamentary victories.

"Poor Yves Guyot has just written to me from the prison of Ste. Pelagie, in dread lest his colleagues of the Municipal Council should fall into the hands of our adversaries in London rather than of abolitionists in seeking information. Mr. Benjamin Scott, who holds a high civic office, that of Chamberlain of the City of London, has presented an address from his own Committee to the Paris Councillors, which I think will have some weight. Mr. Martineau, town councillor of Birmingham, has done the same for his Midland Counties Committee.

"Your daughter Amélie asks for some account of our women's activity during the time of our severest conflict here. I doubt whether such an account might not be a little appalling to your ladies at present, because in England, necessarily, our activities are very strongly directed towards public meetings and election work. Our ladies worked at a number of elections, beginning each conflict with devotional meetings. It was on these occasions that we suffered most annoyance; but we gained great triumphs in convincing Parliament of the power and vitality of our principles. Amélie knows how truly gentle and womanly are the women who take part in this active political work. What you tell me of the women of Switzerland and their increased zeal is most encouraging. If women had votes, there would be less need for them to 'agitate.' Your letters and report of the proceedings of your Grand Council were read at our Federation Council Meeting on Monday. We follow with profound interest every step of your conflict. The 'powers that be' are terribly committed to false principles on this question throughout the world. It is a happy thing when they speak out plainly. When they proclaim themselves aloud in favour of corrupt and immoral institutions, then, and not till then, do slumbering Christians and patriots wake up to perceive that we are indeed in the midst of war, and that our battle is the battle of the Lord against the mighty. We shall be anxious to know how your elections end."

THE GENEVA CONGRESS

As the date of the Congress drew near, the discussions among the members of the different sections became more eager and anxious. Several complications having arisen in regard to the relative importance and position of the different questions to be considered, the Committee in London accepted the offer of Mr. Stansfeld to go in advance to Switzerland in order to meet and confer with all the different Presidents of the Sections, with Mr. Humbert and others. This visit of Mr. Stansfeld had very happy results, in contributing to the harmony which eventually prevailed.

It is not my intention to give any complete account of the great Congress at Geneva. The proceedings were published in two large volumes entitled "Les Actes du Congrès de Genève" (to be had from M. Henri Minod, 6, Rue Saint Leger, Geneva). These volumes contain also all the most important papers and addresses given on the occasion. There were present at the Congress five hundred and ten delegates, representing fifteen different nations. It should be understood that these delegates were all convinced of the necessity of the abolition of all regulations of vice. This was the only condition that was required of them in order to become members.

About 120 papers and reports were presented to the various sections of the Congress, after the reading and full discussion of which, resolutions were formulated and submitted to the different sections for renewed discussion, amendment and final adoption. International Committees had been established several months previously, in which the different sections met periodically for the study and discussion of the subjects to be brought before the Congress. Finally the resolutions adopted by each section were placed before the whole Congress for approval and acceptance. Rarely has there been recorded such a unanimous expression of international opinion, emanating from representatives of so many different countries; nor an expression of opinion, founded upon investigations so extensive and so conscientious. The following are the resolutions of the five sections:—

On the 17th of September, the first day of the Session, immediately after the nomination and election of the Bureaux by the General Assembly of the Congress, the Five Sections in combined Session passed the following resolution:—

"The Congress recognises the many-sided character of the question which it has assembled to discuss.

"It acknowledges that its solution is only to be sought in the collation of the results arrived at by the labours of each of the Five Sections, in such manner that the conclusions of each particular Section may finally be accepted from the point of view of all the Sections; and it is with this understanding that it proposes to contribute, by its decisions, to the general conclusions at which the Congress desires to arrive."

Towards the close of the Congress the Section of Hygiene affirmed—

I.

That self-control in the relations between the sexes is one of the indispensable bases of the health of individuals and communities.

II.

That prostitution is a fundamental violation of the laws of health.

III.

Being convinced that the province of Public Hygiene should not be restricted to the surveillance and prevention of specific maladies which affect populations, we declare that its true function is to develop all the conditions which conduce to Public Health, whose highest form is necessarily included in Public Morality.

IV.

The Section of Hygiene condemns, in view of their complete failure, all systems of Police des Mœurs whose object is to regulate prostitution. The Section bases its condemnation on the following amongst other grounds, namely: that the obligatory examination of women is revolting to human nature; that it can only be carried out in the case of a certain proportion of women; that it is impossible to rely upon this examination to discover the most serious constitutional form of venereal maladies, or to hinder its progress ; and that, consequently, it gives a false guarantee of the health of the women who are subjected to it.

V.

The Section of Hygiene desires especially to see removed all obstacles which at present prevent venereal maladies from being as extensively treated as every other form of disease in the hospitals which are controlled by municipalities and other public bodies, as well as in those which are supported by private liberality.

VI.

The Section of Hygiene also expresses the hope that the ordinary police will strictly maintain order and decency in public streets, and repress every public scandal, whether caused by men or women.

The Section of Morality affirmed—

I.

That impurity in men is as reprehensible as it is in women.

II.

That the regulation of prostitution tends to destroy the idea of the unity of the moral law for the two sexes, and to lower the tone of public opinion in this respect.

III.

That every system of organised prostitution encourages profligacy, increases the number of illegitimate births, develops clandestine prostitution, and lowers the standard of public and private morality.

IV.

That the compulsory medical examination of women, the basis of every system of regulation, is an outrage on woman, and tends to destroy, even in the most degraded, the last remnant of modesty which she may retain.

V.

That the registration of prostitutes is contrary to common law, and to the principle of liberty.

VI.

That in regulating vice the State forgets its duty of affording equal protection to both sexes, and in reality degrades the female sex and corrupts both.

VII.

That the State, whose duty it is to protect minors and to assist them in every good effort, on the contrary, incites them to debauchery, in so far as it facilitates it by regulation.

VIII.

That in authorising immoral houses, and in raising a reprehensible trade to the rank of a regular profession, the State sanctions the immoral doctrine that debauchery is a necessity for men.

IX.

That it is desirable to address an appeal to all authors, editors, printsellers, and booksellers in Europe and America, urging them to lend no encouragement to the sale or circulation of pictures or works of a corrupting tendency.

Questions proposed by the President and answered by the Section of Social Economy.

I.

Are the economic interests, rights, and independence of women sufficiently respected and guaranteed at the present day by the law, by opinion, and by the customs of society?

Answer (unanimous).—No.

II.

Is the continuous exercise by a woman of a profession involving manual labour consistent with the proper performance of her domestic and maternal duties?

Answer.—That depends upon the profession and the individual circumstances of the woman.

III.

Is the pay accorded to the manual labour of women sufficient to satisfy their legitimate wants?

Answer (by majority).—No.

IV.

1. What are the principal causes of the insufficiency of women's wages in industrial occupations?

Answer (by majority).—The inequality established between men and women by the law, the customs of society, general ignorance, and the regulation of prostitution.

2. Is it possible to remedy this inferiority in women's wages·?

Answer.—Yes, by equal laws, by the improvement of morals, by the abolition of regulated prostitution, and by the spread of general and professional education for women.

V.

What are, or will be, the consequences in regard to the economic and moral condition of women of their employment in manufactories?

Answer.—The consequences will vary according to circumstances. The Section considers that no industrial employment should be closed to women which may enable them by their own labour to protect themselves from want and prostitution.

VI.

Should Government interfere to prevent the labour of women in factories?

Answer (with two dissentients).—**No.**

VII.

What advantages can women gain from the principles of union and co-operation among themselves?

Answer (unanimous).—The same advantages as are gained by men.

VIII.

How can women's education be organised so as to contribute most effectually to the amelioration of their social and economic condition?

Answer.—By throwing entirely open to women every branch of education, and by assuring an equal expenditure by the State and by society on the education of the two sexes.

The Section of Preventive and Reformatory Work affirms—

I.

That the ideas which are involved in the system of the regulation of vice are entirely incompatible with the work of rescue.

II.

That it is proved that the Regulation of prostitution is a great hindrance to the success of works of Rescue and Reformation, inasmuch as registration and medical examination are opposed to all sentiments of feminine modesty, which are never absolutely extinguished in any woman, and inasmuch as they render more difficult the moral restoration which we can and ought to hope for in the case of every fallen woman, however abandoned she may be.

III.

It is desirable to have widely established homes, in which the system should be as little as possible of a penitential character, inasmuch as sympathy and Christian love are the only efficacious means of rescuing and reforming young women.

IV.

It is desirable to establish a system of intercommunication between all countries in order to prevent the trading in women and girls for immoral purposes, and in order to protect friendless women who are seeking employment in various countries.

The Section of Legislation declared—

I.

That the State has not the right to regulate prostitution, for it ought never to make a compromise with evil, nor to sacrifice constitutional guarantees to questionable interests.

II.

Every system of official regulation of prostitution involves the arbitrary action of the police and violation of the legal guarantees against arbitrary arrest and imprisonment which are assured to every individual, not even excluding the greatest criminals. The compulsory examination of women is equally contrary to the law. Inasmuch as this violation of the law is solely to the disadvantage of woman, there is made between her and man an excessively unjust distinction; the woman is lowered to the rank of a mere chattel, and is placed beyond the pale of the law. Moreover, by the regulation of vice the State directly violates its own penal law, which forbids incitement to debauchery, by making itself the accomplice of such incitement, in so far as it is offered by the houses and the women sanctioned by its own authority. The State herein also violates its duty of affording protection to minors.

III.

The system of regulation does not attain the object desired, for regulation fosters and develops prostitution instead of diminishing it. The increase of clandestine prostitution in the towns where the system exists suffices to show that the regulations are eluded with increasing frequency. The development of venereal maladies and the number of indecent assaults in these same towns prove also that regulation does not accomplish the desired results.

IV.

It results from the preceding that the State should renounce the project of pursuing the hygienic aim, the more so that in this case there is no question of an external danger such as an epidemic menacing the general public health, but of a danger to which those who expose themselves do so knowingly and of their own free will. The State ought, therefore, to abandon this arbitrary administrative procedure, and to recur to law alone. It should confine itself to the protection of minors and to repressing by legal and judicial means all that is contrary to public order.

V.

The State should continue to punish incitement to debauchery when directed towards minors of either sex, and should treat procurers with special severity. It should punish the decoying of minors for immoral purposes. It should prohibit every collective organisation of prostitution by punishing the offence of keeping an immoral house open to the public, and that of letting apartments for such uses. An analogous case is that of gambling houses, which are prohibited by penal enactment in almost all countries.

We would retain unchanged the penal enactments concerning outrages on public morality, and particularly *public* solicitation and indecent assaults, and the illegal confinement and detention of women and the decoying of those who are under age.

VI.

As to the causes of prostitution, from a legal point of view, the State might punish the seduction of a minor, when that seduction has been effected by means of false pretences.

A question which merits consideration is whether the State should not re-establish the right of affiliation in those countries where it has been abolished, in order to equalise the position of the man and the woman in relation to their illegitimate children.[1]

The following is a personal reminiscence in the form of a letter addressed by myself to a relative, towards the close of the Congress:—

"I can only give you a brief sketch of the past week; full reports will be published. The anxiety which we could not but feel went on augmenting up to Friday. On Friday we began to see daylight, and all has ended well. Many of us are tired and stupefied for want of sleep, but at the same time inwardly giving thanks to God. This Congress has been a wonderful event. There were 510 inscribed members, besides the numerous public which attended the meetings. It is, they say, the largest Congress that has ever been held in Geneva. On the first days people continued flocking in from all nations. There were Greeks who came from Athens; and Russians from St. Petersburg and Moscow. There were Americans, Belgians, Dutch, Danes, Germans, Pomeranians, Italians, French, and Spaniards. Senor Zorilla, the late

---

[1] Owing to the great pressure of time at the close of the Congress, and to the variety in the laws in this respect in different countries, the Section was unable to give an exhaustive discussion to this question; but several members of the Congress, after the framing of this resolution, signed and handed into the Bureau at the Public Meeting the following declaration :—A Congress which has, at the outset, admitted the principle of equality of the two sexes before the law has, in virtue of that admission, affirmed the equal responsibility of the man and of the woman in respect to their illegitimate offspring. Though it may defer for the present the consideration of the possible and practicable means of establishing the right of affiliation, it has in reality already admitted this principle.

THE CONGRESS OF GENEVA

President of the Spanish Cortes, spoke on Wednesday, and was nominated as one of a Committee to consider what action could be taken in Spain. On Sunday, in the Cathedral, Pastor Rörich preached a powerful sermon to a very large congregation on the question before the Congress, and in all the churches we and our work have been prayed for.

"We always anticipated that when the final resolutions should come to be voted upon, then would be the real war, and so it was. On Thursday morning the voting began. Our faithful bands of ladies worked and watched in their different sections quite splendidly. First we had a considerable conflict in the Social Economy Section. Then came the voting in the Legislative Section, in the smaller Hall of the Reformation, which was densely crowded. Professor Hornung presided. The discussion lasted three hours. Some lawyers were present who are now busy in the prospect of the revision of some parts of the penal code of Switzerland, notably a young Jurist, an able man, who spoke well, but as a downright opponent. There followed a stormy scene, which the President with difficulty controlled. People of many different languages stood up at the same moment, each with a finger stretched out, demanding to speak. "Je demande la parole," sounded from all sides of the room. Mr. A——, the young Jurist, made the President indignant by asserting that a resolution drawn up by him was not *juridique*. Seeing that M. Hornung is Professor of Jurisprudence at the Geneva University, and possesses the very highest reputation, this was rather strong, and I do not wonder it irritated him. But it did good, for it stimulated him to come out on the last day of the Congress with a splendid judicial speech, by far the best and clearest utterance of the kind I have ever heard in any country. We shall translate and circulate it. Hornung is a delightful man. He has that good gift of God, an enlightened intellect, as well as a pure heart, together with great refinement and gentleness of manner.

"At one o'clock, when we were all feeling the need of food,

and our throats were dry with the dust of the room, an Italian Advocate got up and declared there had not yet been enough discussion of each point. The Chairman was aghast. He had expected the voting to be got over just at that moment. A kind of barking, House of Commons cry arose of 'Vote, vote!' while the President stood open-mouthed, attempting to read the resolutions so as to be heard. A sort of stampede seized some of the German and Swiss members, and they made for the door. Half the meeting would have gone out, and so damaged the worth of the voting. So I ventured to shut the door and set my back against it, declaring that no one should have any food until he had voted! This half startled and half amused the assembly, and they all sat down again obediently. After another half-hour of discussion, it was agreed that we should meet again for a final voting at half-past six the next morning.

"On the same day the resolutions of the Moral Section were passed very satisfactorily. Then came the Hygienic Section. The discussion here was so long that it was also adjourned until an evening hour.

"At eight o'clock that evening we all went to the Hall of the Hygienic Section, and there sat crowded together, or stood, amidst a scene of intense interest, till midnight. Dr. Bertani, of Rome, took a leading part. Our ladies all went to the meeting; but they had been up so early, and had worked so hard all day, that by eleven p.m. this is the scene which one of my sons described as having observed at the back of the hall: 'A long row of ladies *all sound asleep*'; but they had appointed a watcher, Mrs. Bright Lucas, who sat at the end of the row, and whom they had charged to keep awake, and to give them the signal whenever voting began on each clause of the resolution. Mrs. Lucas was wide awake, with eyes shining like live coals!

"We had prayed that God would direct this meeting, and it was wonderful and beautiful to see how the truth prevailed.

"Dr. de la Harpe, the President, acted well throughout.

At the end I shook hands with him and Dr. Ladame, thanking them for their excellent words. Dr. de la Harpe replied, 'You owe us nothing; it is you and your friends who must be thanked, who have brought us so much light.'

"At the end of the Congress all the Resolutions came out satisfactorily. We owe a good deal of this result to Professor Stuart's tact and patience in talking to the different presidents individually. We think our resolutions are, on the whole, excellent as a statement of principles—clear and uncompromising; and shall we not thank God for this? His hand has been over us for good all this time, convincing men's hearts and consciences, and controlling their words and actions. The earnest daily prayers offered up have not been in vain.

"These resolutions will be sent to every Government, and to every Municipal Council throughout Europe. They have been telegraphed to the English press *in extenso*. My son George was charged with the work of telegraphing, and had necessarily to exercise much alertness and activity; M. Humbert is impressed with the excellence of whatever work he undertakes.

"In the Legislative Section we had an energetic discussion over the seduction laws of different countries, and the *réchérche de la paternité*, subjects not immediately in our programme, but closely touching it. The discussion became so hot that it seemed difficult for some of the members to remain calm at all. Signora Mozzoni, a delegate from Milan, burst into tears over it, and one or two of our good gentlemen lost their tempers a little. One cannot wonder, for this is one of the important questions upon which people of different nations and creeds hold very different views. Miss Isabella Tod and Mrs. Sheldon Amos took a line on the point of the age to which protection should be given, in which I could not quite follow them, and I felt obliged for once to oppose my own countrywomen. Professor Hornung was pleased with what I said, as it seems it accorded with the views of most Continental Jurists. The young advocate who had opposed us called yesterday to say that he had come round to our views, chiefly influenced by that desperate little impromptu legal discussion among the ladies. He had imagined, he said, that we were a number of 'fanatical and sentimental women,' but 'when he heard women arguing like jurists, and even taking part against each other, and yet with perfect good temper *like men* (!), he began to see that we were grave, educated, and even scientific people!' He came afterwards to every meeting, and, as he said, weighed all our words.

"I think I have not mentioned the resolutions at the Section of Bienfaisance, under good Pastor Borel's presidency. Those also were very satisfactory,"

CHAPTER IX

"When the necessary revolution in the mind of the people is completed, that in the institutions of the country will follow as the day follows the night."—W. LLOYD GARRISON, the leading abolitionist of negro slavery.

A GREAT extension of our work followed the Congress of Geneva. As the cause was taken up in several countries of Europe and in British and other Colonies, its history comes naturally to be less of a personal record. My own reminiscences become more limited in proportion as our principles were gradually extended by the force of their own vitality, throughout the world. The originators of the movement could not be everywhere at once. Many stirring scenes and events connected with our work only came to our knowledge through correspondence or press notices, while we continued to direct the work to some extent from our central Committees in London and Geneva, with occasional journeys to and work in, other countries.

It was at the Congress of Geneva that we first made the acquaintance of M. Pierson, of Holland. I lately asked him to remind me of some of the circumstances connected with his first entering into the work, to which he has been so great a strength. (I have already said that M. Pierson was the successor of the well-known Pastor Heldring.) He wrote, in reply to my request, from Zetten, as follows:—

"I saw Heldring first in 1847, and went with him to spend some days in his family. Heldring was forty-three years old, and I thirteen. He was then building his Refuge of Steenbeck. On January 1st, 1848, he opened this Refuge. A lady, Miss Petronella Voûte, of a well-known family in

Amsterdam, descendants of French refugees in the reign of Louis XIV., was placed at the head of the Refuge. She worked with Heldring till his death in 1876, and died the following year under most remarkable circumstances. There were various branches of Heldring's great work. Before his death he had founded institutions for the aid of women and girls in different circumstances. I myself have added to these two smaller homes for young girls, and the Magdalena House for unmarried mothers, with a house for the children born there. For some time my relations with Heldring had been somewhat less intimate, though we were always friends. I had been first, for some years, a minister in a rural district, among staunch Calvinists, and afterwards for seven years in Bois-le-Duc, a town of 25,000 inhabitants, thoroughly Roman Catholic, where Protestants were as one to ten against the Catholics. During this time Heldring now and again expressed strong doubts as to the regulations of vice, which had been silently and slowly introduced in several of our towns in 1852 and after. He felt instinctively that there was something rotten in the State which allowed the introduction of such measures, and as soon as he heard of your first endeavours to attack the system he took note of it, and expressed his hope that a new era was approaching.

"He wrote to Van den Bergh (afterwards my son-in-law), in March, 1870, some words which, as coming from an old man of seventy-one years, show a little uncertainty, but which, taken in connection with his declarations at former periods, prove that he had always seen the true bearing of the question. He stood quite alone in Holland in this matter. He and a friend together had published in 1852 an anonymous pamphlet, in which every kind of regulation is condemned. That pamphlet was lying in a bookseller's garret. I bought the remaining copies, some hundreds, in 1858 for £2.

"In July, 1876, Heldring died, and in January, 1877, I came here in his place. Miss Voûte, the Directress of Steenbeck, had been a friend of my wife and myself from our childhood, and was very happy that we should take Held ring's work. But some five or six weeks after my arrival it became evident that her physical forces were giving way. Once—it may have been in March, 1877—speaking of Heldring and of me, she said to me, 'I feel such strange forebodings, I don't know why; but it seems as if the whole work of Steenbeck will be changed and begun anew.' 'In what sense?' I asked. 'In every respect,' she replied ; 'but I don't know how.' On the 14th April I went to see her, because we thought her end was approaching. After having prayed and spoken some words I left her, but I had not been gone an hour when some one came running to tell me (what, in fact, I already saw) that the Refuge was in flames, and Miss Voûte lying on her death-bed! I spare you the details. It is enough to mention that we brought her to my house. At first it seemed as if the shock had aroused her instead of doing her harm, but four days later she died suddenly.

"Steenbeck was burned to the ground. I had much to do in the following weeks, and when the invitation to the Geneva Congress came, I felt much inclined to accept, simply because it would give me a few days of leisure. But I honestly confess that I had some hesitation; I had always disliked the sanitary measures of the regulations, and abhorred the system of organised houses of shame; but I had the impression that the Congress was not taking up the great and central question, and that it took the humanitarian point of view rather than the Christian. I did not require to be converted by the Congress, for I already agreed with the principles proclaimed by it; but I came back from it persuaded that the question *was much more important* than I had imagined.

"I immediately felt two things : first, that we had been made dupes of by a false and stupid medical science, socalled ; and second, that our question was the ' tendon of the heel of Achilles ' of the whole matter of moral reform. These two points fitted in precisely with my state of mind; for I hate the humbug of false, would-be scientific men (I have seen too much of it); and I enjoy dealing with a question which involves a great many other questions, and which may be said to be a touchstone to try the minds of men.

"So in 1878 our first appeal in Holland was made to the public.

"Steenbeck burnt down ten months after Heldring's death, Miss Voûte dying almost beneath the falling walls, had made a deep impression. Money came in from every side. In five months a large building was erected. Meanwhile the inmates had been lodged in the Church. The work had not been dropped for a moment. On the day of the opening of the new building friends came from every part of the country to assist at the ceremony, and I used the occasion to draw the attention of the assembly to the work of the Federation. There was some opposition. Some thought that I was steering in another direction from Heldring; but as I have said, having discovered that Heldring's pamphlet of 1852 was lying at the bookseller's, I bought all the copies left, for which the good shopkeeper was very glad. It was a strong weapon. I could show that I was only taking up the thread where Heldring was obliged, for want of sympathy, to let it drop.

"I drew up a circular letter, adding with each letter a copy of Heldring's pamphlet, and distributed these. In March, 1878, I invited some four to five hundred persons to a meeting at Utrecht, in the centre of our country. The assembly was numerous. The foundation of our work was laid. A good report of this meeting may be found in the *Bulletin Continental* of June, 1878.

"In recalling those zealous days of our early entering upon the struggle, I instinctively feel the first holy fire rekindling in my heart and mind. God has been with us, and is still blessing his work by his gracious presence. We have not done as much as we wished or could have done; but we have not lived in vain. To him alone the glory, and blessing to our posterity."

M. Pierson adds some words in the same communication which are worthy to be reproduced, inasmuch as they describe a state of mind which we have met with and have had to combat in many countries, and which appears again and again. He writes: " Here in Holland we often find ourselves in enforced opposition to our well-intentioned friends, especially among Christians. In one of our cities some years ago a Committee was formed for promoting purer morals. They were in favour of attacking immorality, but refused to express any opinion about the public regulation of vice. It seems, at the date I am writing, that this Committee sleeps very quietly. I once named them Nicodemites, which much scandalised them. What Christians ought to realise—but seem very much to forget—is that in Christian countries *they are responsible for the spirit in which the laws are made.* Many of them seem to think that the Government, in its very essence, is a worldly, ungodly institution, somewhat in the same way as if they were living in a Pagan land, under the Roman Emperors. The Church, in those circumstances, had nothing to do but to save as many souls as could be brought into the fold of Christ. The Christians were not responsible for the Pagan laws and their destructive influences in those times. But with us it is quite a different thing. It will take a long time to make our principles widely understood, but it is not lost time."

I have gladly hailed at all times, and in all countries, the entrance of our question into its true and necessary political phase. The word "political" terrifies many people, some of them being the best and most earnest Christian people, because they do not, in fact, understand its true meaning. They see the spectre of party feuds, of party political interests in conflict. But there is no question of party in the politics of this sacred cause of ours. It is a question which vitally concerns our social life through all the classes, from the head of the Government down to the poorest toiler for his daily bread. It is a moral question which affects the moral and spiritual life of the peoples of the earth, and through their spiritual individual life, the domestic, social, and public life of the community. *But it must be fought out on the lines of law and Government—on political lines.* Corrupt magistrates, rulers, experts, and profligates of all grades will not look at the standard which the spiritually-minded man or woman holds up to them—the standard of Christian ethics. They pass it by with a smile. They confess no allegiance to any such law. But these rulers, and these inventors and upholders of State-regulation of vice, must bow to the law of the land. They may scoff at Christian teachers, but, sooner or later, they must reckon with that which is at their door, the *Penal Code*, which, though thrust aside, or violated for a time, still stands there, a rock against which they will stumble and fall, or else it will fall on them and crush them out of place and power. And how can we bring the law of the land to bear against an illegal and criminal institution, except on the field of politics, and by means of political action? For my part, I have never been able to hail our salvation from this horrible system as *near*, in any country, until the question has entered into the political stage. While saying this I hold firmly the truth that "our weapons are *spiritual*, to the pulling down of strongholds"; that it is by the faith of the true servants of God, by their persistent prayers and their confidence in Him, that we shall win the victory. But in all matters of human action and conflict we use means. The hand of the warrior grasps the sword, while his heart is stayed on God. We reach out for every lawful means, on every side of us, for the destruction of this iniquity; and a long experience, as well as the lessons of history, prove clearly that the public, political means afforded us by the just laws and Constitutions of our several countries are above all the most effectual means for the destruction of legalised illegality, of the slavery, oppression, greed, cheating, murder, and shames embraced in the institution of State-regulated vice.

A movement in favour of our cause had been energetically promoted in 1878 in Spain by M. Empeytaz and other upholders of our principles in Spain. The " Voice in the Wilderness " was translated and distributed in Barcelona and Madrid. Pastor Fritz Fliedner, the well-known German who founded the deaconesses' institution of Kaiserswerth, was at that time travelling in Spain, and found that the Governor of Madrid had suppressed the Spanish edition of the " Voice in the Wilderness." He called on the Governor, and also procured the intercession of the German Ambassador on behalf of the work, and the prohibition was withdrawn.

In Spain we also found a brave champion of our principles in the Countess de Precorbin (Spanish by birth), who had joined us a few years before. This lady held meetings in several towns and districts of Spain, giving addresses to soldiers, students and others, and was everywhere graciously received. So great was her desire to gain the ear of the working people, that in one district, where a large proportion of the male population was engaged in working in mines during the day, she had herself let down into a mine in a basket. It was a surprise to the miners to see this gentle lady in the midst of them, and to hear her message concerning justice, equality, purity, and the sacredness of home life; they heard her gladly and reverently. A Spanish lady of high rank, Donna Concepion Arenal, continued for some years to advocate our Cause in a periodical edited by herself, *La Caridad*. This ceased at her death. The movement in Spain languished after a few years, yet we continue to hope that it may be revived in some manner in future. During this year we received expressions of personal sympathy and adhesion from several influential Jews. Zadok Kahn, the Grand Rabbin of Paris, wrote a beautiful letter to the Federation, expressing his full sympathy and that of the best men of his people. The Grand Rabbin Wertheimer, of Geneva, gave his adhesion. I had called on the Grand Rabbin Astruc, of Belgium, on my way through that country in the previous year. From that time he became also a firm adherent. Ben Israel, Grand Rabbin of Avignon, also wrote several letters full of sympathy with the work.

Dating from the Congress of Geneva, we began to store up an arsenal of good weapons in the form of literature. Books innumerable had been written by the defenders of regulation, and there was no lack of solid literature on their side. The only Continental work of any consequence which had been used to counteract their influence up to 1878 was the modest little book entitled, " A Voice in the Wilderness ; " this was a collection of my first appeals made on the Continent of Europe, ably edited by M. Aimé Humbert. This work never appeared in English. It was translated gradually from the French into every other European language. This little book was, as M. Humbert rightly said, merely a call to battle, a challenge—and this assertion was reproachfully echoed by our adversaries. " We want," they said, " something scientific, statistical and closely reasoned. We do not want merely the expression of a woman's revolted feelings against a system which we believe to be useful and necessary." They had not long to wait for the scientific arguments and close reasoning which they professed to desire ; for the two bulky volumes published after our Congress of 1877, entitled *Les Actes du Congrès de Genève*, furnished all that could be desired in that direction, being a collection of the weighty utterances, prepared for our Congress, of philosophers, statesmen, medical men, jurists, women of experience in social work, and of thoughtful leaders among the working classes, drawn from many different countries of the world. It may not be uninteresting to my readers to see the relation of our first literary effort to what followed, as expressed in a quotation here given from a letter which I wrote to M. Humbert in reply to his proposal in 1875 to publish in pamphlet form the principal portions of my appeals on the Continent.

"I feel with you every day," I wrote, "that some such *voice* is needed just now. It would, perhaps, have been better had we been able to bring out a complete book as our first—a book which should contain all the scientific and juridical arguments as well as a complete review of historical facts relating to this subject. But such a complete book is at this moment impossible; I therefore beg you to communicate what I now say to Messieurs Sandoz and Fischbacher (publishers). We want statistics and facts—yes,—but would English statistics and facts alone, drawn from a limited experience, be much or generally valued in other countries? I think not, if they stood alone. Facts from a larger area we must have later, and we shall have them, for, thank God, they stand as indestructible witnesses everywhere of the folly and futility of the attempt to regulate vice. How much more powerful, how overwhelming, in fact, would it be for our opponents, and how strengthening for our Cause, if we could show facts and statistics gathered from every country and over a larger period of time. This is precisely what we are now aiming at. We have received all the most recent reports from Italy, France, Germany and other countries. On every hand there is confession of the failure of regulation. Mireur, Jeannell, Diday, Deprès, Pallasciano, Huet, Crocq, all confess to hygienic failure. The proposals of some of these men to insure future success (a success which they confess they have never yet ensured) are of such a wild and ghastly nature that one has only to read their books to see that the beginning of the end is at hand.

"From out these statistics there appear here and there deeply pathetic facts such as this: that four-fifths of the poor girls subjected to this tyranny (according to one writer) are orphans; many are foreigners in the country of their enslavement; many are young widows. Does not our God, who is the God of the Fatherless, of the Widow, and of the Stranger, take note of these things?

"You see that in a year or two we shall have a mass of evidence against this system which will give the doctors and materialist legislators a hard task to refute.

"I care little that men accuse me, as you say, of mere sentiment, and of carrying away my hearers by feeling rather than by facts and logic. Even while they are saying this, they read my words, and they are made uncomfortable! they feel that there is a truth of some sort there, and that sentiment itself is after all a *fact* and a power when it expresses the deepest intuitions of the human soul. They have had opportunity for many years past of looking at the question in its material phases, of appreciating its hygienic results, and of reading numberless books on the subject, statistical, medical, and administrative. Now, for the first time, they are asked to look upon it as a question of human nature, of equal interest to man and woman, as a question of the heart, the soul, the affections, the whole moral being. As a simple assertion of one woman speaking for tens of thousands of women, those two words '*we rebel*' are very necessary and very useful for them to hear. The cry of women crushed under the yoke of legalised vice is not the cry of a statistician or a medical expert; it is simply a cry of pain, a cry for justice and for a return to God's laws in place of these brutally impure laws invented and imposed by man. It is imperfect, no doubt, as an utterance; but the cry of the revolted woman against her oppressor and to her God is far more needful at this moment than any reasoned-out argument. I think, therefore, and my husband agrees with me, that it is better to publish the 'Voice in the Wilderness' simply as the utterance of a woman, and to do it quickly. It will rouse some consciences, no matter how imperfect men may find it. On the eve of a war it may be said that the sound of the trumpet is imperfect because it only calls to the battle, and that we want to see the troops, their arms, and the strength of muscle on either side; yet the call to battle is needed: the close grappling with the foe will follow. It is only when the slave begins to move, to complain, to give signs of life and resistance, either by his own voice or by the voice of one like himself speaking for him, that the struggle for freedom truly begins. The slave now speaks. The enslaved women have found a voice in one of themselves who was raised up for no other end than to sound the proclamation of an approaching deliverance. Never mind the imperfection of the first voice. It is the voice of a woman who has suffered, a voice calling to holy rebellion and to war. It will penetrate.

Then by-and-by we shall come down on our opponents with the heavy artillery of facts and statistics and scientific arguments on every side. We will not spare them. We will show them no mercy; we shall tear to pieces their 'refuge of lies' and expose the ghastliness of their 'covenant with death and their agreement with hell'; we and our successors will continue to do this year after year until they have no ground to stand upon."

There was, and is, of course, this marked difference between the character of the literature of the regulationists and our own—namely, that the motive of all their arguments is that of expediency, based upon the assumption of the necessity of vice; the moral and the higher hygienic aspects of the question are ignored by them. This has been well expressed by Sir James Stansfeld on several occasions. He wrote shortly before the Geneva Congress to M. Aimé Humbert as follows:—" You and I have a great work in hand. Speaking for my own country, I have neither doubt nor fear of the issue of the conflict. There is no case in the history of England of the failure of any movement based upon the moral and religious sense and convictions of the community in which any considerable number of men or of women have had the courage and the faith to persist; and there are men and women enough prepared to spend their lives in this holy cause thus to insure its success. We had the weakness, we incurred the guilt, of borrowing and accepting this unholy and indecent law from France. It stole its way on to our Statute Book under a miserable hygienic pretence. Its contrivers seem to me as men deprived of the consciousness of the unity of the law of God. They would sacrifice morality to health, the soul to the body, the immortal to the mortal part. They cannot look high enough or far enough to see that it is a philosophic, a scientific, as well as a religious truth that there cannot be dissonance between the laws of Nature and the laws of God, and that it is, therefore, inconceivable that the immoral should be a truly sanitary law. Even partially and temporarily applied as these laws are here, they are already a proved sanitary failure, proved upon the figures of the Government Returns."

Besides the more solid works which began from this time to appear in favour of our cause, each country interested in it, beginning to find the necessity of some record of its own activity and that of other nationalities, started a special organ of its own. Beginning with the *Bulletin Continental*, published monthly at Geneva, there followed special organs of the Abolitionist Societies in Holland, Belgium, Denmark, Sweden, Norway, France, and Italy.

Up to this time we had not obtained much support from the Roman Catholic section of the community in different countries, except in individual instances, such as that of Archbishop, afterwards Cardinal Manning, who some years previously had expressed his strong disapproval of the principles of the Regulationists at the Papal Court on the occasion of several of his visits to Rome. Our friend Mme. de Morsier, of Paris, had been prompted by some of the writings of Archbishop Dupanloup on the subject of woman's education to pay a visit to that prelate on behalf of our cause shortly before the Congress of Geneva. I give the account of her visit in her own words written to me at the time.

"We went to the house of Monseigneur Dupanloup. The residence of the Archbishop is situated on the banks of the Loire, in the midst of verdure; on one side there is the college which he superintends, a large building standing close to the woods which descend to the river; on the other side stands an ancient castellated mansion, covered with ivy, climbing roses, and honeysuckle. It is in this house that the Monseigneur himself lives. On the terrace, embosomed in woods, the table was spread for the evening repast. The Monseigneur had just arrived from Rheims, whence he had come expressly to receive me. In spite of his fatigue and the suffering caused by an accident to his finger, he did the honours of his house with graceful courtesy. When he appeared and crossed the lawn, dressed in his purple robe, his white hair uncovered, I must confess I felt surprised. I had only known him by Parisian report, so that I had expected to see a proud and rather pompous old man, receiving his guests amidst the luxury and ceremonial of the cardinals of the Middle Ages. But I saw before me a gentle and holy looking man, so simple in his manner and bearing, that in talking to him I soon forgot his high position and great talent, and felt quite drawn to speak to him freely as an equal. The table spread upon the lawn, and among the flowers, the venerable old man invoking a blessing on the repast, the nightingale which was singing the first notes of evening, and the strains of the 'Angelus' which reached us from a distance, all together formed a striking picture of peace and happiness. It was in the midst of this scene that, summoning courage, I spoke to him of those dark horrors and of that hard struggle in which I had come to claim the support of his sympathy. The Monseigneur listened without remark, asking from time to time some question. Several times he exclaimed, 'Your Congress delights me; that is the important point. It will require a thunderbolt to awaken consciences.' His secretary, an Abbé of great talent, manifested his approbation of our cause. Monseigneur described to me how much the conscience of their religiously educated youth revolted when they learned that vice is actually legalised by the State. He himself had had, he said, only very recently a complete revelation of the state of things, from the work of Parent Duchâtelet which had fallen into his hands. The evening passed in conversation. When I was leaving I offered him my hand (which I afterwards found was contrary to etiquette) and said to him, 'Monseigneur, may I now feel assured of your sympathy for our cause?' 'Yes, assuredly,' he replied. 'Do you authorise me,' I asked, 'to make use of your name as a convinced adherent.' 'Yes,' he said; 'I consent fully.' Then he himself extended his hand to me, and finally, in parting, I said: 'Monseigneur, I recommend our cause to your prayers.' 'You have them,' he said. The carriage rolled away, and I felt my heart full of gratitude to God, and I said to myself, 'Ah! if all Bishops were like this one, and all Abbés like those I have seen at Orleans, the true friends of progress would have little excuse to make war against the Catholic religion."

Up to the time of which I am writing very little progress had been made in Germany in respect of State abstinence from compromise with public immorality. In the year 1876, M. Humbert had some correspondence with eminent members of the German Inner Mission, and from that time onward we had several distinguished individual adherents in Germany, men and women; but they were few.

A Petition had been presented in that year to the Reichstag, signed by Dr. Dorner in the name of the Central Committee of the Inner Mission. It was as follows:—

"BERLIN AND HAMBURG.

"The undersigned Central Committee takes the liberty of drawing the attention of the Reichstag to the following:—

"Upon the occasion of the revision of the Penal Code by the German Empire, upon the 15th May, 1871, there were proposed certain additions, emanating from the Reichstag itself, Sections 180 and 361; additions which would have for their effect to accord in Germany a legal existence to houses of infamy, and to thereby introduce them within certain portions of the limits of the Empire in which they do not at present exist. It is not to be doubted that the motive which has dictated this proposition is that of acting in the supposed interest of the public health, but we are none the less convinced that its adoption would be injurious to the public welfare, and that the moral foundations of our social life, already menaced, would be thereby still more profoundly shaken.

"The trade of the procurer, which hitherto has fallen under the ban of severe penalties, would find itself, by virtue of the observance of certain formalities, with which it would be easy to comply, placed henceforth under the protection of the law. The number of women, especially in the large towns, who practise vice under the supervision of the police would also be materially augmented; once legalised, the trade of the procurer would be given up to a depraved competition, and all this would tend in the highest degree to the public demoralisation. Further, confidence in the Imperial legislation, and consequently in the Empire itself, which has need rather to be strengthened, would experience a serious shock amongst very considerable and important portions of the population; and the supreme authority, which, according to the declaration of the Government and of the Chancellor of the Empire, was to be augmented by the revision of the Penal Code, would find itself instead materially weakened. As regards the sanitary reasons which are put forward in support of the proposition, we believe ourselves authorised in saying that their value has not yet been sufficiently established from the experimental and scientific point of view, and that, on the contrary, in this respect also, the proposition is open to serious objections.

" We will add, lastly, that this proposition is put forward precisely at the moment when we are witnessing, in England and in Switzerland, a movement as profound as it is earnest, which has for its aim, with ever increasing prospects of success, the abrogation of all legalisation of vice, whether on the part of the Legislature or of the Administrative function.

" In virtue of these considerations, we address to the Reichstag the following prayer:—

"'That the Reichstag be pleased to reject every proposition tending to alter the provisions already enacted by the law against the trade of the procurer, or to authorise in any manner whatever the exercise of that trade by placing it under official protection.

"'In the name of the Central Committee of the Inner Mission of the Evangelical Church in Germany, for the President, Dr. Dorner, Member of the Superior Consistory.'"

This petition, it will be observed, was directed, not against the then existing system of legalised vice in Germany, but only against a fuller development of it which was threatened. Then, and up to the present time, in most cities in Germany, a permission to follow their calling was and is given by the police to unfortunate women living in their own lodgings, on condition of their conforming to certain prescribed police and sanitary rules. This is in itself an open, official sanction. A people, having become accustomed to this amount of official license, is easily, and, indeed, logically, carried on to acquiesce in the more complete form of Governmental sanction of vice, namely, the licensed and protected house of shame. There is, therefore, to the convinced Abolitionist, a fatal omission in this otherwise excellent petition, in the absence of an additional protest against the license which was *already accorded* in Germany.

The light which is now falling so fully and steadily upon this question will surely in time reveal clearly to reformers in Germany, as elsewhere, the necessity of attacking any and every compromise with vice, in whatever form. In official compromise with sin there is no standing still; there is a perpetual advance towards more shameless and elaborate organisation of profligacy. The house of ill-fame *never existed* in England as an openly recognised and State-protected institution, but it came by degrees, under the regulations now abolished, to be tacitly permitted, and the English Abolitionists knew well that, unless a blow were struck at the root principle of the whole system, the open recognition of organised houses of debauchery would follow in their own, as in all other countries, where the system of regulation has once obtained a footing. This matter is clearly stated in the Berlin Regulations instituted in 1850. The following words are translated from the German of the *Resolution of the Royal Presidency of Police of Berlin, December* 11*th*, 1850, which precedes the Regulations:—

"The method of tolerance may be twofold: permission may be given to the women to have each a domicile of her own, upon submitting to a stringent regulation; or, on the other hand, they may be confined in special houses, under a responsible householder.

"This last method offers more guarantees and greater security to police-regulation, and facilitates supervision. No doubt the moral sentiment revolts at the idea that the public authority should tolerate and protect houses set apart for purposes of vice, *but experience has proved that this mode is, for Berlin, the least objectionable.*"

In March, 1878, a visit was paid to the district of Torre Pellice, in North Italy, the cradle of the Waldensian Church. The pastors and people of that country were quickly and securely gained to our cause, as is usual with persons who have suffered for a truth for which they have been called to contend.

In 1879 I visited the Ban de la Roche in Alsace, with my husband; here Pastor Dietz and others were won to be warm adherents of our cause. We passed through Colmar and Muhlhausen, but it was not until some years later that we made the acquaintance of M. Schlumberger, Mayor of Colmar, and heard of the unique part which he had taken in the cause of justice and morality.

The principal event on the Continent of the year 1879 was the Annual Conference of the Federation, held at Liége, in Belgium. The following account of that event was written by Mme. de Morsier, of Paris.

"There is an advantage in choosing middle-sized towns for these annual meetings. In large centres like Paris and London our action is partly lost on account of the vastness of the place. No doubt the active members of the Federation feel the benefit of them, but very little impression can be made on the public, whilst in smaller towns, like Liége, we may, as we have seen, produce a great impression, even at an unfavourable season, when the higher class people are away.

"Our public meetings in Liége, Verviers, and Seraing, were attended by a numerous public, chiefly men. The earnest attention with which we were heard convinced us that the good seed did not fall on barren soil. Even the press did us the honour of discussing our question, and some papers published very good articles. However, we had the opportunity of noticing that Belgian editors, like those of other countries, are extremely full of solicitude for *us*, and eager to caution us against many and various dangers. 'Beware the perilous paths;' they seem to say, 'if you take the right one we will follow you; but what is wanted are works of rescue; leave the police alone and create *Refuges*.'

"Well, the Conference of Liége answered in a very categorical manner to this, the constantly repeated suggestion of the over-prudent and timidly charitable.

"The one thing that struck us was how much the question has developed, how much enlarged is the view taken of the subject—the really essential aspect of it, *i.e.* the defence of individual liberty and right. And this is the result of the *logic of facts*. The strength of a principle lies in this, that it gradually imposes itself upon all true and serious minds, and leads them to accept its logical and necessary consequences. I have no hesitation in saying that, in my opinion, the main fact of the Conference in Liége has been this unity of feeling among the Delegates present on the great question of the sacredness of personal liberty and individual right.

"This is the firmest basis upon which to act, our best security against inconsistency. If we deny to the police the right of sitting in judgment upon the morality of women, we must be ready to refuse this right also to every form of arbitrary rule, whether it be the arbitrary rule of an Assembly of well-intentioned people, or the arbitrary rule of corrupt agents or officials. Our experience during our struggle for this cause has opened our eyes to the fact that all the great struggles of the present day, whether political, social, economic or religious, may be summed up as one great war between the two principles, Compulsion and Liberty, and if the first principle is still so powerful in countries boasting of liberal institutions, is it not to some extent be-

THE CONFERENCE OF LIÉGE

cause the partisans of the second principle have thought it prudent to temporise with the first; being led astray by the beautiful modern invention—*opportunism?* It was, therefore, with double satisfaction that I saw the Federation fortifying itself more and more by relying upon absolute principles. I will quote as an example the energetic speech of Mr. Benjamin Scott, Chamberlain of the City of London, at the public meeting of the 22nd August in Liége. Mr. Benjamin Scott regarded the subject from an extremely elevated point of view, and showed himself as daring as truth itself.

"'You are not free,' said he to the citizens of Liége. 'Liége is not free; Brussels is not free; and Paris is not free, though she has battered down the Bastille, and placed the statue of Liberty on the column of July. . . . It could never be said that the United States were free so long as they held four millions of negroes enslaved. Paris, Brussels, and your fine city of Liége are not free so long as any woman may be deprived of her civil rights at the caprice or tyranny of a police agent, or through the denunciation of a scoundrel.'

"You may be sure that M. Yves Guyot did not fail to fling many keen shafts at the Police des Mœurs, on the ground of its illegality and violation of individual liberty, enforcing his powerful arguments by quotations from the Belgian Code, which fell like battering-rams on the hypocrisies of the system. M. Humbert traced in broad outlines the history of the Federation in all countries. With the readiness of mind and tact of a man accustomed to act as chairman, he took the opportunity of a rather violent speech from M. O―― B――, of Liége, to re-affirm the large and independent point of view maintained by our Association. 'We are not here to enter into any political or religious polemics,' he said, 'we seek to recall your minds to those humanitarian truths and principles in which all those who desire justice and respect the rights of human beings can unite.'

"M. Pierson, Director of the Asiles of Zetten, Holland, gave some interesting details of his special work, and declared that his experience in such practical endeavours had convinced him of the truth of the principles maintained by the Federation.

"Let the editors of papers be at rest; we also approve and encourage works of rescue and reformation, and especially when their founders understand the duty of thus publicly proclaiming the lessons they have learned through such private experience.

"The public meeting of Liége will take its place among the brilliant successes of our cause. Seven hundred people expressed their adherence to our principles by their enthusiastic cheers. M. Nicolet, President of the Committee of Liége, must have been well satisfied with his countrymen.

"On the Thursday evening we held a women's meeting The schoolroom placed at our disposal was full, and, notwithstanding the warnings as to the necessity of *prudence* which had been given us, we stated the question plainly and frankly. The expression of mingled curiosity and amazement, which we first observed on the faces of the listeners, was soon succeeded by an expression of attentive sympathy.

"The Baroness de Stampe spoke of Denmark, the Countess Schack of Germany, and Mme. de Morsier related some facts which she had witnessed in Paris. A hearty vote of sympathy was granted to us, and on our leaving the room, many hands pressed ours, and heartfelt words of encouragement were spoken.

"We had also the great satisfaction of seeing many young men of Liége, students, etc., at our business Conference, where we invited them to a private meeting at the Hotel de Suède. A great many came, students, and some workmen also. That evening's reunion will remain one of the best souvenirs of Liége. Nothing moves me more deeply than to see on the faces of young men the expression of noble impulses and generous enthusiasm. Whatever the struggles, the failures, or the wreck of illusions which life may bring, a spark of the

THE CONFERENCE OF LIÉGE

true fire will always linger in the soul of the man who sincerely believed in justice and in true love when he was twenty.

"M. Humbert's words found ready response when, in a splendid improvisation, he drew for them the picture of a truly noble, active, and useful life, and spoke to them of the march of humanity on the path of progress, guided by the light of the two beacons of science and faith.

"M. Testuz and M. Durand of Liége, spoke also some heart-stirring words to this youthful assembly.

"On Sunday 21st, the delegates of the Federation were invited to a friendly tea-party, in the *Presbytère de la Chênée*, by M. Nicolet, which was rendered delightful by the feeling of true fraternity which united us through sharing the same moral aspirations and hopes, in spite of our many differences of opinion upon other points. We may construct systems, found religious sects, or analyse scientific facts, but the focus of true life, the lever elevating humanity to noble aims, will always be the spirit of *Love* and *Justice*.

"On Sunday we were awakened by the sound of the funeral bell, which announced the death of the Archbishop of Liége. We were invited at four o'clock to visit the Pastor Nicolet, at Chênée. About the same hour M. Yves Guyot gave a conference in his own name, personally, to the Associations of *Libre Penseurs*, and the Countess Schack accompanied him. Some of us took the route to Chênée in a carriage. The presbytère (pastor's house) is situated in the middle of the village— a pretty little house, the ground floor of which is the chapel. Above is the drawing-room, which opens upon a wooden balcony with a charming view. Next to the house is a garden extending to the bank of the Canal de l'Aurte; beyond, to the right, a little village with its bell-tower and church. On the left the great furnaces of the Vieille Montagne;[1] further down, and all round, wooded hills.

"Nature here is as amiable and peaceful as the charming

---
[1] One of the largest iron foundries in Belgium.

hosts who received us. M. Nicolet offered to have a service in the chapel in English for the English workman delegates. Those of us who remained on the little balcony enjoyed the sound of the manly voices singing their beautiful hymns. The setting sun was covering the west with gold, and a light mist slowly rose from the valley. In the drawing-room there was conversation, grave and gay. Mr. Stuart was compelled to pay a fine in aid of the Maison Hospitalière. He had made a bet that the English working men delegates would not find their way to Chênée; but they, setting off on foot at the moment that we entered our carriage, had arrived at the door of the presbytery before us. Mme. Nicolet proposed that we should all visit the Chapel. It is charming, this little chapel in its great simplicity, with its iron pillars and its Gothic windows, which open upon the garden, the river, and the hills.

"There was a harmonium; why, we said, should we not sing? M. Nicolet brought his violin, and took the shoulder of M. Pierson as a *chevalet*, young Gustave took the harmonium, and the singers grouped themselves round the window. The sweet melody rose and fell like a wave, and our souls were quieted and elevated by this flood of harmony. The last rays of the sun, broken by the lattice work, bathed the group of singers in their golden light, playing round the white hair of the venerable violinist. At the same moment M. Yves Guyot and the Countess Schack silently entered the Chapel, and took a seat on one of the benches.

"We shall not soon forget the peaceful presbytery of Chênée, the balcony garlanded with flowers, the group in the chapel, lighted by the setting sun; and above all, the kind pastor and his wife, whose loving Christian friendship gained every heart. Whenever I may hear again Luther's hymn, the Hallelujah of Beethoven, or the sorrowful melodies of Calvary, I shall see again, in thought, the chapel of Chênée, and the friends who were assembled there that Sunday evening, the 24th of August, 1879.

"Gustave and Clement accompanied us to the railway

station. The pale crescent moon rose above the horizon, and the furnaces of the Vieille Montagne flung their flames into the cool evening air.

"On Monday, at 3 o'clock, the Federation was under arms; it was time to go to Verviers, where a conference had been prepared. Verviers is a pretty little industrial town; the houses have a comfortable look, which is somewhat reflected in the faces of the citizens. At 7 o'clock we were at our places in the Hall of Emulation; the public alone was late. This, however, allowed us to enjoy upon the balcony a magnificent spectacle. The town had just been inundated by a storm of rain, the western sky was on fire, here and there clouds torn asunder revealed calm expanses of the heavens, of a pale blue or green, which harmonised with the purple tints of the evening. The wet pavement reflected the burning sky, and the whole place seemed illuminated. Some of us admired in silence, while others analysed every changing effect.

"The meeting began coldly. We were told that the hour fixed was too early, and that the workmen had not yet left the foundries. By degrees, however, the hall filled; there were a great number of men, and some women—a very attentive audience, though less enthusiastic than that of Liége.

"M. Yves Guyot, Mrs. Butler and M. Pierson spoke. Mr. Lucraft, a delegate of the London workmen, improvised a speech full of fire; the ardour of his manner and voice captivated those even who did not understand what he was saying. Mme. de Morsier translated for him. Mr. Bonjean, a citizen of Verviers, in a brief speech, thanked the Federation.

"The hurry to reach the train at night was not very favourable to the orators; nevertheless, the meeting was good. As we entered the railway carriage, M. Humbert complained bitterly of the blows which he had received in the back from ladies' fans, which they thus made use of to remind the speaker that the time was getting late! He demanded that at Seraing fans should be prohibited!

"On Tuesday our partings began. The representatives of the North disappeared from amongst us, with the Baroness de Stampe and Dr. Giersing, of Denmark. M. Testuz (from Sweden) disappeared like a shooting star. Those who had exchanged thoughts with him at the dinner table of the Hotel de Suède, would gladly have once more shaken hands with him before his departure. Why did M. Testuz disappear like a shooting star?

"M. and Mme. Pierson next took their departure, and the Parisian deputation also began to be dismembered. Nature seemed to wish to soften our regrets, for the weather was beautiful, the heavens blue, and the bright rays of the sun tempered by an autumnal breeze.

"It was pleasant to linger in the Botanical Gardens where underneath the canopy of pines, the gentle breeze carried to us the scent of the heliotrope, roses, white campanula and giant daisies flowering together in the beds in that beautiful disorder which is more agreeable to the eye than the mosaic horticulture which is now the fashion.

But it was time to start for Seraing. We went by the river, the whole party—at least, all who still remained. The wind had risen, it fluttered the ladies' veils, and it seemed that the classical hat of the Cambridge Professor had a design to make acquaintance with the waves of the Meuse. Madame de Morsier, depositary of the precious Belgian Code, carried the volume with a respectful awe, which caused her to be charged with fetichism. The Belgian Code! It is the Krupp cannon of our artillery! Madame de Morsier asked what certain orators would do that evening if, putting out their hands to take it for quotations, they should find it had disappeared.

"The boat flew quickly through the water. We glided past wooded hills, at the foot of which the furnaces, with their blackened walls and tall chimneys, launched out columns of smoke mixed with flames. Here and there were workmen's villages nestling in the woods. Nature and industry were united in a powerful harmony; it seemed like a key-note of our age. Those who despise the romance of the Rhine might enjoy themselves here. At every moment the scene changed; it was a succession of little pictures of varied style : here a slope of dark woods, against which rises a great furnace; there an island in the middle of the river, in which one caught glimpses of mysterious paths; further on, a meadow of brilliant green, meeting at its horizon line the western sky all decked in gold; here, a boat, whose brown sail stood out against the sky, while lower down on the horizon, clouds of capricious form, lighted up by the departing rays of the sun, presented the most varied tints, or, tearing themselves asunder, revealed to our sight the transparency of a boundless horizon. Occasionally the boat stopped to take in passengers. We saw on the shore a friend waving his hat in our direction, the wind blowing back his silvery hair. It was the good pastor of Chênée and his excellent wife, standing on the little pier, ready to join us.

"At last we reached Seraing, coquettishly seated upon the two shores of the Meuse, bound together by a bridge of iron which is not wanting in elegance. Opposite the place of debarkation, in the middle of a little parterre, stands the statue of Cockerill, the founder of these vast ironworks. Around the pedestal are grouped figures representing the workers in the foundries with their various implements of toil; their countenances and their marked features have something noble and proud about them; one reads in them the character of men who feel themselves masters of their art. We walked through the streets of the village, women and children gazing at us with curiosity from the door steps.

"On this occasion we had no time to lose, only just time to take a cup of coffee at the little Inn, before going to the hall placed at our service by the Society of Seraing. We found all the seats already occupied, but there was no gas lit; it was not the custom to light up before a quarter past seven. We took our places upon the platform whilst attempts were made to light up. The patient audience interested itself much in this operation, and gave advice. At last a few burners consented to be lighted, and the meeting began. There was a crowd of workmen and women who listened attentively. We found here a more complete sympathy than at Verviers. The enthusiasm was not so loudly expressed as at Liége, but there was something convinced and quiet in the audience; whenever the smallest noise occurred, the meeting demanded silence. These people we saw had not come to be amused, but to be instructed. The speakers were MM. Minod, Humbert, Guyot, and Mrs. Butler. Mr. Stuart concluded a brief speech with the words, 'The police of morals is the greatest mystification of our age. It is a servant which has never fulfilled its task. Dismiss it.'

"We had this time leisure to go quietly to the station through the beautiful air; the moon and Jupiter were shining brightly in a deep blue sky. We passed along the side of the great foundries; immense jets of fire were flung out from the chimneys; we heard the dull heavy blows of the steam hammers, and then a roaring sound like the breaking of a great wave. It was the flowing out of the boiling fountain of metal into the mould, accompanied by the shouts of the workmen announcing the success of an operation. A mighty spectacle, but one which has its melancholy side, when one thinks of those men compelled to such hard nocturnal labour, exposed to the heat of that burning lava, condemned to a life apart from other citizens, and only coming out from the foundries in order to go to rest, when others are awaking up. The eternal problem of social industry—will it ever be solved?

"But here was the train, and the last joyous return to our hotel. Once more a repast together: to-morrow the great adieu.

"Wednesday morning, the 27th August, the friends who remained re-assembled once more for conversation in the drawing-room of the Hotel de Suède. The conversation took that tender and serious tone which often precedes the hour of parting. Each one traced back the thread of his or her memories, and recounted the events or circumstances which brought them first in contact with the great idea which unites us. Strange coincidences some of them appeared to be. 'The chances of life' one said. 'Perhaps something more than that,' said another. Yes! there is something here more than chance.

"That same day the trains for Paris, for Antwerp, for Cologne, and for Calais carried away the last of our band. A farewell grasp of the hand, a parting smile, a bouquet of flowers presented, and then all is said.

"Each one drove away towards his destination, and to the encounter with new duties.

"And now, little town of Belgium, sitting on the banks of the Meuse, surrounded with green hills, let me take one parting look at you! We have only known you a few days and now you live in our memories a luminous point in the past. Many of us arrived within your walls strangers to each other, and have parted friends; some arrived sorrowful, discouraged, asking what will be the end of all this? They return peaceful, and fortified with the conviction that work is happiness, and conflict a duty.

"*Manet alta mente repostum.*"

M. Lecour, the well-known chief of the Morals' Police in Paris, had been advised in 1878 to retire from his post, and was appointed chief *marguillier* (bell-ringer) of Notre Dame.

On the 23rd and 24th January, 1879, the editor of the *Lanterne* was prosecuted by the Government for a series of letters published in that paper containing charges against the administration of the police, including the Police des Mœurs. The editor was condemned to three months' imprisonment and a fine of 2,000 francs.

The disclosures made at the trial of the *Lanterne* induced M. Gigot, the Prefect of Police, to beg M. Marcère, the

Minister of the Interior, to appoint a Commission of Inquiry.

M. Naudin, M. Lecour's successor, was heard before this Commission on the 7th April. Nothing could be more shallow than his deposition; a *rechauffé* of administrative phrases, uttered with an air of conviction, as if they were novel truths. His evidence was to the effect that " all the officials hitherto employed at the Prefecture had but one idea—to maintain appearances; avoid mistakes in arrests; exercise the greatest prudence in the most delicate functions; and, above all, prevent public scandal, and maintain the secrecy of their operations."

The Commission had arranged with the new Prefect of Police, M. Andrieux, to hear his deposition. They met and waited some hours, to be told afterwards that he had forgotten his appointment. A fresh appointment was made, when the Prefect again insulted the Commission in the same manner.

Soon after the celebrated articles published by the *Lanterne* (M. Yves Guyot), under the signature of a " Vieux Petit Employé," were resumed, and they pointed out that the greater number of the officials who were implicated in the atrocities brought to light at the trial of the *Lanterne* were still in office, while those of their subordinates who had dared to speak the truth had been summarily dismissed the service without compensation.

The Appeal which had been made in the case of the *Lanterne* was decided, and that courageous journal was again condemned by French law, and victoriously absolved and applauded by French public opinion.

The damning evidence brought against the Prefecture of Police had caused the retirement of M. Gigot, the chief members of his staff, and later, of the Minister of the Interior, M. Marcère. In more than one country, the light which our crusade threw upon men and deeds caused many a man in office to disappear, to melt away out of sight. The new Prefect continued to countenance the same abuses, and the *Lanterne* continued its public censure of them. M. Andrieux then calumniated that journal in his place in the Assembly, declaring it to be the centre of a Bonapartist plot, of which the "Ex-Agent des Mœurs," "The Vieux Petit Employé," and the "Médécin," were the leaders.

CHAPTER X

> 'What though the cast-out spirit tear
> The Nation in his going,
> We who have shared the guilt must share
> The pang of his o'erthrowing;
> Whate'er the loss,
> Whate'er the cross,
> Shall they complain of present pain
> Who trust in God's hereafter?"

IT was in the year 1880 that we first began to see that we were approaching a turning in the long road which we had traversed for ten years, and were facing towards victory, the victory which we had always, even in the darkest hours, believed we should one day see. I have described in a former chapter the chill which fell upon our hopes for a time in the year 1874, when the General Election of that year resulted in the return of a reactionary or indifferent Parliament from which we had little to hope for our cause. The seven years' existence of that Parliament having expired, and our principles having meanwhile gained ground, through our unceasing efforts, in the public mind, the new Parliament of 1880 was hailed by the Abolitionists with a hope which was not destined to be deceived, although there were yet five years more to run before we saw the virtual demolition of the hated tyranny against which we had so long made war, and six years before the seal was put upon its legal abolition by Queen Victoria's signature to its death warrant, given on the 13th of April, 1886.

Younger workers in other parts of the world may, we hope, be encouraged and fortified in present or future conflicts against injustice, by a knowledge of our seventeen years of labour, crowned at last by complete success. A first or a second defeat sometimes causes a sense of dismay in the minds of those who have had as yet a limited experience in such warfare. Such may perhaps take courage by looking into the deeper meaning of our long struggle. Had our victory been more quickly or more easily won, it would not have been a solid or durable victory. An early success based on a partial awakening of the public conscience would have left us an easy prey to renewed designs for the reestablishment of the evil system, based on the old corrupt traditions. God, in His providence, had a far deeper and wider work in view than we had any conception of when we first arose at His call to oppose an unjust Act of Parliament. His purpose embraced also our own education, the education of those who were called to the front, and for whom a prolonged and stern training was needful to enable them to "endure hardness," and to become worthy representatives of the truth which was to be handed on by them to the people of other lands and to their own descendants. He brought them through all the trials and vicissitudes which were needful for the strengthening of their faith, the maturing of their judgment and the perfecting of their patience.

A Parliamentary Committee of Inquiry on the subject of the vice-regulating Acts have been appointed by the late Government. Its proceedings were necessarily closed by the dissolution of the Parliament which had appointed it. Its Report was printed, which contained a recommendation of the appointment of another and similar Committee by the New Parliament, with the same objects in view, *i.e.*, to take evidence on the subject from all sides. This new Committee was appointed, and some of our best friends and leaders were elected members of it. The scope of the inquiries and examinations made by it was of a much wider and more comprehensive character than that of any former parliamentary inquiry on this subject.

It was in January of this year, 1880, that a deep impression began to be made on our English public by the revelations coming to us from time to time of the extent and cruelty of the white slave traffic between our own country and several Continental cities, more especially Brussels, Antwerp, and other towns of Northern Europe.

I cannot and need not here undertake to give at length the story of the noble and self-denying enterprise of Alfred Dyer and his friend George Gillett. Their work has already been described in a brochure [1] published by the Abolitionist Committee of the City of London, under the auspices of the late Chamberlain, Mr. Benjamin Scott. The two men who undertook this difficult and heroic research were members of the Society of Friends, men of the highest character; and it may be imagined what such men had to suffer for their boldness in entering personally the Belgian prison houses of cruelty and shame, with the design of rescuing young English girls who had been betrayed by the merchants of vice, and sold to these institutions. They not only risked their lives through the violence and rage of the keepers of these slave dens, but bore to be ridiculed, traduced and slandered on account of their action, by persons in high position whose own lives and theories of life were a constant denial of the possibility of virtue in man. I realised some of the outward and tangible results of this courageous action (considered independently of its far deeper moral effects) eleven months later, when I received, at midnight, on the 15th of December, the following telegraphic message from Mr. Alexis Splingard, an advocate of Brussels, written on leaving the Court in that City, where a number of the *Tenanciers* and Slave-traders of Brussels had been tried. "All condemned, Regnier to three years of prison, Roger two, Parent twenty-two months, Landre eighteen months, Perpéte eighteen, Andronnet eighteen, Mayer ten; five others to different terms of penal servitude." I sent this telegram

[1] "The European Slave-trade in English Girls. A narrative of Facts." Dyer Brothers.

the next morning to my sister in Naples, accompanied by the following words, in a letter which she returned with others to me: "This news will strike incredulous people perhaps a little as corroborative of our statements concerning the cruelty and guilt of these men, statements which, in my own case, my friends sometimes think to be coloured by my sympathy for the victims. We are thankful to know that some of these prison doors are now opened, and some of the slaves set free; but alas! for the thousands who are gone, dead, murdered, who found no deliverer!"

"Sometimes I feel like Dante, who fell prone 'as one dead' on witnessing inexpressible human woe. I do not find in ordinary evangelic teaching anything which meets this mystery of wrong and pain, this woe of the murdered innocents, (for indeed many are innocent, mere children, having no choice, but thrust violently into hell). But God is above all human teachings. If *He* would reveal Himself more clearly to me, I feel sure I should be stronger to act. Religious teachers never lead us to hope that God makes up hereafter to these outraged creatures of His for all they have endured, *unless* they have gone through a proper repentance here below. Some day I believe He will tell me Himself what He has done, and is doing for them. The winter is long and dark; but summer will come, and will bring more light."

One of the most important meetings which had been held upon our subject in France was held in the Salle Lévis, Paris, in April of this year. The room was crowded to excess. The following report was written by one of the principal assistants :—" The chair was taken by Dr. Thulié, a former president of the Municipal Council, who, in an extremely eloquent address, explained the aim and action of the Federation, of which the existing French Association regarded itself as a section, and showed the immorality and utter uselessness of the Police des Mœurs.

"'These English women,' he said, 'are the apostles of this great cause; they have the virtue, the self-abnegation, and the daring of apostles. Now, for the first time, woman comes forward to plead her own cause, instead of awaiting the *bon plaisir* of man. She has a right to life; she has therefore a right to liberty. If it should be attempted ever to apply to men the cruel and exceptional measures that are applied to women, all the world would cry out. For one act of self-abandonment to evil, you impose upon a woman a whole existence of torture, while you leave man irresponsible for his libertinage. We must begin by replacing woman under the protection of the Common Law, and thus restoring her to her true dignity.'

" Professor Stuart spoke shortly and ironically against the Police des Mœurs, and the stupidity, uselessness, and false pretences of those who were always ' going to stamp out the disease,' but who, during the hundred years that they had been going to do so, had never yet so much as begun to succeed.

" Mr. Benjamin Scott said that he had been commissioned by the City Committee to congratulate them on their having obtained the right of public meeting; but he regretted to find the congratulation was somewhat premature, the admission to the present meeting having been, he found, limited to those bearing tickets. He hoped, however, that this great right would soon be theirs; liberty of the press and liberty of speech were as the air we breathe; without it we die.

" Mrs. Butler followed. Her speech was thus described in *La France*: ' It was a prayer, an urgent appeal, to this popular audience so accessible to generous emotion.' ' M. Lecour argued with me,' said she, ' that as the regulation of vice was established by law in England, and we English have so much respect for the law, we were bound to respect this law. M. Lecour spoke in profound ignorance. It is because we respect the law that we desire to have our laws worthy of respect. This law is not worthy of respect—it will be abolished.'

" M. Yves Guyot followed. He concluded by moving the following resolution based on the principles of the ' Declaration of the Rights of Man.' It was carried by acclamation, the audience rising to their feet.

"'Considering that the principles of 1779 form the basis of our Common Law:

"'That the proclamation of the rights of man applies equally to the rights of woman:

"'That article 1 of that proclamation declares all citizens equal before the law:

"'That article 5 declares that no action that is not forbidden by the law shall be interfered with officially.

"'That article 7 declares that the law shall be equal for all, whether it protect or punish:

"'That the same article 7 declares that no one shall be accused, arrested, or imprisoned, save in such cases as are specified by the law, and according to the forms prescribed by the law:

"'That those who solicit, facilitate, execute, or cause to be executed any arbitrary act, are liable to punishment:

"'That the creation of all or any exceptional laws being contrary to the principles of the Common Law, it is *a fortiori* impossible to tolerate those police regulations which are in flagrant violation thereof:

"'That the Common Law is sufficient to repress all violations of public morality or order:

"'This meeting, approving the objects of the Association for the Abolition of Regulated Prostitution, requests the representatives of the people, Municipal Councillors, Deputies, and Senators, to put an end as speedily as possible to the system known as the Police des Mœurs, a system illegal in its origin, arbitrary in its application, and immoral in its effects.'"

"This resolution was voted with an enthusiasm, which sufficiently proves that the abolition of the Police des Mœurs interests a large portion of the honest and industrial population of Paris.

"The Prefecture of Police comprehends this, and attaches the greatest importance to the meeting of yesterday, they having sent to it a considerable number of their agents. Lurking behind a pillar was the *sous-chef* of the Police des

Mœurs, Remise, taking notes and listening with an impatience he could not dissemble. A certain number of his agents were in attendance.

"The Chief of the first brigade of the detectives had sent the Inspector Guyot de Lencleuse, who M. Brissaud had formerly charged with the surveillance of the *Lanterne*. The second brigade of detectives was represented by the Seigneur Antonny, who took more than twenty pages of notes. There were other police officers of lower grade scattered over the room. If M. Andrieux did not obtain the most completely detailed and faithful accounts of the meeting, he had, nevertheless, taken all the precautions for that purpose."

The distinguishing event of this year was our second great International Congress, which was held in Genoa at the end of September. In August the Hon. Depretis, Italian Minister of the Interior, issued from Rome a Circular to all the Prefects of the Kingdom, requiring them promptly to "send in their observations as to the results of the provisional regulations now in operation, in order that they may be considered in the compilation of the permanent regulations." So, "a month before representatives of the civilized world," said one of the Journals of Rome, are to assemble in Congress to prove by facts that every form of Governmental regulation of vice is noxious, the Hon. Depretis proposes suddenly to enforce a new regulation in Italy by a simple royal decree."

The *Dovere* of Rome published the following eloquent defiance addressed to the Minister :—"From the 27th of September to the 4th of October next a Congress will be held at Genoa to discuss the principles of the Federation. You, sir, hold in your hands and at your orders the countless phalanx of those interested in the revolting system of officially regulated and patented vice. Despatch all those persons to Genoa at that epoch, bid them take part in the Congress, and bid them defend the system which you are still striving to uphold. Let them advocate your cause, and to them will make answer those men and women of conscience and of

MOVEMENT IN ITALY: GENOA CONGRESS

science who have sacrificed time, thought and labour to this great question. The conscience of the people will decide between the two, and, be assured, that to the decisions of that conscience you, whether you will or no, will have to bow down sooner or later."

The *Liberta* of Genoa and the *Nazione* of Florence had articles or addresses to the Minister in the same spirit.

A delegate to that Congress wrote to friends in England as follows:—

"It would be impossible to give you within the scanty limits of a letter any adequate idea of the really imposing character and the splendid success of the second Congress of the Federation. Full details will be furnished later, which will afford you the means of publishing matter of deep interest to our friends in England. There can be no doubt that a great step in advance has been made, and that a real international progress must have taken place in public opinion before so unanimous a declaration of principles could be formulated—one might almost say without discussion—inasmuch as the complete accordance of principles which existed among the delegates from Associations and Committees of so many distinct nationalities was evident at the first great public meeting—and not merely in the Executive Committee and the Conseil Général. The formal public declaration of those principles at the popular meeting in the vast Hall of the Carlo Felice Theatre, was voted over again by acclamation by the people. The Federation found itself in a city of friends and believers in their principles. It was unnecessary to argue those principles out in detail. The various orators who ascended the tribune in turn were greeted by the Genoese as old and tried friends, whose services they were met together, not to discuss, but to approve. It was almost confusing to those who had gone to the meeting prepared to prove their case to find it already understood and judged by a public as intelligent as it was enthusiastic.

"You are probably aware that the Syndic and Municipality of Genoa had already freely granted the use of the huge Opera House to the Italian Committee of reception, and that the Syndic himself was among the first to inscribe his name among the Genoese adherents to our principles.

"The various *ordres du jour* will give you a general idea of the course of the proceedings on each day, but I have only time to tell you now of the winding-up. The Government appears to have become alarmed at the vast concourse of people from all parts of Italy that had signified their intention of thronging the theatre on the last morning. Delegates from the Working Men's Associations of all the towns of Italy were to arrive and join the Working Class Associations of Genoa in procession with their various flags and bands of music, and the Prefect at the last moment forbade the opening of the vast theatre of the Opera House to the public. It soon appeared that this was an injudicious act on the part of the Prefect; for the demonstration was far grander in consequence. The Hall of the Carlo Felice Theatre opens upon an enormous stone balcony, the whole length of the building, which looks upon the largest square in Genoa. To that square the crowd proceeded, in perfect order, each Association arriving in turn, with flags flying and trumpets sounding, and ranged themselves in a compact mass underneath, awaiting the public announcement of the final Resolutions of the Congress. All the members of the Federation went out in a body on to the long stone balcony; a platform was hastily improvised for Professor Bovio, Deputy of the Italian Parliament, whose magnificent voice could be heard from one end to the other of the immense piazza, and absolute silence was maintained while he read, one by one, to the people, the Resolutions which had just been voted in the Hall within. Each Resolution in turn was voted by acclamation by the multitude with deafening cheers, which ceased as if by magic when he again held up the paper in his hand as a sign that he was about to read again.

"He then addressed a few stirring words to the people, and on his retiring, Signor Brusco Onnis—the oldest living friend of Mazzini—was called for. He is a great favourite

THE CONGRESS OF GENOA

with the people, whom he has done much to educate in the principles of true equality and morality. Mr. and Mrs. Butler took the opportunity of going down among the people during Signor Brusco's speech, and on their return reported that so perfect was the silence and order maintained that every word he uttered was distinctly audible to the furthest extremity of the immense square. A business meeting of Delegates was held on the morning of the 4th, and a friendly banquet of the Foreign Delegates, the Commissariat and the Members of the Italian Committee took place on the evening of that day in the Restaurant of the Café Roma, a pleasant conclusion to a week's work which will not soon be forgotten by those who had the privilege of sharing in it."

Our President at this Congress was Signor Aurelio Saffi, who had been associated with Mazzini and Armellini, the Triumvirate who governed in Rome for a short time after the Revolution.

His presidential address was very eloquent, philosophical, and closely argued, its colouring here and there heightened by flashes of personal recollections of the years of exile he had spent in England, and by touches of deep emotion. Among his closing words were the following : " Let us arise, let us arise, with the courage that wins every battle against this doctrine (of the necessity of vice), the accomplice of tyranny, and against the guilty policy of those Governments who have made use of it to legalise their false authority. Let us arise, in the name of humanity, to protest against such abominations as those which we have recently seen to be sanctioned by the vice-protecting laws of Belgium, which permit base wretches to corrupt innocent, betrayed children. Let us not permit the power of truth and the sense of right, the fire of Prometheus, to be extinguished in the soul at the bidding of the high priests of vice and the pontiffs of tyranny. Let us fight against them to the death. The protest of a single victim of the guilt and selfishness of the whole world has, in the end, more influence on the course of human affairs than all the crimes—armed and decorated though they be—which outrage and crush all that is immortal and sacred in the human being."

Several recollections of those bright days in Genoa stand out in my memory with a vividness of which, perhaps, they may not seem quite worthy, when compared with the great and serious work done at that Congress. The weather was brilliant; the beautiful city was bathed in unbroken sunshine; and the hearty welcome given to us by our Italian friends was cheering and grateful beyond words. Numbers of the poor industrious Ligurian working people, as well as some of the sunburnt seamen and captains of merchant ships lying in the harbour, managed to find time now and again to attend our meetings, following with intelligent interest all that was said.

I recall the devotional meetings, morning after morning, in the Church of the Scottish Minister, a warm friend, and the words of encouragement and inspiration spoken there by my husband and M. George Appia, of Paris.

The brilliant appearance of the city was enhanced by the enthusiasm aroused by the fact that Garibaldi was then staying at his daughter's house in Genoa. He invited the leading members of the Congress to pay him a visit there, as he was then failing very much in health, and unable to move without the help of his faithful servant, a tall, dark Nubian. He received us in his room, with some of his children around him, and spoke to us cheering words concerning the ultimate triumph of our cause, which was the cause of truth and justice. It was his habit to take a daily drive, reclining in a large easy carriage. One day he passed thus along the Acqua Sola, and down the Via Nuova. The streets were a living mass of human beings, every window filled, and even the housetops covered with people, eager to see and greet the old hero. On this occasion his carriage stopped for a moment in front of the Hotel Isotta, where some of the English members of the Federation were staying. One of my sons, who was at the window of our salon, said to me, "I think he is asking for you, mother." I went to the window, and

Garibaldi, looking up and smiling, raised his poor crippled right hand with a movement of salutation. He was disabled in almost every limb by rheumatism.

On returning one evening from one of our sessions, we found around the door of the Hotel Isotta a group of women of humble rank, some with babies in their arms. The Master of the Hotel said that this was a deputation, which had waited for more than an hour to see me. He bade them enter the hall, where these poor women presented to me a formal and neatly written petition, evidently prepared with extreme care, and slightly ornamented. This was a respectfully worded request that I would, before leaving Genoa, come and address them in their own " People's Hall."

Wishing to know more particularly the object of the request, I asked them if they desired that I should speak to them on the subjects which were before the Congress. [Some of them had been at our meetings, and had caught some words of sympathy concerning the wrongs of the daughters of the poor.] One of them came forward, and speaking for the deputation, replied : " We beg, Signora, that you will come and speak to us of the *Man of Nazareth.*" " Of Christ our Saviour ? " I asked. " The same," they said, bowing their heads. There was a patient, grave self-restraint, and a look of trouble in those poor faces which went to my heart. It was not in me to resist such an appeal, and I said I would come. Some evenings later two workmen came to conduct me, the Countess de Precorbin and Signora Schiff, of Milan, to their Hall. I find a letter, in which I wrote of that meeting as follows :—" It was an excellent meeting, and in a certain sense more practical than any of the others. Though I had been invited to address women, when we arrived we found a number of men also gathered round the door. One of the women said, ' Many of our brothers, husbands, and sons are waiting outside, and are very desirous to be allowed to enter with us to hear your words.' Too gladly did we welcome them ; I always prefer mixed meetings ; and among the working people, separate meetings are never asked for, nor desired. The audience understood perfectly the question dealt with by the Federation. There was no need for us to point out to them the cruel injustice and shame of the vice regulations. They knew all that only too well; and in a conversation with a group of them afterwards, we felt that many a story of wrong and woe lay behind the quiet tears that were shed. I did not forget their special request, and took as the basis of my address several incidents in the life of Jesus, in which he especially showed himself as the great Emancipator, the friend of womanhood, and of the poor and the weak; the only absolutely Just One, the Saviour of all. The faces of the poor women evidenced deep but quiet emotion. At the close they all, men and women, crowded up to the platform to pour out their pennies on the table. There was quite a little mountain of pennies, and of little soiled papers of *Una Lira*. This was a contribution towards our Federation work. I often observe how much more readily in general a poor audience offers a contribution than a richer or higher class audience. I was much touched by it. They then wrote out and passed unanimously a resolution of adhesion to the principles of the Federation, which was signed, later, by the whole assembly."

I must not omit to record that the whole of the Catholic Press of Rome, and almost of Italy, wrote that week in support of our cause.

The imposing and affecting demonstration of sympathy given by the concourse of representatives of Operative Societies from every part of Italy was one of the most striking features of the Genoa Congress. This result was mainly due to the missionary efforts of Giuseppe Nathan, and to the confidence in and love for him which prevailed among the people of his country. He wore himself out in the cause; his whole heart and soul were in it. He died only a few months after the Congress of Genoa. He had been already suffering and weak before the Congress. We had written from England to his mother, Signora Sarina

Nathan of Rome, to ask her to use her influence with him to persuade him to take greater care of himself. Her reply was worthy of a true Roman matron of the old times: "The cause comes first," she said, "my son's life second." She did not long survive that beloved and revered son.

And now we are still waiting to see this yoke of legalized vice removed from the necks of the people of that beautiful country. They have been deceived again and again by promised or partial reforms. In some parts of their country the system is falling to pieces through its own corruption. But the victory is not yet. Revived energies and a leader are wanted. Poor Italy! when troubled about her I recall the words of Dr. Commandi of Florence, who, after speaking of her poverty, her weakness and her many difficulties, said, "But we know that our God will have the last word, and that word will be *Salvation*."

I must turn to a darker page in my memory of this year's events.

On the 1st May, 1880, I published in England a statement which was afterwards reproduced in French, Belgian, and Italian Journals, in which occurred the following words :— "In certain of the infamous houses in Brussels there are immured little children, English girls of from ten to fourteen years of age, who have been stolen, kidnapped, betrayed, carried off from English country villages by every artifice, and sold to these human shambles. The presence of these children is unknown to the ordinary visitors; it is secretly known only to the wealthy men who are able to pay large sums of money for the sacrifice of these innocents." There followed a recital of incidents which had been sworn to by witnesses, but which I need not repeat. I concluded with the words: "A malediction rests on those cities where such crimes are known and not avenged."

Much indignation was felt by certain persons, and especially by some of the chiefs of the police in London and Belgium, at the audacity of these assertions. Many of my friends cautioned me not to publish such statements, declaring that all sensible persons would say that the writer of them was mad. I persisted, however, in giving them publicity.

In the autumn after the appearance of these statements, M. Levy, a " Juge d'Instruction " of Brussels, instigated probably by the police of that city, challenged me to prove a single case in Brussels of outraged childhood in any house of the kind referred to. This challenge was sent through the " Procureur-Général " to our Home Secretary, Sir William Harcourt, and took the form of a demand that I should be required, under the Extradition Act, to make a " deposition on oath " before a magistrate. There was considerable hesitation amongst my friends as to whether I ought to accept this challenge or not, as the legality of the demand made by the Belgian authorities was questionable. I quote the following from a letter written to my sister in Naples: " We are still in suspense about this affair. There is a doubt as to whether I should submit to the Home Secretary's demand, and answer all the questions, or whether I should refuse to answer, and so incur the full legal penalty. On Saturday last my husband, travelling to Oxford, met in the train Mr. Stamford Raffles, the stipendiary magistrate before whom I should have to make my affidavit. Mr. Raffles appeared very nervous about having to take my statement. I was not well that evening, and retired to rest early; but I was not allowed to be quiet very long, for before 5 o'clock in the morning I was awakened by a loud knocking at our front door. It was a confidential messenger from the Chamberlain of London. He said he had travelled down from London through the night with a sealed packet, containing a message for me, which it was not desirable to trust to the post, and which was to be delivered as quickly as possible. It was quite dark. I lighted my candle to see to read the letter, and Jane made a fire downstairs and prepared some tea, etc., for the messenger, who was shivering with cold. He was to return to London again by the first train. I felt a little confused in the cold and dark morning, reading a mysterious letter from the Guildhall, which contained also a telegram in cypher from Brussels, warning me that there was some trap being laid for us, and probably some collusion between the police of London and that of Belgium. I do not think that this latter is the fact, but I suspect that certain enraged Belgian authorities have prompted this arbitrary act on the part of the Home Office with a malicious purpose, and also, no doubt, in the desire to clear themselves from the charges of the crimes which we have imputed to them, and with which I mean to continue to charge them. I am sure that neither at our Home Office nor at Scotland Yard, shall I or our cause meet with sympathy. This early-morning letter, which enclosed several communications from friends in Brussels, implored me to refuse to give evidence, adding, 'it would, if you declined, be worth everything to the cause for you to suffer the full legal penalty of refusing to answer. This would arouse the public as nothing else could.' I appreciate this point of view, but on the other hand, if I refuse, the Belgians and our opponents elsewhere would naturally say it was because I had no positive charges to make against them. Moreover, I am longing to make known in the most public way, those terrible cases. We wish these iniquities to be known. It has been said to me several times, 'You may be prosecuted for libel,' but my Counsel says, ' Who are the persons who would prosecute? Not the keepers of these houses or their clients. Perhaps the Procureur du Roi on their behalf, but would he dare to do it? I scarcely think he would.'

"Such days as these must come, we know, sooner or later, for us or our successors, and it is not for us to draw back. M. Humbert writes to me beautifully as follows:—'The father of lies will employ all his strategy in order to parry the blows of your denunciation. I am persuaded that at Brussels the police have strict orders to cause all the proofs (including persons) to disappear which could afford justification of your statements, and those of Mr. Dyer. In the face of all, advance courageously, even into the jaws of the dragon if need be, and even if the monster is concealing himself in the sacred precincts of the Hotel de Ville or the Palais de Justice. It was inevitable that this phase in our history should arrive. Primitive Christianity itself needed, in order to become known, that its adherents should be dragged into the Judgment Hall and before the Tribunals.'

"Mr. Scott had received a carefully sealed letter from a friend in Brussels, who wrote, 'Do you know that you are walking into the jaws of hell?' Mr. Scott answered, 'I know it. How is it possible but that hell should be moved to its depths, now that its right to swallow up its thousands of yearly victims is questioned?'

"M. Bosch, a good man and honourable magistrate in Brussels, said to our colleague, Pasteur Anet, 'Oh, take care what you do, especially in the matter of the children found in these houses. You know not the depths and bitterness of the infernal hatred you are rousing against yourselves.' This is true, but then the cry of the children is sounding in our ears, and also those words, 'Take heed that ye offend not one of these little ones.'

"The words of the 94th Psalm come often to my mind :— 'They slay the widow and the stranger; they murder the fatherless; yet they say, the Lord shall not see it.' And also the tenth chapter of Isaiah :—'Woe unto them that decree unrighteous decrees, and write grievousness which they have prescribed; to turn aside the needy from judgment, and to take away the right from the poor of My people, that widows may be their prey, and that they may rob the fatherless.' When half awake at night, I feel anxious and sad; and sometimes I am impelled to get up, in spite of the cold, to arouse myself, and kneel and pray; and then sometimes a great calm takes the place of the waves of troubled thought, for I see clearly that God is working, and that we are only like little flies, so very small, though His instruments, in the midst of the great events which may be about to be evolved.

"I am writing to try and encourage Mme. Splingard; her

son Alexis has been with us, and has returned to Brussels. His life has been threatened, and he might one day be a victim to malice."

I made my deposition in the month of November, in the Room of the Chief Magistrate. There were present, besides my husband, half-a-dozen of the most solid and honourable citizens of Liverpool, who were deeply interested in the whole matter, my Counsel, Dr. Commins, and a reporter. My deposition was forwarded to Sir William Harcourt, and by him to the Procureur du Roi, at Brussels. *From that time forward there were no more attempts to deny the charges I had made.* The proofs of everything I had said were too strong to be set aside, while Mr. Dyer's action, and the facts cited in my deposition, produced results in Belgium for which all the friends of Justice were thankful.

Besides the facts which I stated on oath, others had been published in Belgium, in spite of efforts to hush them up; among them was the following:—

"On the 19th January last, two persons, Constance Delvaux and Catherine Reniers, were brought before the Correctional Tribunal of Brussels, charged with the offences indicated in the following narrative:—Madame P——, of an honourable family of Brussels, had placed her little daughter at a school in that city. She was accustomed to call for her child at the end of the week, and to take her home to spend the Sunday with her. On a certain Saturday she called as usual, and on asking if her daugher was ready, she was met by a look of astonishment from the ladies at the head of the establishment, who replied, 'But, madam, you sent for your daughter some days ago, and she went to you, accompanied by your messenger.' It transpired that a woman had called, bearing a letter, apparently signed by Madame P——, saying that owing to special circumstances she wished to have her daughter at home that week, and had, therefore, sent a servant to bring her. This letter was a forgery. It was proved in the trial that the Baron de Mesnil Herman, of the rue des Arts, No. 17 (why should I spare him the publicity he deserves, and had attained?), of forty-three years of age, had somewhere set his adulterous eyes upon this child, and that he had engaged the women above named to bring her to him. The child was taken to the notorious Café Riche, a place of assignation much resorted to by gentlemen of high society, councillors, diplomatists, military officers, etc. Thérèse Daubremist, called as witness, said that Constance Delvaux had asked her to write the fraudulent letter; 'I thought she was the child's mother; I wrote the letter.' Constance Delvaux replied, 'I caused the letter to be written in order to oblige the Baron de Mesnil.' Catherine Reniers stated, 'I had gone previously to the school to ask for the young girl, but the directress required that a letter should be brought to her from Madame P——. It is so natural that we should wish to oblige Monsieur le Baron de Mesnil.' The Public Prosecutor commented on the depth of immorality revealed by the conduct of the two women, and demanded a severe application of the law. The two women were condemned to seven months of prison. *The Baron de Mesnil was not even summoned as a witness at the trial?* The poor child, after having been introduced to 'indescribable scenes' at the Café Riche, was sent with one of the women above named to Aix-la-Chapelle. Her mother went immediately in pursuit of her (this lady is a widow), but her child had been hastily removed thence to some other city, and no trace of her could be discovered. Silence on the subject was for a long time maintained by the press, on account of the high position of the Baron de Mesnil. Then there came a rumour of the young girl having been found in Paris, whence, it was said, ' the police will return her to her native land.'" Return her! but in what condition? I republished this story in an appeal to the mothers of England, in which I said:—" Reflect what it would be to you, to have one of your pure and tenderly cherished darlings returned to you, after having been forced to witness and take part in such unspeakable horrors—ruined in body and mind, the poor young brain never more able to get rid of the spot blacker

DARK DEEDS BROUGHT TO LIGHT

than death, which no tears from the heart, nor even a mother's love, can efface! Reading these things, you will not be among those who blame me for 'wounding the susceptibilities' of persons in high office, perverted judges, luxurious livers, who condone and even take part in such horrors. If we mothers were to hold our peace the very stones would cry out."

Similar revelations of this kind began to come to us from France and other countries. I wrote to my sister:—
"The present time resembles an era of incendiarism, in which fires are breaking out with lurid light on all sides, north and south, east and west. We have scarcely taken breath after hearing of one tragedy before the post brings us tidings of another. It is well it is so. For long years past the slaughter of the innocents has been going on. We knew it not, or only had a partial knowledge of it. Now we know, and before God we are responsible for that terrible knowledge."

From Bordeaux, in France, there came to us a terrible story of the two little children Delemont. The scandal in this case was so great that several gentlemen of high position were arrested and tried, among them being Commandant A——, a man of advanced age, and another, a Colonel C——. The former was condemned to ten years' imprisonment. The latter was acquitted, on the ground of his having fought bravely at Metz. The Minister for War, M. Ranc, however, did not deem it a brave action to have taken part in the destruction of a little child, and shortly afterwards expelled him from the army. The evidence given by the children was tragic and heart-rending. They identified the criminals at once when they were brought before them with a number of other men. Very awful must have been the steadily pointed finger of those innocent victims for any culprit not wholly reprobate. These men, however, were past shame. But a judgment day awaits them, when the pointed fingers of the children will be worse for them than the heaviest judgment of any earthly tribunal; for

"The child's sob curseth deeper
Than the strong man in his wrath."

In the late autumn, the trial to which I have before alluded took place, resulting in the condemnation of large numbers of the slave-dealers and slave-owners of these modern times. The evidence brought against them was of the most awful kind, showing that the exaggeration with which we were sometimes charged had had no existence; and, in fact, no words could have been strong enough in which to describe or denounce the atrocities perpetrated in these bastilles of shameless vice. One young girl, having escaped from one of these houses in Brussels, came to us, and was a refugee in our house for some time. She was taken with another English girl to Brussels, under the kind care of Mrs. Steward, to be witnesses against their tormentors. I was not present at those trials, but was told that they gave their evidence with firmness, and sometimes with an indignant *brusquerie* which was not unbecoming. These events certainly had a purifying effect for a time on the moral atmosphere of Brussels, and the publication of the sentences pronounced on the culprits conveyed a kind of electric shock throughout the infamous world of slave-dealers, both in Belgium and other countries, which we believe, for a time at least, to have materially lessened the evil.

The Public Prosecutor wrote kindly concerning our poor young English witnesses, saying that Pasteur Anet and Mrs. Steward would have permission to sit by their side in the Court. One of these girls, on returning to my house, told me that the brutal creature Roger, afterwards imprisoned, meeting her in a passage of the Court, fell on his knees before her to beseech her not to give evidence concerning his violent treatment of English girls, of which she had been both a witness and a victim.

Another of the poor refugees helped by Pastor Anet to escape from Brussels came to our house in Liverpool. She appeared to be in pain, and on being questioned she replied that she was suffering from unhealed stripes on her back and shoulders from the lash of this tyrant. I called in our physician, Dr. William Carter, of Rodney Street, Liverpool, to certify to the truth of her declaration; and, in very deed, we found the livid marks of the stripes of which she had spoken. We seemed to stand before a victim of some cruel overseer of slaves in the cotton plantations of one of the Southern States of America in the past times. I drew from her, when alone, the story of her martyrdom. The keeper of this house in Brussels, enraged with her because of her persistent refusal to participate in some exceptionally base proceedings among his clients, had her carried to an underground chamber whence her cries could not be heard. She was here immured and starved, and several times scourged with a thong of leather. But she did not yield. This poor delicate girl had been neglected from childhood; she was a Catholic, but had had little or no religious teaching. She told me with much simplicity, that in the midst of these tortures she was "all the time strengthened and comforted by the thought that Jesus had Himself been cruelly scourged, and that He could feel for her." Before her capture she had one day seen in a shop window in Brussels an engraving of Christ before Pilate, bound and scourged. Some persons, no doubt, may experience a little shock of horror at the idea of any connection in the thoughts of this poor child between the supreme agony of the Son of God and her own torments in the cellar of that house of debauchery. We often sincerely mourn over these victims as "lost," because *we* cannot reach them with any word of love or the "glad evangel." But *He* "descended into hell," into the abode of the "spirits in prison" to speak to them; and I believe, and have had many testimonies to the fact, that He visits spiritually these young souls in their earthly prison, many a time, He alone, in all His majesty of pity, without any intervention of ours.

And yet we continue to mass all these victims under one great ban of social excommunication; to treat them as a *class*, to make exceptional rules and laws for them; and in our various police codes we continue to call them all by the ugly name of *prostitute,* and to pile on fresh penal clauses in order to deal with them more and more severely, in the idea that we are "repressing vice." The Judgment Day will reveal some astonishing things.

At the close of the year I wrote to my sister in Naples as follows:—" I received some weeks ago a letter from the Editor of the *National,* of Belgium, telling me that he was summoned to give evidence before the Commission now sitting at the Hotel de Ville on the complicity of the police in the crimes divulged in the late trials, and asking me to send him all the information I could, and especially, for his own use, my deposition made before the magistrate. I sent him this, having already sent one copy to the Bourgmestre of Brussels. I imagined he would make use of it in some way, but not exactly as he did. He took this document to the Hotel de Ville, read it all through before the Commission, and next day published it entire in his paper, with all the names. I had had it printed, you understand, simply for private or judicial use. It seems that the editor of the *National* is an enterprising man, and no doubt he would like to gain some notoriety for his paper, as I have been told he wishes to become a *Grand Seigneur de la Presse,* but in a good cause. I dare say his motives are somewhat mixed. He gave the whole evidence, with a fine summing-up on the principle. 60,000 copies of his paper were sold before the evening; a second edition was called for, and the next day 20,000 more were sold. Of course, at once his life was threatened, pistols were levelled at him, prosecutions for libel were in preparation, of which he is the object, as the publisher in such a case is prosecuted and not the author of the accusations; his office was besieged, and is still so, by people threatening him, and by a yet greater crowd of persons pouring out their griefs and wrongs which they have suffered through the Police des Mœurs, revealing many terrible tragedies. For the moment this editor is a great man, and the agitation throughout Belgium is considerable. About two-thirds of the Press of that country, they tell me, are now warmly on our side. The *Journal de Mons* thanks the English for this 'chastisement.' All honest and decent people are aroused, many are indignant, many more are incredulous. The *Courrier de Bruxelles* speaks of 'profound emotion,' and of 'the conscience of the people being aroused as by a thunderbolt.'

"You can imagine that on first hearing of this I felt a little troubled, and as if I had been 'given away.' Also, persons friendly to us, such as Lambillon, Hendrick and others, who had given us information from a good motive, were angry at seeing their names published as having had any knowledge whatever of these evil things; and I was pained to think of *their* pain.

"I was pondering all this one evening, when I suddenly recollected that on New Year's Day of this year, and many days after, I had taken upon me to make a special and definite request to God for light to fall upon these 'dark places of the earth wherein are the habitations of cruelty.' Some strong influence seemed to urge me to make this request. I used to kneel and pray, 'O God, I beseech Thee, send light upon these evil deeds! whatever it may cost us and others, flash light into these abodes of darkness. O send us light! for without it there can be no destruction of the evil. We cannot make war against a hidden foe. In the darkness, these poor sisters of ours, these creatures of Thine, are daily murdered, and we do not know what to do, or where to turn, and we find no way by which to begin to act. Send us light, O our God, even though it may be terrible to bear.' I had made a record of this petition, and then I had forgotten it. But not so our faithful God. His memory is better than mine! He did not forget, and He is now sending the answer to that prayer. Then I thought of the words;—'O fools, and slow of heart to believe.' Here is the very thing I had asked for, brought about in a way I had not dreamed of.

'We cannot ask the thing that is not there,'
'Blaming the shallowness of our request.'

"The Journals speak of that number of the *National* as 'a flash of lighting,' and use almost the language of my own soul about it, and I bow my head in thankfulness, seeing the hand of God in all.

"M. Humbert wrote to me in the early days of this year:— '*I begin this year under a sense of awe; I can but hold my pen obedient to the dictation of incalculable events.*' It is interesting to know that some of these slave-owners of Brussels shut up their houses and fled on reading the accusations in the *National*. 'The wicked flee when no man pursueth,' but only the echo of a far-off woman's voice! M. Humbert quotes a German proverb, '*the dead fly fast*.' Long-lasting corruption, when ripe for dissolution, is not slow in suiciding. But alas! the poison has spread far and wide. There is an infection in the presence of deathlike corruption which even the best can scarcely escape; and we may ask, 'Can these bones live?—Ah, Lord God, Thou knowest.'

"I have been a little troubled by an article published in a Brussels newspaper by an ardent young Belgian friend, who makes it seem that his own generous, but too violent, and even fierce expressions convey my own feelings. One cannot be too indignant or too full of scorn in such a case, but I never in my life spoke of *physical* force! 'Our weapons are not carnal, but spiritual, to the pulling down of strongholds.' Nevertheless I can forgive people longing for pistols who have not experienced the superior power of moral weapons. Indeed, at some moments I do also!

"Events have followed each other rapidly. M. Lenaers, the famous Chief of the Police des Mœurs in Brussels, and his second in office, Schroeder, were both summoned to the Hotel de Ville, and at a secret sitting of the *Echevins* Schroeder was censured. These two worthies, however, instituted a prosecution against the Editor of the *National* for libel, on account of the statements regarding them. The Editor was jubilant. He took no advocate, but pleaded his own cause, and accepted the whole responsibility of his publication of my accusations. I asked myself, 'Will his jubilance endure if he is condemned to imprisonment, poor man?' We have the Catholic Press largely on our side, but our best individual champions are not Catholics. His Majesty the King looks on! Parliament has taken up the matter. Reuter's telegram announced in our *Daily News* that 'the Minister of the Interior had been questioned on the misconduct of the Police des Mœurs.' A short debate took place. M. Jacob, a deputy, spoke gravely and well 'amidst a deep and significant silence.' He solemnly called on the Minister to take a bold step and dismiss certain functionaries. The Minister replied that the accusations published in the *National* were 'probably a libel,' whereupon a great hubbub arose in all the Journals of the two following days.

"One evening, before her departure for Brussels, Mrs. Stewart was with us, and when we were gathering for family prayer she asked, 'Shall we not pray for those wretched men now in prison? What must their thoughts be, waiting for the earthly judgment, in anticipation of the awful judgment to come?' My husband replied, 'Yes, we may indeed pray for mercy for them;' but his heart bleeds, as mine does, for their victims."

A Memorial concerning this traffic in child slaves had been drawn up at the Guildhall by the City of London Committee, addressed to Lord Granville, our Foreign Secretary at that time. The City Committee commissioned me in October to present a similar Petition to the Bourgmestre and Echevins of Brussels, enclosing also a copy of the Memorial to Lord Granville. I went with these to the Hotel de Ville, where I was courteously received. After presenting the Memorials I ventured to request the Bourgmestre to dismiss the officials and other persons in the room, which he did, looking a little troubled; for my heart urged me to speak to him face to face concerning his own reponsibility in all this matter. It proved to be rather an affecting interview—rather terrible even. I think I trembled, and the Bourgmestre covered his eyes with his hand. He treated me with courtesy and gentleness.

Some time later, two or three official personages, to whom these revelations of evil had come forcibly home, found that the state of their health required them to visit the South of France. In one case it was found necessary greatly to prolong this residence in the south, for he never returned; 'his place knew him no more.' MM. Lenaers and Schroeder, Chiefs of Police, were dismissed from office. But the system of Government-patented and regulated vice *continues to exist*, and the friends of Justice continue to work and to wait.

Looking back over the ten or eleven years of our crusade, and observing the admirable organisations which had arisen in that time, I felt impelled to point out a danger, which often threatens the success of vital work, though seldom recognised as a danger, namely, the tendency to lean too much on a perfected organisation, which sometimes in itself cramps the life within it. I sent out a circular to my friends on this subject, in which occurred the following, which I reproduce, because the same tendencies may arise again. "This international work of ours seems to have entered upon a phase through which all movements of the kind are liable to pass, and to point to the danger which there is even in the attainment of a high and satisfactory organisation. This high organisation is often reached at the expense of individual initiative and independent personal effort. We are now incurring the risk of substituting stereotyped office work for the vitality of missionary zeal. M. Humbert lately wrote to me that he considers our propagandist activity is at the present moment somewhat paralysed, and I think we must ourselves confess that the individual activities of the members of our League are not on the increase at present. Some of the prominent members of our Central Committee are unable to give more than a small fraction of their time to our work, being heavily charged with other business of a public or political kind, and this necessitates to a great degree their reliance on the regular machinery and steady work of a bureau.

"In the winter of 1874, taking counsel only with my own

ORGANISATION AND INDIVIDUAL EFFORT

heart, I started, as you know, on a mission for our cause to the Continent. In the summer of 1876 our two able comrades, Mr. Wilson and Mr. Gledstone, went forth to America, to stir up a spirit of watchfulness there. More recently, Mr. Dyer and his friend undertook a difficult and hazardous enterprise in Belgium. I cite these incidents as cases in which there was no danger of sacrificing missionary zeal to system. These missions and others of a similar nature have proved to be very fruitful, and I am deeply convinced that our cause will cease to make such rapid progress as heretofore if individual propagandism of this nature is altogether abandoned, while we, sitting at home, or largely absorbed in other business, leave the cause mainly to the working of office machinery, and expect its triumph to be achieved by agencies established in London and in Switzerland, however perfected those agencies may be, and however skilled the agents. It is not by official machinery that we shall conquer, though that is necessary *as a scaffolding of operations*, but by self-sacrifice and unwearying missionary zeal, without which no great cause was ever won. I have observed that we are sometimes even betrayed into the error (unconsciously probably) of discouraging the initiative of honest and humble persons who have been filled with the desire to do something independently for the cause. Their ardour must have been checked rather than stimulated by being directed to follow in the path of a centralised organisation, the very existence of which tends to make people think their own personal efforts are not required. We cannot, of course, dispense with our valuable organisations and bureaus, but it is quite possible at the same time to welcome the efforts of every individual, however humble, and to stimulate independent activity on all hands. We need missionaries in all countries. The discovery of these, and the impulse to be given to them, must greatly depend on the maintenance of a vigorous correspondence of an informal, personal kind, wherever there is an opportunity for it; and when such persons are found, a generous confidence as well as prudence may well be exercised in the amount of encouragement given to them to go forward, even if their plans and methods may not be wholly familiar to, or approved by us. The essential is that they should have a clear grasp of our principles."

CONCLUSION

"BEING in the line of Duty, and realising my oneness with Omnipotence, I cannot possibly fail of success; for Omnipotent Love is pledged for the accomplishment of *that for which I trust.* The zeal of the Lord of Hosts shall perform it. 'Thou shalt decree a thing,' He hath said, 'and it shall be established unto thee.' There is no room for doubt. Because of the imperativeness of duty and the faithfulness of God, I am fully equipped with power to fulfil that duty."

IN concluding this volume of personal reminiscences, I am reminded of the survey of the work of the decade which expired in 1880, which I was asked by our friends to bring before them on the occasion of the Annual Meeting of the "Ladies' National Association" of that year. The thoughts which rose to my mind then, come again vividly before me now. I may fitly close this record by some extracts from that address, as follows:—

"The fact that a Select Committee of Parliament is now sitting to inquire into the working of the system which we oppose, produces a certain lull in the more public and demonstrative action of the Abolitionist movement. Our question is again placed *sub judice* by the House of Commons, and our Parliamentary leaders consequently have their lips closed. For five years past successively, we have had the support of the eloquent voice and powerful arguments of Sir James Stansfeld, who always on all occasions asserted that, amidst all his convictions, deep and strong on this question, he had none deeper or stronger than this—that women must continue to stand in the forefront of this battle, and that, if they should cease to do so, the battle would be lost. Mr. Stansfeld is now, however, a member of the Parliamentary Committee of Inquiry, and cannot be with us here. Sir Harcourt Johnstone, our Parliamentary leader, is in the same position, being also a member of that Committee.

"We are this evening called once more, therefore, to plead publicly our own cause; and this happens to be the case just at the close of a decade of labours, as if to call us, as women, to look back and record what God has done for us, perfecting His strength in our weakness, in these past ten years.

"These circumstances seem to prompt us to an attitude of grave retrospect, and of calm and deliberate preparation for the future.

"We must remember that the principal labours of a great movement do not consist in those public demonstrations and exciting parliamentary debates in which they culminate. Thought leads, after all, and the intellectual battle must continue to be waged by solid argument, by repeated assertion of principles, and by the unwearying pursuit of the multifarious fallacies and falsehoods to which a retiring cause inevitably betakes itself. Above all, ours is a spiritual warfare, and the victory must be won by the deepening of our own convictions, by increased faith in the permanence of the eternal principles of justice, and by a more absolute trust in Him in whose cause we are engaged.

"Since our first uprising in 1869, we have been gathering around us an increasing number of adherents of the medical profession, the breadth of whose views has led them to take a foremost place, not only in our crusade, but in the ranks of scientific teachers; they have set forth, not only the true medical aspect of this question, but also its far higher scientific aspect, in its relation to ethics and jurisprudence.

"The Society of which Elizabeth Fry was a distinguished member was, as we might naturally expect, among the first to welcome the public action of women in this matter; and the earliest public meetings addressed by women on this question were held in Quaker meeting houses. I cannot refrain from expressing my gratitude to those who, while most persons were scandalised by women's action in those early days of our conflict, frankly gave me the right hand of fellowship, asking for no credentials whatsoever, except my own assertion that the cry of the oppressed and the voice of God within me were calling me to this work.

"It would be impossible for me, in this brief hour, to enumerate the succession of conferences, debates, mass meetings, and stormy election conflicts in which we have taken part during the last ten years; and my address to you this evening is not in any sense a report of work done, but only a most brief and imperfect survey of the rapid expansion of our cause. . . .

"Let me lead you on to the spring of 1874. At that date we became aware of a vast enterprise, conceived and planned by the advocates of regulated vice,—an enterprise which involved a world-wide scheme for bringing under this degrading system all the nations of the earth. In order to meet this international action, it seemed to us that we must ourselves make an appeal to all the nations of the earth.

"A few of us—very few—met in York in June, 1874; our small number seemed utterly incommensurate with the vastness of the scheme before us. Faith enough was found, however, in that little band to welcome the suggestion of one member of it that she should go whither God would send her on the Continent of Europe.

"On the eve of her departure a company of friends assembled at Birmingham to commend to God this mighty enterprise in its small beginnings. The conference of that evening began by the reading of those prophetic words—for, in fact, they proved to be prophetic—'I will say of the Lord, He is my refuge and my fortress, my God, in Him will I trust;' 'He shall give His angels charge over thee to keep thee in all thy ways;' 'Thou shalt tread upon the lion and adder' (violence and treachery).

"The history of that winter's journeyings and labours is known to you, as well as something of the subsequent progress of the work on the Continent. This being the anniversary of the Ladies' National Association, I may fitly mention that women on the Continent are faithful to the call they have received. Indeed, the hearts and consciences of women, especially of women of the humbler classes, bear the same witness in every land, concerning this question. At a meeting of women lately addressed by the Baroness Stampe and the Countess Moltke in Copenhagen, the poor women crowded up to sign their names, and pay their little contributions as members of our great League. One, who was very poorly clad, said, 'If I have to sell my shawl in order to become a member, I will do it.' If every woman in the more favoured classes of life were willing to make a sacrifice in proportion to this which the poor Danish woman was ready to make, we should have a mighty force added to our army.

"Another important feature of our progress is that of the establishment of a branch of our work in the United States of America, to prevent the encroachments of the Regulationists there, who are making constant efforts to introduce this system. Every great cause is propagandist in its spirit. Mr. H. J. Wilson and Mr. Gledstone went over as delegates from England to America, to arouse the lovers of virtue and freedom there. The seed they sowed has been very fruitful.

"The great event of the Geneva Congress, in the autumn of 1877, is well known to you all. I may remark, however, that an important element in our success has proved to be the importation into England of Continental opinion on this subject, opinion which is the more weighty as our Continental neighbours have had a prolonged experience of the regulation system, which has been comparatively recently introduced here. We have now in our hands a powerful weapon to employ for this work; I mean the published *Actes* of the Congress of Geneva. The conspiracy of silence of the press has done us this service—in that it has forced us to create a literature of our own.

"If we ask ourselves what are the results which we have gained, in the form of the actual abolition, in any part of the world, of the regulations against which we contend, we must confess that they are small. But the approach of victory is signalised not so much by the definite results which we are able to record in the shape of abolition as by the attitude and manœuvres of our opponents, accompanied by the progress of public opinion everywhere, on the question of morality and of the equal application of the moral law to both sexes. The Spartan general Brasidas, surveying the ranks of his enemies, said, 'I see by the shaking of their spears that the rascals are preparing to run.' We see as clearly by the ungraceful and eccentric dance now being performed by our opponents that they are preparing for a forced retreat from the position they have so long and so proudly maintained. The whole army of Regulationists have changed their front during these past ten years, having introduced the most extraordinary alterations in their tactics; and, as is generally the case when a bad cause begins to fall, they are introducing changes in the most opposite directions; on the one hand exaggerating all their pretensions and demands, and on the other hand making concessions, with the hope of prolonging their own existence.

"I may enumerate the concessions which have already been made to the advancing force of public opinion in the form of committees or commissions of special enquiry into this question: First, the Royal Commission appointed in 1870, the report of which was contradictory and inharmonious, resembling the confusion of tongues at the tower of Babel. Secondly, the Italian Parliamentary Committee, which sat in Rome, and which, at the close of its inquiry, proposed some kind of compromise. Thirdly, the Commission of the Municipal Council of Paris, now sitting. Fourthly, the Hong Kong Commission, which reported unfavourably of the Government establishment of vice in that colony, but gave way practically to the urgency of medical men in maintaining an amended form of the system. Fifthly, the Parliamentary Committee actually in session in London.

"Through all the cycles of human history, certain crimes and cruelties have in a great measure succeeded in hiding themselves, but now the fierce light is bursting in upon them on every side. The horrors and agonies of sensual sin are appearing in view. We continually receive from all parts of Europe revelations such as men had never guessed of before. The international slave traffic in human souls (that *necessary* adjunct of State-organised vice) has prospered in silence and secrecy; but *it* also is now coming to the light; it has been and is carried on on a larger scale and in more horrible ways than is generally suspected or can be easily conceived.

"It is possible, even probable, that the most anxious and difficult days of our struggle are yet to come; that when the upholders of the existing regulations of vice in various lands shall see it necessary to abandon their present position, they will come to us with offered compromises; and then there will be a sifting-time; our principles will be tested, and our integrity severely tried. That such compromises, various in kind and more or less subtle in their nature, will be proposed, and that they are already being concocted, I cannot doubt. We shall require clearness of insight to discern their nature, and firmness of purpose to deal with their propositions.

"We have experience enough to demonstrate that, whenever a practical victory awaits us, we may look for a corresponding attempt on the part of the Regulationists to re-establish the evil principle in, it may be, an extremely modified form or in a misleading guise; hence the supreme importance of clearness of discernment on our part, of wisdom and penetration, of skill to separate the old leaven to its last particle from every plan for the future, and to reject, at the risk of being deemed vexatious irreconcilables, every proposal which bears within itself the theory that prostitution is a necessary evil, and the consequent admission that a certain number of God's creatures are doomed, also by a fatal law of necessity, to be transformed into mere instruments for the basest and most unholy purpose."

1897.

And now, my dear Friends and Fellow-workers who have followed so far with me this record of our first ten years of conflict, my concluding words shall be addressed to you.

As I look back through our long warfare there rise before my mind not only our united band in untiring conflict with injustice, but many pleasant adventures, social gatherings, and sweet friendships, taking their rise in a common aim, cemented by fellowship in trial and in hope, and ripening, year by year, for the higher communion of the life to come. Many pleasant memories are revived, and some sorrowful ones. Ties have been riven, ties so dear and so familiar that when they vanished our weak hearts were rent. Fair households amongst us have been scattered. Some who were active in the work are now disabled by permanent physical weakness or approaching age; and we daily feel that our dearest communion fronts the hour of death. We have mourned together when some of our ablest helpers and boldest champions fell in the heat of the battle. But we have had strength given us to rise again, to put on our armour, and to turn our face to the foe.

We are of those (it has been said) who represent the imperishableness of principles, one of the many assurances of immortality. Let us be of good courage, then! He who has helped us hitherto will be with us to the end. More than twenty-seven years ago, while we were but a small, feeble company, and few cared to give ear to our appeal, much less to join in our aggressive action, we may have said in our hearts, 'Who will rise up for me against the evil doers, or who will stand up for me against the workers of iniquity?' and, indeed, I may say for myself, 'Unless the Lord had been my helper, my soul had almost dwelt in silence.' But the heavy curtain of darkness was lifted up at last, and we now see that there were celestial warriors on our side, and more for us than against us. The event foretold by Christ is coming to pass; the secret sins of Europe are beginning to be proclaimed from the housetops; the light of truth is already falling upon the dark places of the earth, full of the hideous habitations of cruelty; the hidden things of darkness can escape the dreaded light no more.

Looking forward, as we must, to another term of conflict, and considering what may, and probably will be, the special trials which await us, I counsel you, Friends, to be strong. Cultivate a sound judgment. Take this question into the solitude of your chamber; let the light from God's presence penetrate your inmost thoughts; see clearly and act firmly.

> Let this be all our care
> To stand approved in sight of God, though worlds
> Judge us perverse.

God forbid that we should ever trifle with the righteous conditions of success, for we know that every compromise is a loss of power, and would force us to begin all our work over again! May He grant us the disciplined conscience whose unfaltering logic shall hold its own against every fallacy, and continue to pierce through an iniquity which has corrupted more or less all the Governments of Europe, and blinded even the Churches, in which there can be no real health until they have openly taken their stand on God's side in this matter.

Our opponents continue to tell us that 'something must be done.' True! practical effort is wanted on every side, economical, industrial, social; legal reforms are required, as well as moral and spiritual forces. We do, in fact, already combat, from all these sides, by means of the many collateral organisations which have gathered around us, the great evil of prostitution itself. It is true we had long neglected this work; but let those who blame us look round now, and survey the array of forces and agencies which have sprung up in many countries during these last twenty-seven years, animated by our protest, and working hand in hand with us.

Let them regard these efforts and their results, and say whether we have not fully recognised the fact that 'something must be done,' and whether we have not faithfully endeavoured to do that something. But what some men mean when they call for something to be done, is that some provision of some sort must be made, whereby impurity may be divested of its unpleasant physical consequences,—that some organisation must be planned, based on the recognition of prostitution as a necessity of our social condition. To these we have but one reply: while it is our turn to remind those persons that 'something must be done,' and that that 'something' is that men must learn to live virtuously; that is the only possible remedy for the physical plague. But there are men who do not like to hear this; they will try everything rather than this. The end, however, will be the failure of their every effort to separate the moral and the physical laws of the universe, and the confirmation of this truth—that the only cure for the evils which they so much dread is *purity of life*.

O! that men would turn from the evil of their ways, for then, though their sins should be as scarlet, they shall be as white as snow, and they shall find themselves in the hand of a Saviour who is able to save *to the uttermost!*

Let holy charity continue, dear Friends, to be the inspiration of all our work. Pity for the suffering; justice for all; the oppressed to be delivered; the slave to be set free; the moral law to be obeyed to the last tittle; the soul of the poor to be delivered from the hands of the spoiler; and the Governments of the world to be warned of that logic of retribution whereby men and nations reap as they have sown. Such has been our programme in the past; such it will continue to be in the future.

THE END.

Butler & Tanner, The Selwood Printing Works, Frome, and London.